# Palgrave Macmillan Series in Global Public Diplomacy

*Series editors:*

Kathy Fitzpatrick, Quinnipiac University, USA
Philip Seib, University of Southern California, USA

*Advisory Board:*

Mai'a K. Davis Cross, ARENA Centre for European Studies, Norway
Nicholas J. Cull, University of Southern California, USA
Teresa LaPorte, University of Navarre, Spain
Donna Lee, University of Kent, United Kingdom
Jan Melissen, Netherlands Institute of International Relations Clingendael and University of Antwerp, Belgium
Abeer Najjar, American University of Sharjah, United Arab Emirates
William A. Rugh, Former U.S. Ambassador to Yemen and United Arab Emirates, USA
Cesar Villanueva Rivas, Universidad Iberoamericana, Mexico
Li Xiguang, Tsinghua University, China

At no time in history has public diplomacy played a more significant role in world affairs and international relations. As a result, global interest in public diplomacy has escalated, creating a substantial academic and professional audience for new works in the field.

This series examines theory and practice in public diplomacy from a global perspective, looking closely at public diplomacy concepts, policies, and practices in various regions of the world. The purpose is to enhance understanding of the importance of public diplomacy, to advance public diplomacy thinking, and to contribute to improved public diplomacy practices.

The editors welcome submissions from scholars and practitioners representing a range of disciplines and fields (including diplomacy, international relations, international communications, public relations, political science, global media, marketing/advertising) and offering diverse perspectives. In keeping with its global focus, the series encourages non-US-centric works and comparative studies.

*Toward a New Public Diplomacy: Redirecting U.S. Foreign Policy*
Edited by Philip Seib

*Soft Power in China: Public Diplomacy through Communication*
Edited by Jian Wang

*Public Diplomacy and Soft Power in East Asia*
Edited by Sook Jong Lee and Jan Melissen

*The Practice of Public Diplomacy: Confronting Challenges Abroad*
Edited by William A. Rugh

*The Decline and Fall of the United States Information Agency: American Public Diplomacy, 1989–2001*
 Nicholas J. Cull

*Beyond Cairo: US Engagement with the Muslim World*
 Darrell Ezell

*Collaborative Public Diplomacy: How Transnational Networks Influenced American Studies in Europe*
 Ali Fisher

*Religion and Public Diplomacy*
 Edited by Philip Seib

*Communicating India's Soft Power: Buddha to Bollywood*
 Daya Kishan Thussu

*European Public Diplomacy*
 Edited by Mai'a K. Davis Cross and Jan Melissen

*The Challenge of Public Diplomacy*
 James Thomas Snyder

*Shaping China's Global Imagination: Branding Nations at the World Expo*
 Jian Wang

*Front Line Public Diplomacy: How US Embassies Communicate with Foreign Publics*
 William A. Rugh

*China and Taiwan in Central America: Engaging Foreign Publics in Diplomacy*
 Colin R. Alexander

*Turkey's Public Diplomacy*
 Edited by B. Senem Çevik and Philip Seib

*US Public Diplomacy and Democratization in Spain: Selling Democracy?*
 Edited by Francisco J. Rodríguez, Lorenzo Delgado, and Nicholas J. Cull

*Understanding Public Diplomacy in East Asia: Middle Powers in a Troubled Region*
 Edited by Jan Melissen and Yul Sohn

# Front Line Public Diplomacy

## How US Embassies Communicate with Foreign Publics

William A. Rugh

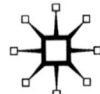

FRONT LINE PUBLIC DIPLOMACY
Copyright © William A. Rugh, 2014.

All rights reserved.

First published in hardcover in 2014 by PALGRAVE MACMILLAN® in the United States—a division of St. Martin's Press LLC, 175 Fifth Avenue, New York, NY 10010.

Where this book is distributed in the UK, Europe and the rest of the world, this is by Palgrave Macmillan, a division of Macmillan Publishers Limited, registered in England, company number 785998, of Houndmills, Basingstoke, Hampshire RG21 6XS.

Palgrave Macmillan is the global academic imprint of the above companies and has companies and representatives throughout the world.

Palgrave® and Macmillan® are registered trademarks in the United States, the United Kingdom, Europe and other countries.

ISBN: 978–1–137–58937–8

The Library of Congress has cataloged the hardcover edition as follows:

Rugh, William A.
    Front line public diplomacy : how US embassies communicate with foreign publics / William A. Rugh.
      pages cm.
    Includes index.
    ISBN 978–1–137–44414–1 (hardcover : alk. paper)
    1. Diplomatic and consular service, American. 2. United States—Foreign public opinion. 3. United States—Foreign relations administration. I. Title.

JZ1480.A5R84 2014
327.73—dc23                                                    2014007054

A catalogue record of the book is available from the British Library.

Design by Newgen Knowledge Works (P) Ltd., Chennai, India.

First PALGRAVE MACMILLAN paperback edition: January 2016

10 9 8 7 6 5 4 3 2 1

*This book is dedicated to*
*Andrea Rugh*

# CONTENTS

| | | |
|---|---|---|
| *Acknowledgments* | | ix |
| *List of Abbreviations* | | xi |
| Introduction | | 1 |

## Part I   The Context

| | | |
|---|---|---|
| One | Legacy: Public Diplomacy's Philosophy and Legal Basis | 7 |
| Two | Public Diplomacy Professionals | 23 |

## Part II   Field Office Management

| | | |
|---|---|---|
| Three | The Public Affairs Officer | 43 |
| Four | Contacts and Personal Networking Techniques | 65 |

## Part III   Information Programs

| | | |
|---|---|---|
| Five | Traditional Information Channels | 81 |
| Six | Social Networking Media: Use by Field Posts | 95 |
| Seven | Social Networking Media: Factors to Consider in Their Use | 113 |

## Part IV   Cultural and Educational Programs

| | | |
|---|---|---|
| Eight | American Cultural Programs | 129 |
| Nine | Centers, Libraries, and Other "American Spaces" | 145 |
| Ten | Educational Exchanges | 161 |

## Part V   Pentagon Communications

| Eleven | Defense Department Communications: Changing Role | 181 |
| Twelve | Defense Department Communications Abroad Compared with Public Diplomacy | 201 |

## Part VI   Conclusion

| Thirteen | Changes and Enduring Principles | 221 |

Notes  235

Index  269

# ACKNOWLEDGMENTS

Many people have helped with the research that is cited in this book.

First, I want to thank the students in the graduate seminar on American public diplomacy that I taught for several years at the Fletcher School of Law and Diplomacy of Tufts University. The term papers they wrote were superb and made significant contributions to our understanding of the actual practice of public diplomacy (PD) because they interviewed American PD professionals currently serving at US embassies in many countries about their work. Although I helped with contacts, their original work made their papers unique and valuable. Some were later published, but with the authors' permissions, I have cited many that have not been published. I have quoted dozens of them and their names appear in the endnotes. I am grateful to these students and to all of my students at Fletcher, including my foreign students, who made teaching there intellectually rewarding.

Numerous Foreign Service Officers (FSOs) now working in public diplomacy at the State Department gave me their time to answer my questions related to my study of public diplomacy. Among them were Ambassadors Adam Ereli, Alberto Fernandez, and Rich Schmierer, as well as Walter Douglas, Pat Kabra, Haynes Mahoney, Matt Lussenhop, Duncan MacInnes, Michelle Rubayda, Rick Ruth, Kathy VandeVate, and Donna Winton.

I owe a special debt of gratitude to two currently serving FSOs who are public diplomacy professionals, Bridget Gersten and Elise Crane. Dr. Bridget Gersten is a mid-career FSO who served in several different public diplomacy positions since 1999. She was the public affairs officer at the US embassy in Saudi Arabia and the US mission in Vladivostok, Russia; the information officer (IO) at the US embassy in Bogota Colombia; the assistant IO in Moscow; and a senior PD advisor at the US embassy in Kabul, Afghanistan. She was also a senior PD officer at the State Department. She reviewed the entire book manuscript. Elise Crane is also a PD officer who in 2011–2013 served as an IO at the US embassy in Uganda, and is preparing for her next assignment in Bogota, Colombia. She reviewed several key chapters of the book. Both of them helped me by checking facts and making sure my information was up-to-date. As experienced and successful field officers, their advice was invaluable but they are in no way responsible for any errors of fact or interpretation that may remain in the book. I also want to thank Ambassador Brian Carlson, a retired PD officer, and Tim Niblock, a currently serving PD FSO, both of whom have had extensive experience with the Pentagon, and who reviewed and commented on my chapters on the Department of Defense (DOD). They also have no responsibility for any remaining errors in the book.

In recent years I have also benefited from discussions with many friends and colleagues who have had professional experience in public diplomacy and whose wisdom has helped inform this book, although they are by no means responsible for its contents. Among them are: Mike Anderson, Len Baldyga, Kathy Brion, Jim Bullock, Mike Canning, Bill Cavness, Steve Chaplin, Fred Coffey, Bob Coonrod, Jeremy Curtin, Evelyn Early, Bruce Gregory, Bob Heath, Alan Heil, Bud Jacobs, Joe Johnson, Bill Kiehl, Peter Kovach, Pat Kushlis, Michelle Kwan, Bill Maurer, Sherry Mueller, Donna Oglesby, Marjorie Ransom, Chris Ross, McKinney Russell, Katie Schaeffer, Mike Schneider, Stan Silverman, Pam Smith, Dan Sreebny, and Tom Tuch.

Finally I am grateful to Professors Philip Seib and Kathy Fitzpatrick, the editors of the Palgrave Macmillan Series in Global Public Diplomacy, for their unwavering encouragement to me in this project, and their support over the years for my efforts to help analyze the practice of public diplomacy. They could not have been more helpful.

# ABBREVIATIONS

| | |
|---|---|
| ACAO | Assistant Cultural Affairs Officer |
| AFRTS | Armed Forces Radio and Television Services |
| AIO | Assistant Information Officer |
| BBG | Broadcasting Board of Governors |
| CAO | Cultural Affairs Officer |
| COIN | counterinsurgency |
| CPI | Committee on Public Information |
| DCM | Deputy Chief of Mission |
| DOD | Department of Defense, also called "the Pentagon" |
| DVC | Digital Video Conference |
| ECA | Educational and Cultural Affairs bureau, Department of State |
| FIS | Foreign Information Service |
| FSI | Foreign Service Institute |
| FSO | Foreign Service Officer |
| GWOT | Global War on Terror |
| IIP | International Information Programs bureau, Department of State |
| IMET | International Military Education and Training program |
| IO | Information Officer |
| IVLP | International Visitor Leadership Program |
| LES | Locally Employed Staff, formerly called Foreign Service Nationals (FSNs) |
| MSP | Mission Strategic Plan |
| NGO | Nongovernmental Organization |
| OIG | Office of Inspector General, Department of State |
| OSS | Office of Strategic Services |
| PA | Public Affairs |

| | |
|---|---|
| PAO | Public Affairs Officer, the senior PD officer at a US diplomatic mission |
| PAS | Public Affairs Section at a US diplomatic mission |
| PD | public diplomacy |
| PSYOP | Psychological operations |
| QDRR | Quadrennial Defense Review Report |
| RELO | Regional English Language Officer |
| RRU | Rapid Response Unit |
| UN | United Nations |
| USG | United States Government |
| USIA | US Information Agency, created in 1953, abolished in 1999 |

# Introduction

This book is about public diplomacy as it is practiced by American diplomats at US embassies around the world. The focus is intentionally on field operations, since that is an aspect of public diplomacy that has been neglected in the literature. The book shows how American diplomats cope with the challenges of criticism—and correct misunderstandings—that foreign publics have about US foreign policy and American society and culture. It discusses the techniques they use to engage in a dialogue with people from different cultures. Some of these techniques are new, designed to cope with new technologies, and some are older and have been tested over time. The book it takes the reader inside American embassies to show how public diplomacy specialists work with ambassadors and other American officials as part of a team representing the United States.

This book is based on extensive original field research into actual cases of public diplomacy operations as conducted abroad in the twenty-first century. Much of the research has never been published before. The book uses empirical evidence to formulate written and unwritten rules that have been followed by experts and it highlights their best practices. It is also informed by the author's personal experience of thirty-one years in the Foreign Service, including two ambassadorships and several tours as public affairs officer (PAO) or assistant PAO. This book will therefore be useful for students and scholars of US policy, diplomacy, and international relations, as well as foreign service officers (FSOs) and prospective FSOs.

A few books and articles have been written about field practices, but they have mostly been narrow in scope. Some books focus on one geographic area.[1] Two recent books have presented case studies of field operations but they have necessarily been selective in which countries they have analyzed, but they have not tried to present a comprehensive picture.[2] The book by Hans Tuch, written in the heyday of US Information Agency (USIA) and updated in 1990, remains a classic study of field operations and is still unique in the literature, but it has become dated because much has happened since it was published.[3] Nicholas Cull's books about the USIA are excellent histories up to the end of the twentieth century.[4] This book's focus is on current practices but it provides some brief historical background that is relevant today and shows how some past practices have been adapted to fit modern conditions. The book makes appropriate references to publications in the existing literature but it is best seen as a complement to that literature rather than as a recapitulation of what has been published.

This book gives special attention to several special concerns that have arisen in the twenty-first century confronting public diplomacy practitioners trying to do their jobs at field posts around the world.

One is the dramatic growth globally of social networking media. On the one hand this development presents a serious problem for American officials as they try to deal with the cacophony of international communications that now exists 24/7, much of which is either hostile to the United States or misinformed about America and needs to be addressed. On the other hand since these new communication channels have become widely used in some countries especially by the youth, they offer new opportunities to reach out to the public using the means the public prefers.

A second concern for public diplomacy professionals today is security. The recent growth of terrorism directed at American embassies and other official installations has led to new security measures at these installations that did not exist in the past, and that hamper access by US officials to the public. Traditional public diplomacy depended heavily on personal contact and on free access to our libraries, centers and offices, but in some countries these contacts are now much more difficult. American diplomats are struggling to deal with this problem.

A third new development is the significant expansion since 9/11/2001 by the Department of Defense (DOD) into efforts to communicate directly with foreign publics. Before the 9/11 terrorist attack on America, DOD confined its communication programs to Americans and the only significant communication with foreign audiences were the psychological operations directed at the enemy during wartime. Now, starting with the wars in Iraq and Afghanistan, and the Global War on Terrorism, the Pentagon has expanded its communications to civilian noncombatant populations in many countries. Some of this effort looks like the information work that civilian public diplomacy professionals have been doing for decades.

This book devotes special chapters to each of these new challenges to show how public diplomacy officers have faced them and come up with techniques—some new, some old—to deal with the new situations.

One of the difficulties of writing a comprehensive book about field operations—and a reason why such writing is rare—is that every post is different. Indeed, one major point of this book is every American diplomat who carries out public diplomacy programs in an embassy abroad must start with the premise that his or her working environment is unique and must be understood before any activities can be undertaken. The diplomat must know what issues related to US interests are of concern to the local public, and what the public thinks about them. He or she must know how best to communicate with them using the most suitable local means. Local restrictions on the diplomat's communication efforts, caused by the host government or by local social norms and cultural practices, must be taken into account before programs can be developed and implemented. That process is explored in this book.

The definition of public diplomacy used in this book is that it is a function of a government, in this case the US national government. That definition has been in use in the United States since 1966 and is the one that has always been used by American officials. In recent years, some scholars have argued that the proliferation of cross-border communication has been so significant that non-state actors must be included in the definition of public diplomacy. No one is more aware of the huge amount of communication across borders by non-state actors than the public diplomacy professionals in the US government. They must cope with comments and assertions about US policy and American society and culture that appear in communications 24/7 and are intentionally or unintentionally incorrect. But they do not call communications by non-state actors public diplomacy, a term that seems more suited to the communications efforts of official government agencies. The rest is simply "private communication" that comes in many varieties, serving many different purposes.

The first two chapters of the book set the stage by reviewing briefly the fundamental philosophy and legal underpinnings behind public diplomacy, and showing how PD professionals fit into the Foreign Service. The book then analyzes the role of the public affairs officer (PAO) at the embassy, the person who is in charge of the American official public diplomacy program in that country, and the important role that personal networking and personal contact play in the success of that program. Three chapters then focus on the work of the information officer (IO), who is responsible for "fast media"—the traditional media outlets like newspapers, radio and television—and for the new social networking media. The next three chapters analyze the work of the Cultural Affairs Officer (CAO), in developing cultural programs in country. Two chapters then deal with an issue that has become very important since 9/11, namely the rapidly growing international communication efforts in support of our conventional wars and our unconventional war on terror. These two chapters are devoted to the efforts by the DOD to communicate with foreign publics, that have expanded significantly since 9/11, and that to some extent overlap with the work of the public diplomacy civilians at the State Department.

Note that these chapters do not deal with international civilian broadcasting because the Voice of America and other services that are now managed by the Broadcasting Board of Governors have nothing directly to do with the field work of the public diplomacy professionals who are working at our embassies abroad.

The final chapter briefly summarizes some main points and indicates where the profession may be headed in the future. It concludes by offering thirteen principles that have been derived from best practices in PD field operations.

# PART I

*The Context*

CHAPTER ONE

# Legacy: Public Diplomacy's Philosophy and Legal Basis

## The Concept of Public Diplomacy

The term "public diplomacy" was coined in 1966, but as far back as 1776 American leaders were thinking about the concept. America's forefathers believed then that foreign public opinion was important and that American views are not always well understood, so it serves our interests to make an open explanation to foreign audiences of our country's views. The Declaration of Independence therefore stated in its Preamble:

> When in the Course of human events it becomes necessary for one people to dissolve the political bands which have connected them with another...a decent respect to the opinions of mankind requires that they should declare the causes which impel them to the separation.

Then the first paragraph of the Declaration, before presenting a long list of grievances, offers this explanation of its purpose:

> The history of the present King of Great Britain is a history of repeated injuries and usurpations, all having in direct object the establishment of an absolute Tyranny over these States. To prove this, let Facts be submitted to a candid world.

The idea of explaining ourselves to the world remains in the twenty-first century as the fundamental rationale for public diplomacy. Before World War I the principle was only a declaration, without institutional expression. And until then it only applied to foreign policy explication, but after that the idea expanded to include an understanding of American society and culture, and later the promotion of mutual understanding.

America's focus on public diplomacy has always has been sporadic. Concern about wars and foreign threats to the United States has been the main stimulus attracting attention to the need to employ public diplomacy to communicate with foreign publics and influence foreign public opinion. World Wars I and II, the Cold War and then the twenty-first–century Global War on Terrorism (GWOT) all focused American interest on public diplomacy, but after these crises seemed to subside, that interest declined.[1]

Institutionalization of public diplomacy began under Woodrow Wilson who established a Committee on Public Information (CPI) led by George Creel. The CPI was the US government's first formal government agency for providing information to foreign publics. It initially began as a program to inform domestic opinion but, starting in 1917, it was given a mandate to address foreign audiences as well. Creel called it "the fight for the mind of mankind." The CPI had a foreign section which produced news and picture services, and arranged for foreign journalists to visit the United States. It also disseminated Hollywood films abroad. Those were clearly public diplomacy projects, antecedents of today's programs. But the CPI ended in 1919 when the war ended; Congress withdrew funding, saying it had been too partisan.[2]

In 1935, motivated by the growing threat from Germany and a desire to counter Nazi propaganda against the United States, the State Department began to transmit a daily bulletin of news to overseas posts. In July 1938, the State Department created the Division of Cultural Relations that worked with American academics to provide cultural programs to Latin America. In 1940, President Franklin D. Roosevelt appointed Nelson Rockefeller as Coordinator for Commercial and of Cultural Relations, renamed in 1941 as the Coordinator of Inter-American Affairs. His staff opened libraries and bi-national centers and established exchange programs, sponsored traveling musical presentations and art exhibitions, and published a magazine. Roosevelt's prewar public diplomacy was therefore focused on Latin America.[3]

But in 1941, while the United States was at war with Germany, President Roosevelt broadened the concept. He established the Office of the Coordinator of Information (later the Office of Strategic Services, OSS), that had a "Foreign Information Service" (FIS). Roosevelt appointed Robert Sherwood, his speechwriter and a playwright, to head FIS. The new FIS opened ten information offices around the world, each called the US Information Service (USIS), a name that was used throughout the rest of the century. In February 1942, three months after the Japanese attack on Pearl Harbor, the State Department started a broadcast service called Voices of America, soon renamed The Voice of America (VOA). It began with the announcement, "Today and every day from now on we shall be speaking to you about America and the War. Here in America we receive news from all over the world. This news may be favorable or unfavorable. Every day we shall bring you the news—The Truth."[4] This concept became a revered VOA principle and is fundamental to the practice of public diplomacy today.

In June 1942, Roosevelt created the Office of War Information (OWI), and made the FIS its overseas arm. OWI operated VOA and an expanding chain of information centers around the world. It also published and distributed magazines and books abroad and worked with Hollywood to produce and distribute films abroad. It worked with the US military to help defeat the enemy by providing leaflet drops and broadcasts calling for the Germans to surrender. In 1944, OWI's Division of Cultural Relations moved into the State Department. By then State's International Information Division was distributing American media products around the world, including films, newsreels, and magazines such as *Reader's Digest*. During the war, OWI set up field posts abroad, first in London, then in liberated cities, so that by the end of the war in 1945 they existed in forty countries. Also, by 1945 OWI was distributing a news service product of 100,000 words each day to sixty US diplomatic posts worldwide.[5]

### *Postwar Organization*

President Truman abolished OWI in 1945 at the end of the war, but transferred its overseas information activities including information, broadcasting and exchanges to the Department of State. Psychological operations continued separately under the Department of Defense. That year, Congress authorized spending for educational exchanges, when Senator J. William Fulbright, a Rhodes Scholar, proposed that proceeds from the sale of surplus property be used to fund educational exchange programs. In August 1946, Congress passed an act to amend the Surplus Property Act of 1944, authorizing expanded educational exchanges. The first agreement was signed in November 1947 to bring Chinese students to the United States, and the first American "Fulbrighters" left for Burma in the fall of 1948.[6]

The Cold War that began in 1946 revived interest in what was later called public diplomacy, but Americans wanted to distinguish it from the negative connotations of "propaganda" being deceptive, as employed by Nazi Germany. In April 1947, Secretary of State George C. Marshall expressed the philosophical basis of today's public diplomacy when he urged the use of information to counter the Soviet Union. He said: "The use of propaganda as such is contrary to our generally accepted precepts of democracy and to statements I have made. Another consideration is that we could be playing into the hands of the Soviets who are masters in the use of such techniques. Our sole aim in our overseas information program must be to present nothing but the truth, in a completely factual and unbiased manner. Only by this means can we justify the procedure and establish a reputation before the world of integrity of action."[7]

As the Cold War intensified, Congress saw this as reason to pass new legislation supporting public diplomacy. In January 1948, Truman signed Public Law 402, informally called the Smith-Mundt Act. It has been amended since 1948, but it remains today the most important legislative foundation for the US government's entire public diplomacy program. Its purpose was "to enable the Government of the United States to promote a better understanding of the United States in other countries, and to increase mutual understanding between the people of the United States and the people of other countries. Among the means to be used in achieving these objectives are... an information service to disseminate abroad information about the United States, its people, and policies promulgated by the Congress, the President, the Secretary of State and other responsible officials of Government having to do with matters affecting foreign affairs." The Act said that information dissemination should be accomplished "through press, publications, radio, motion pictures, and other information media, and through information centers abroad."[8]

In 1972 and 1985, Congress amended Smith-Mundt explicitly to ban domestic distribution of materials produced for foreign audiences. This ban became its one controversial provision, challenged on the grounds that it was anachronous and unenforceable because it is impossible to separate domestic from foreign information, especially now that new information technology has made international communication so easy that almost anything that is done for public diplomacy purposes is accessible to Americans now.[9] In practice, no one was ever prosecuted for violating the ban, and although over the years it was of concern to lawyers in Washington, it has not affected the daily operations of public diplomacy practitioners abroad who tended to regard it as irrelevant to their daily tasks and not an important issue to worry about.

In 2012 Congress passed the Smith-Mundt Modernization Act that basically lifted the domestic dissemination ban in Smith-Mundt, and in January 2013, President Obama signed it into law. The act now permits Americans to view taxpayer funded material intended for audiences abroad and allows the dissemination of that material inside the United States. However it retains the original provision in Smith-Mundt that emphasizes that such dissemination must not compete with existing domestic media.[10]

## USIA 1953–1999

Under President Eisenhower, Congress in 1953 created the US Information Agency (USIA), a foreign affairs agency that managed America's public diplomacy until 1999.

Eisenhower's Secretary of State John Foster Dulles disdained consideration of public opinion in foreign policy and he wanted to move information, education and culture out of State so he could focus on traditional diplomacy.[11] Senator Bourke Hickenlooper (R-IA), chair of the Senate Foreign Relations Committee, also supported the idea of a separate agency, but for different reasons. He explained that the goals of an effective overseas information program "could hardly be met within the outlines of a cautious, tradition-bound, bureaucratic foreign office."[12] (Hickenlooper's comment has found an echo half a century later in criticism of the decision to merge USIA back into the State Department.) Senator J. William Fulbright of Arkansas, a prominent Democrat on that committee (and later chairman, 1959–74) who had sponsored the exchange program that carried his name, agreed to a separate, new agency provided it only dealt with information and did not include the educational and cultural functions he cared so much about. He wanted them kept instead at State, and the new law did that. This anomaly mattered little to USIA's public diplomacy professionals working at embassies, however, because they handled education and culture along with information matters. In 1979, under the Carter administration, these programs were transferred to USIA headquarters.

In 1961, Congress passed the Mutual Educational and Cultural Exchange Act of 1961, informally called the Fulbright-Hayes Act. This act consolidated existing programs, added initiatives in book translations, exhibitions and American studies, and provided for new cultural centers abroad.[13] It said its purpose was "to strengthen the ties that unite us with other nations by demonstrating the educational, cultural interests, developments and achievements of the people of the United States and other nations, and the contributions being made toward a more peaceful and fruitful life for the people throughout the world; to promote international cooperation for educational and cultural advancement; and thus to assist in the development of friendly, sympathetic and peaceful relations between the United States and the other countries of the world." It authorized funding for educational exchanges for study, research, instruction, and other educational activities, and it authorized cultural exchanges in music, arts, sports, or any other form of cultural expression. It also authorized exchanges of books, periodicals, and translations, the establishment of cultural centers, and the promotion of research and language training.[14]

In these early years, various terms were applied to the US government's communication efforts abroad, including international communication, educational and cultural exchange, or both. Then in 1966, Edmund Gullion, a retired foreign service officer (FSO) who was the dean of the Fletcher School at Tufts University, proposed the term "public diplomacy" and it stuck. Although Gullion's original formulation did not confine the term to activities by the government, US officials have consistently used it to mean only the US government's efforts to communicate with foreign audiences.[15] Note also that the public diplomacy professionals who serve abroad work in the "public affairs section" of the embassy, that is headed by a "Public Affairs Officer," although when the term "public affairs" is used in Washington it usually refers to the function of communicating to an American domestic audience.

Professor Joseph Nye added to the discussion by coining the term "soft power," which he defined as "the ability to shape the preferences of others" by attraction rather than coercion, which is the use of "hard power." He said that soft power "rests on a country's culture, values and policies."[16] Soft power is not the same as public diplomacy but the two are connected. To the extent that America's culture, values and policies are admired and respected abroad, they are beneficial to the United States and support American public diplomacy. Public diplomacy can benefit by communicating their positive aspects to foreign audiences.

But to the extent that these attributes are seen in a negative light, they are harmful to the US and American public diplomacy needs to try to correct any misunderstandings about them and show them in a more positive light.

## Programs

Since the middle of the twentieth century, public diplomacy professionals working at embassies under USIA Washington's direction had a variety of resources and program possibilities. Some of these programs have been replaced or modified over the years but their basic public diplomacy purposes have remained to this day.

### *Wireless File*

The "Wireless File" was, throughout the twentieth century, the most important fast media instrument in the public diplomacy officer's toolkit. Established in 1935 as series of radio-teletype bulletins, and transmitted from Washington by radio, it was received on teleprinters in US diplomatic missions around the world. An unclassified daily bulletin, it included texts of policy statements by US officials, plus excerpts from American newspaper editorials and reports useful to PAOs, notices of programs and some cleared commentaries. Ambassadors and PAOs consistently rated the Wireless File as the most useful of all tools. PAOs selected portions of the File and sent them to local media for possible placement, editing some pieces before they were distributed. They used official US texts and officially authorized comment to help correct distortions and provide context, especially for local editors who only had wire service reports of US policies that were incomplete and possibly misleading. The Wireless File was a main source of information for the ambassador and other embassy officers. In the 1950s, the Wireless File was split into five geographic versions that allowed for some customizing. French and Spanish versions were added later, then Arabic, Russian and Chinese. In 1994, USIA added thematic and geographic sections written by special teams. Editors in the central newsroom and in the regional branches provided feature items to lighten the load of serious policy statements. The File also developed the practice of occasional exclusives to local newspapers of op-eds by senior US officials.[17] In the 1990s, it was renamed "Washington File" and although it was subsequently discontinued, its basic type of content can be found today on the Internet and on Embassy websites or social media so that users can readily access this information in a timely manner.

Although the wireless file no longer exists, the concept behind it remains. In the twenty-first century, texts very similar to the types that used to be delivered by the Wireless File, now arrive at the embassy electronically, and although the local editor and other embassy contacts may receive them at the same time, the PAO and other embassy officers can make use of them with their contacts as talking points and in other ways, including via SMS alerts, because the local media may not have published the material.

### Printed Materials and Film

During the twentieth century, before the age of the Internet, USIA produced a wide variety of printed materials including pamphlets, reports, books, posters, and paper shows (small traveling exhibits). These included sets of materials with fundamental information on various aspects of US society and culture, and practical material such as how to study in the United States. Most of these were translated into the several foreign languages. Some of the pamphlets were for specific purposes, such as for students and visitors coming to the United States, or for occasions such as the death of President Kennedy. Usually these publications were given away free, and attempts to sell them usually were not very successful. In the 1960s and 1970s, USIA maintained its own printing plants in Beirut, Mexico City, and Manila, with a smaller plant in Vienna to serve European posts. Beirut shut down in 1976 because of the Lebanese civil war and Mexico City shut down in 1985 because of an earthquake, while Manila is still operating.[18]

USIA also created and produced a variety of magazines and journals and used them as major public diplomacy instruments. They contained articles from diverse sources: some were written by USIA editorial staff, some by outside experts commissioned to write on a specific topic, and others were reprinted from publications. By 1960, USIA produced 57 magazines in 20 languages worldwide, with a total circulation of 110 million copies. More than two-thirds were produced abroad. Some were global publications, edited in Washington, printed in special US government printing plants located abroad, and intended for worldwide distribution. They were sent to PAOs abroad, who gave them to their audiences, usually free of charge. *Economic Impact* started in 1973 when it seemed that economic issues were especially important to the US national interest; it continued into the 1990s. *English Teaching Forum* was a professional publication for English teachers, with articles from both American and international contributors. *Problems of Communism* was a small-circulation magazine about the Soviet Union, China, and other Communist countries, whose scholarly articles were written by experts. Published bimonthly in 20,000 copies starting in 1952, it appeared in English and in select foreign languages. *Problems of Communism* continued to be published until 1992, when it was discontinued because of the fall of the USSR. The quarterly journal *Dialogue* contained reprints from reputable American journals and was published for intellectuals in several languages.[19]

There were several one-country and regional publications. In India, *American Reporter*, a newspaper written for an elite audience, was one of the first magazines. Later, the public diplomacy staff at the US embassy produced a glossy popular magazine called *Span*, similar to *Life*, which was very successful. Now, SPAN is available online and also available for viewing in Hindi and Urdu. In Serbia, during the Cold War, USIA printed a general interest magazine in Serbo-Croatian called *Pregled* ("Overview").[20] *Markin Parikama* (American Panorama), a magazine in Bengali for East Pakistan, had a circulation of 30,000, the largest paid-circulation in East Pakistan at the time.[21] From the 1950s until the 1967 war, USIA produced al *Hayat fi Amrika* in Arabic, and then it began publishing *al Majal*, in Arabic.[22]

Among the most successful one-country publications was *Amerika*, a Russian-language picture magazine that was edited and produced by USIA and distributed in the Soviet Union during the Cold War, when Moscow strictly controlled all incoming information. Published monthly from 1944 until 1994, the magazine did not deal directly with foreign policy, but focused instead on describing life in the United States. It relied on images as much as words because the Soviet public tended to distrust words, so simply showing photographs of well-stocked super markets sent a message to an audience used to scarcity of consumer goods. It responded to Soviet propaganda, albeit indirectly. The US embassy sent copies of *Amerika* to elite Soviet audiences, and it was at times distributed under a Washington-Moscow agreement that allowed in 50,000 copies that reached an estimated one million readers. The agreement brought Moscow's *Soviet Life* to the United States where it was largely ignored by the American public because it was not interesting.[23]

In the twenty-first century, embassy public affairs sections still use the basic concept of distributing texts of various kinds, but they now receive them electronically and either sends them on in that form or they print them locally if a printed format is useful.

USIA for decades supplied field posts overseas with a variety of documentary films, some screened at posts using 16mm projectors. In its heyday, USIA films reached 500,000 people each year and USIA TV programs were seen in 47 countries.[24] It also produced award-winning films including "Night of the Dragon," a tough film supporting the Vietnam war effort narrated by Charlton Heston, and the Oscar-winning *Nine from Little Rock*. Cultural diplomacy programs sent abroad included the New York City Ballet, the Philadelphia Orchestra, Louis Armstrong, and Duke Ellington. Exhibits sent abroad included the moon rock and a "space lab," and the Moscow exhibit arranged under a US-Soviet agreement that featured the famous Nixon-Khruschev "kitchen debate."

In the 1960s, a PD officer might show an American film in a remote village using a 16mm projector on a mobile van. This practice has disappeared but the same concept applies to a PD officer in the twenty-first century who uses YouTube to communicate with the local audience. In both cases, the PD officer has made use of a visual aid, and selected its content and means of delivery based on local interests and practices at the time. Only the means of delivery changed.

These activities were unclassified and open, not to be confused with the clandestine propaganda activities that the Central Intelligence Agency has carried out, and that USIA directors took pains to explain were completely different from public diplomacy.[25]

## Budgets and Staffing

USIA's peak years were in the 1960s, during the height of the Cold War. In 1967, USIA had 12,500 employees, of whom 7,500 were working in embassies abroad. After that, the numbers slowly declined. One decade later, USIA had 8,700 employees including 4,700 working abroad. Another decade later there was some increase in the budget and staffing (9,500 employees, 4,000 abroad) largely due to the efforts of USIA director Charles Wick, a close friend of President Reagan's. Under Wick's leadership, the USIA budget increased 1981–84 from $201.9 million to $659.7 million and that became the high water mark of USIA funding. But in the 1990s, the size of USIA declined rapidly, reaching 8,000 employees (3,500 abroad) in 1995 and 6,600 employees (2,700 abroad) in 1999, USIA's last year.[26]

The rapid decline during the 1990s was due to several factors. The end of the Cold War diminished Congressional and public support during the Clinton administration for public diplomacy. The "peace dividend" was supposed to mean budget cuts—and they hurt USIA. For half a century the confrontation with the Soviet Union had been a major motivating factor persuading presidents and members of Congress to devote time, energy and funding to public diplomacy. In the absence of that perceived major threat from the Soviet Union, it was difficult to convince the political leadership in Washington—at either end of Pennsylvania Avenue—that public diplomacy was necessary.

The administration and Congress saw the end of the Cold War as the end of major challenges facing America, but the practitioners saw the period as just the beginning of a new phase in which public diplomacy remained a vital tool to protect our national interests. Many of the practitioners felt that Washington's intense focus on countering Moscow and the threat of international Communism, while necessary, had been a distortion from a more balanced approach to the world in which many other issues were important locally and therefore affected bilateral relationships with the United States and should be addressed more effectively. They hoped that with the end of the Cold War, a more nuanced approach to foreign affairs would emerge, that would take into account local issues and views as they affected US interests. They felt the need for PD programs and people was increasing rather than disappearing. So they were dismayed to see the Congress decrease funding and personnel levels for public diplomacy, on the assumption that it was only vital because of the Cold War.[27]

Some members of Congress also thought that the new technology would eliminate the need to have so many American personnel working at embassies abroad. They thought that with the Internet in addition to faxes and better phones, Washington could send information out around the world without much help from people on the ground. This view reflected a fundamental misunderstanding of public diplomacy and the central importance of personal contact in doing it successfully, which practitioners were all well aware of.

In fact, as its practitioners knew, the information revolution that accelerated in the 1990s with the spread of satellite television and the Internet everywhere actually made US public diplomacy more necessary than ever, since it created a more competitive information environment in which American officials had to operate. The new technology did of course help spread American ideas and views across borders, but it also helped spread misinformation and criticism, whether based on ignorance or deliberate hostility. Public opinion in many countries around the world was becoming even more of a factor in influencing public policies toward the United States, as the new technologies helped more people express themselves and gave them access to information they did not have before.

## Programming Changes

The decline in budgets and staffing negatively affected programming. Because of the post–Cold War cuts, cultural presentations and exhibits that had been so important during the Cold War almost disappeared altogether by the late 1990s.[28] Also, all of the Washington-based US government magazines and journals, plus most of the local-focus ones (except *Span*) were discontinued in 1994 as a result of budget cuts at USIA, when the entire magazine division was shut down.[29] For example, the Arabic language *al Majal* magazine was eliminated in 1994 as part of Vice President Al Gore's "reinventing government" effort. *America Illustrated* produced for the USSR was eliminated because the Cold War was over and many Western commercial publications were available in the former Soviet Union, and that helped lead to the elimination of other magazines, now thought to be unnecessary. In the 1990s, *Problems of Communism* came to an end and was replaced by a new publication *Problems of Post-Communism*, edited at George Washington University and distributed by a New York publishing firm, but that did not survive. The publications cancelled in the 1990s were replaced only to some extent by electronic journals (see chapter six).[30] In 2002, the George W. Bush administration launched a new Arabic language magazine for the Arab world called *Hi*, but it was not successful. Posts in Arab countries tried to sell it at a subsidized price, but few bought it. Because it failed to attract a readership, *Hi* was later cancelled.

Most of those products in those formats are gone today, but the basic concept behind them remains in the many electronic products that public diplomacy professionals produce in the twenty-first century. The concept is essentially that public diplomacy professionals working at embassies abroad can make use of US-made communication vehicles, to convey to foreign audiences an accurate picture of US foreign policy and of American society, culture, and values. These communication vehicles can be created by government employees or by private American companies, but their selection and use is basically controlled by public diplomacy professionals working at US embassies abroad, because those who know the local audience well and who know how to design a package of programs to reach them.

## The Merger

A major change in the organizational structure of American public diplomacy took place in 1999 when Congress passed legislation abolishing USIA and merging most of its functions into the State Department. Part of the reasoning behind this decision was the perception in Congress that with end of the Cold War, public diplomacy was no longer necessary. But there were other factors as well. Some members of Congress and the administration believed that public diplomacy should be brought closer to the policy makers in the State Department, and a merger would do that. A leading proponent of a merger was Senator Jesse Helms, the powerful chairman of the Senate Foreign Relations Committee. Secretary of State Madeleine Albright was not a strong defender of public diplomacy, and she had other issues with Senator Helms that she considered more important. She reportedly agreed to the merger in a deal with Senator Helms to overcome his objections to a Chemical Test Ban Treaty and to achieve funding for the US contribution to the United Nations (UN), both of which he opposed.[31]

President Clinton signed a law implementing the USIA-State merger, and it took effect on October 1, 1999.[32]

USIA-State negotiations over the details of the merger lasted from 1997 to 1999, and USIA professionals were not pleased with the result. Many were uncomfortable with the fact that USIA's regional bureaus that directly supervised PD field posts were abolished, as was USIA's management bureau. These functions were absorbed into the existing State structure. Moreover, as one USIA participant noted, "great damage had been done to USIA confidence that a new State environment might bring public diplomacy closer to the heart of foreign policymaking."[33] USIA Director Joe Duffy believed that Secretary Albright's support for the merger was motivated to support the merger in order to augment the State Department budget. But he and others at USIA apparently saw that it would not be possible to stop the merger entirely so they worked to mitigate some of its worst consequences.[34]

The most significant accomplishment of the USIA negotiators was that a new Bureau for Education and Culture Affairs (ECA) was created, headed by an Assistant Secretary, and that funding for these matters was walled off in the State Department budget so it could not be used for other purposes. Another new bureau, for International Information Programs (IIP), was created to manage media matters, but it was only headed by a "coordinator," not an assistant secretary, so it had less bureaucratic clout. The personnel from USIA's regional bureaus were scattered around State's regional bureaus where they reported to the regional assistant secretaries, and other USIA personnel, such as administrative and public opinion specialists, were assigned to the relevant State bureaus. A new position of Undersecretary of State for Public Diplomacy and Public Affairs was created, that was the most senior PD position in the State Department, but this position had none of that authority of the former USIA Director. The USIA director had had direct supervisory responsibility over the career PD professionals at USIA, and ultimately controlled all public diplomacy budgets and personnel assignments. This new undersecretary did not have any of that authority. Moreover, the new undersecretary reported to the Secretary of State and had no direct access to the president.

The new law put international broadcasting under an autonomous agency, the Broadcasting Board of Governors (BBG), which made it functionally independent of the State Department. The VOA had been under the supervision of USIA since USIA was created in 1953, but now it was under the Broadcasting Board of Governors. This arrangement was worked out in a separate deal between the Congress, the White House and the Secretary of State.[35] The BBG has a nine-member board of governors, appointed by the president with the consent of Congress, that includes four Democrats and four Republicans with a ninth seat reserved for the representative of the Secretary of State. In practice, the BBG acts quite independently of the State Department and the new Undersecretary for Public Diplomacy and Public Affairs, so that the link between PD professionals and broadcasting that existed under USIA was broken. They have no real influence in practice over VOA or the other US government broadcast channels.

The vast majority of public diplomacy practitioners who served with USIA regard the merger as a mistake. One of them put it this way: "The dismantling of the USIA, the dissolution of its personnel and functions with the State Department bureaucracy, and the creation of a BBG responsible to no one (not the Secretary of State, not even the President) is a compound and nearly fatal blow to the ability of the United States to project a global information strategy."[36] A survey of over 200 former senior USIA officials, many of whom served at State after the merger, found that only 4 percent thought the dissolution of USIA was a good idea, while 79 percent rated the merger into

State as a "disaster." A majority of 91 percent said the merger did not enhance USIA's advisement role.[37] This despite the fact that enhancing the advisement role had been major reason used to justify the merger.[38] (The personnel consequences of the merger are discussed in chapter two.)

In the first years after the merger, some veterans of USIA, including several former directors, argued that the organization should be revived in its original form as an independent agency, because "shutting down USIA has been a major mistake."[39] Even Robert Gates, when he was secretary of defense, regretted the merger, saying, "the U.S. Information Agency was abolished as an independent entity, split into pieces, and many of its capabilities folded into a small corner of the State Department."[40]

However, there was little or no interest in Congress or the administration to undo the merger legislation. Senator Richard Lugar, a powerful voice on Capitol Hill, put it succinctly in one of his reports: "Re-creating USIA, or something similar, is neither feasible nor affordable in today's budgetary environment."[41] That has meant the end of the discussion.

## Conclusion

During the 1970s and 1980s, USIA had abundant budgets and large staffs all over the world. In the 1990s, the size of its budgets and staffs declined precipitously due to several concurrent factors. The belief that there should be a "peace dividend" in substantial financial savings because the Cold War was over, and the misconception that the information revolution would take the place of public diplomacy professionals posted at embassies abroad, plus the Clinton administration's agreement to abolish USIA, all undermined the effectiveness of our public diplomacy effort.

By the end of the twentieth century, many print media items that had been the mainstay of USIA efforts were cancelled and cultural presentations and exhibit programs almost disappeared entirely. Professional public diplomacy officers were apprehensive that the changes, including the downsizing and the merger, would do harm to United States interests because the basic rationale for public diplomacy programs had not gone away with the end of the Cold War. During the first decade of the twenty-first century, many media items became electronic vehicles so in effect they survived in a different form (see chapters that follow), but the cultural and exhibit programs never fully recovered. And the culture of the USIA, as a small but cohesive and highly focused group of professional specialists in public diplomacy, was diluted in the larger and more bureaucratic State Department.

At the same time, a legacy for twenty-first-century public diplomacy practitioners remains from the experiences of the twentieth century, in the principles and concepts that motivated them then. The following chapters will discuss and analyze how the practice of public diplomacy has developed in the current century, and will show how basic approaches and rationales have remained the same, although the forms and many of the means of communication have changed. As we shall see, many of the basic operational principles followed by professional PD officers working at embassies abroad, that have stood the test of time, have been maintained and enhanced.

CHAPTER TWO

# Public Diplomacy Professionals

This chapter analyzes the role of public diplomacy professionals working abroad in the context of an American embassy.

## The Foreign Service

American Foreign Services Officers (FSOs) at the Department of State are divided into five career "tracks" or specialties (formerly called "cones"). One specialty is designated for public diplomacy officers, and the others are for political, economic, consular, and management officers. Each new entrant into the Foreign Service is required to choose one of these five specialties, and is expected to spend the bulk of his or her career, although not all of it, in that specialty. Transfer between tracks is rare, although as explained below, cross-assignments have become common. In addition, at the beginning of their careers, FSOs often are required to do a consular assignment, even if their track is not consular.

The number of positions allotted to public diplomacy is quite small, less than one-tenth of the Foreign Service. This is to an extent a reflection of how the Department regards the role of public diplomacy. In 2013, there were 1,552 public diplomacy positions at State. These positions constituted only 8.4 percent of the total number (18,540) of State's American diplomatic and consular positions. The 1,552 PD positions were distributed as follows: 780 in the regional bureaus, most of them deployed to embassies abroad; 422 to the Educational and Cultural Bureau (ECA); 285 in the International Information Programs bureau (IIP), and 65 to various functional bureaus.[1] This is a significant decline from the past. In 1960, the US Information Agency (USIA) employed 3,771 American public diplomacy officers and 6,881 local hires for a total of 10,652 public diplomacy personnel.[2]

The Foreign Service itself is actually quite a small part of the US government. One comparison is with the Department of Defense (DOD), which has 1.3 million employees and an enormous budget.[3] As Robert Gates noted when he was Secretary of Defense: "Consider that this year's budget for the Department of Defense—not counting operations in Iraq and Afghanistan—is nearly half a trillion dollars. The total foreign affairs budget request for the State Department is $36 billion—less than what the Pentagon spends on health care alone."[4] Also, DOD normally bases only 21 percent of its personnel abroad, while 68 percent of the Foreign Service is deployed abroad, so it has no surge capacity. And training is relatively shortchanged. State's vacancy rate recently was 21 percent overseas, 30 percent in Africa. Nearly 25 percent of Foreign Service vacancies are for one-year assignments or "tours" in places so dangerous that they are unaccompanied by family. Thirty years ago there were only 2 danger pay posts, while today there are 28.[5]

Public Diplomacy professionals are in many respects like all Foreign Service Officers, although they also have some different functions that require different skills.

All Foreign Service Officers including public diplomacy officers enter the Service through the same process. They must pass a highly competitive written exam, write a series of personal narratives, pass an oral assessment, pass medical tests, and undergo a security clearance investigation process before they are eligible to be hired.[6] Approximately 2 percent of all applicants to the Foreign Service are successful in this process. (Between 2001 and 2006, for example, more than 100,000 applied for FSO positions, but only 2,100 became Foreign Service Officers.)[7]

The entire career of an FSO is highly competitive. Upon entry, a new FSO is considered untenured and tenure must occur within five years of the initial hire. This requires the officer to, among other things, get off language probation by passing foreign language tests or serving in a language-essential position. Tenured FSOs then are evaluated annually by their supervisors and the evaluations go to independent "promotion panels" of other FSOs who rank-order each member of each class. Dismissal ("selection out") can occur as a result of repeated low ranking, while high-ranked FSOs ones can be promoted. FSOs can also be selected out for "time in class," if they are not promoted by a designated time limit or deadline that is tied to the number of years since their last promotion. This process specifies the number of years an individual can remain in at one rank or pay grade. It is therefore an "up or out" system that requires FSOs to continue to be promoted or they are out.

All FSOs agree to support and defend US national interests and all agree to be available for world-wide placement, meaning the government can send them anywhere abroad, depending on the "needs of the Service." There are more than 250 embassies and consulates abroad, but some posts are less desirable than others, for example because they are dangerous, and spouses, partners, and children are not allowed accompany them. Another factor that makes a post less desirable is an unhealthy local environment or one that lacks many of the amenities of the United States. FSOs all agree to accept these conditions when they join. Moreover, married couples who are both FSOs are "tandem couples," who face additional hurdles in finding suitable assignments at the same post at the same time.

It is important to note also that the human resources roster at every US diplomatic mission includes personnel who are hired locally. They are called "Locally Employed Staff" abbreviated to LES or LE Staff, who were previously known as Foreign Service Nationals or FSNs (The term FSN is still used informally at some embassies, especially by long term employees, some of whom dislike the term LES because it sounds like "less"). In 2009, for example, the State Department had more than 40,000 Locally Employed Staff at US diplomatic missions abroad.[8] The LE Staff are hired by the US mission and they are essential to its efficient functioning. In most cases, they must be bilingual in English and the local language, and they are usually bicultural, capably of explaining local circumstances to the American officers and otherwise bridging cultural gaps (in some cases, spouses of FSOs who do not speak the local language are hired as LES). Typically the Public Affairs Section (PAS) of the embassy has more LE Staff than the other sections.

## Public Diplomacy Officers' Skills

The skills an FSO should have in a public diplomacy assignment differ in several respects from the skills required in non-PD assignments. A successful public diplomacy officer must be good at program and personnel management, interpersonal and communication skills, as well as reporting, and at staying informed on a wide variety of issues and topics.

### Communicators

Public diplomacy is essentially a communication function. Every FSO carrying out a public diplomacy function should be an excellent communicator because a major part of his or her job is effectively communicating American policy, society and culture to a wide variety of people across cultural barriers. The PAO or IO also is often called upon to be embassy spokesman, and to organize press conferences for the ambassador, embassy officers, and visiting US officials or guest speakers. FSOs in other assignments normally do not do those tasks, although the State Department has recently put more emphasis on all officers "doing public diplomacy" as part of their job.

PD officers must write well. Although other FSOs, especially political and economic officers, are sometimes called "reporting officers," public diplomacy professionals must also be able to write clearly because they must report to the ambassador and country team, as well as to Washington, on local trends in public opinion and the media, as well as on program results.

### Linguists

Fluency in the local language is more likely to be necessary for those FSOs in a public diplomacy function than for others in the embassy because they deal regularly with a variety of local contacts who tend to lack English proficiency. A PD officer who has a working level oral command of the local language (a ranking of at least 3 on the State Department's Foreign Service Institute [FSI] scale of 1-to-5) can carry on a professional conversation with contacts, making the engagement more productive than one in English and showing respect for the local culture and its people. The State Department pays for language training to prepare FSOs going into language designated positions.

Because language barriers to communication exist in most posts abroad, Locally Employed Staff are especially important to the Public Affairs Section, more than to other sections, because translation and cultural interpretation are central to its efficient function. However, the incremental advantage for an American officer with fluency in the local language is quite substantial, adding to the benefit the local staff has to offer. Local staff members usually do most of the writing in the local language because that is the most difficult and sensitive language task. But American PD officers who can read and converse in the local language are a great asset. It allows them to make direct assessments of the local situation by following what is in the local newspapers and on local radio and television since the most important media to monitor are usually in the local language. Following local media, and speaking with local citizens, provides them with a window into the local culture that is vital for their work—allowing them to report their insights back in the office and to the country team through the PAO. Fluency in the language always is helpful in making and maintaining local contacts, even if they speak English. If the American does the work of speaking a foreign language, the contact is more comfortable and is usually more willing to have an ongoing relationship. Moreover, making the effort shows respect for the local culture.

It would be impossible for every PD officer at the embassy to be fluent in the local language, so most public affairs sections make do with less than that. Some hard languages such as Arabic and Chinese take a long time to develop fluency (the normal Foreign Service Institute course for Arabic and Chinese is two years, while for French it is six months). Some languages are spoken only in a single country so a diplomat with a single tour of only two or three years there will prefer not to spend a year or so studying that language.

The State Department labels some embassy positions as "language designated" but many of these go unfilled for lack of candidates or a language waiver is granted to allow the employee to go overseas without the requisite, desired Foreign Service Institute proficiency score. It is important that public affairs section has at least one FSO with a professional level in speaking, to be able to engage with the contacts who have no English at all. In my career, I always had better access because I spoke the local language (Arabic) well enough to carry on a professional conversation, and my interlocutors were pleased that I did not bring a local interpreter with me who would be privy to our conversation.

In 2006, President Bush announced a $114-million National Security Language Initiative to teach more Americans critical languages, with several government agencies—State, DOD, and the Department of Education—participating. Its focus is on eight critical languages: Arabic, Chinese, Japanese, Korean, Russian, Hindi, Persian, and Turkish. By 2006, the study of Chinese in the United States had already almost doubled since 9/11 and the study of Arabic quadrupled, but the number of Americans studying Spanish was still almost thirty-five times as many as studying Arabic (746,267:21,168), and fifteen times as many as studying Chinese.[9]

One report in 2006 found that in Baghdad during our occupation of Iraq, "All of our efforts in Iraq, military and civilian, are handicapped by Americans' lack of language and cultural understanding. Our embassy of 1,000 has 33 Arabic speakers, just six of whom are at the level of fluency. In a conflict that demands effective and efficient communication with Iraqis, we are often at a disadvantage. There are still far too few Arab[ic] language–proficient military and civilian officers in Iraq, to the detriment of the U.S. mission."[10] State and Defense tried to remedy the situation but later interest tapered off, and many students dropped out before becoming professionally proficient which takes time.[11]

### Management

All public diplomacy professionals must be good program managers because they are responsible for developing and carrying out programs—as well as providing Washington with reporting via short "highlights" or "results" reports and through the cable reporting channel. They must know how to evaluate the program environment accurately and draw on Washington resources as well as local ones. They must draw up budget requests based on accurate assessments of needs and resources. They must be able to identify opportunities to work with host nation institutions that often provide space and other support for programs, attracting a good audience and enhancing local relationships. These activities all require a level of strategic planning and knowledge of the local community beyond that which other embassy officers are required to have.

PAOs assist in setting up partnerships between local institutions and American ones. These may lead to collaborative partnerships between American and foreign universities, for example, or partnerships between NGOs or individuals who have common professional interests. Ideally, the relationships that are facilitated become self-sustaining and do not require the continued expenditure of resources by the embassy. When working in partnership with other organizations, both United States and foreign, good practice involves securing cost sharing for any given program, as well as considering fund raising, within the confines of official regulations on doing so.

Public diplomacy officers must also be good personnel managers because the Public Affairs Section (PAS) normally has many more Locally Employed Staff than any other section of the embassy, and the supervision of personnel from another culture is often difficult. Typically every FSO in the section, even the most junior one, supervises some local staff, and if it is the FSO's first tour abroad, he or she may be supervising older local staff who have been with the embassy for many years and know more about public diplomacy operations than the American does. That presents a challenge that American PD professionals are well aware of.

As one experienced PD officer explained:

> [One] significant difference among public diplomacy FSOs and other State FSOs (especially economic and political officers) is the level of managerial responsibilities that the former have. PD officers are expected from their first assignment to supervise numerous... Foreign Service Nationals (or FSNs), in tasks both intricate and basic, since they usually head an office of several persons or, sometimes, a whole range of operations (such as [an] American cultural center director). [The] public diplomat's contact work is often wider ranging than that demanded of typical State officers, requiring an ability to communicate convincingly across a broader segment of contacts. Beyond usually demanding solid language competence, such contact work requires subtle readings of local contexts and empathetic understanding of local mores. It demands not just pronouncing policy positions, but actively listening to others in an ongoing dialogue which enriches both parties through what is a cross-cultural conversation. Of course, the best State political officers also possess these capabilities, but their ultimate output—pertinent analysis and assessments rather than direct programming activity—is not fundamentally dependent on it. Some of this bent for contact work can be taught; much of it is innate.[12]

Another FSO put it this way: "A good PD officer combines skills in persuasion, empathy, logistics, setting priorities, and tracking details—among other competencies. Often such an officer is not the medium of the exchange that takes place, but the mediator between an American presence (e.g., a visiting expert, teacher, performer, or VIP) and a foreign contact, i.e., the person who sets up a conversation, but then lets it take its course between the new interlocutors—and follows up on it later."[13]

### Interpersonal Skills

Public diplomacy professionals must have excellent interpersonal skills, not only to develop and maintain useful contacts in the local society, but also to mobilize other members of the embassy to help the public diplomacy effort.

All FSOs at the embassy are expected to develop personal contacts as part of their work, but the public affairs section's contacts are more extensive and varied. Political, economic, and consular officers, and the ambassador and DCM, tend to devote most of their time to contacts with host government officials, and their encounters are classified and reported in classified channels. Commercial officers deal primarily with the business community. FSOs serving in public diplomacy positions, on the other hand, must develop a wide and diverse range of contacts, including radio, television, and newspaper editors and reporters, university students and faculty, USG exchange program alumni, NGO leaders, independent writers, artists and some officials such as the ministries of information and education.

An experienced FSO put it this way: "traditional diplomats usually deal with foreign officials and government representatives, both to assess foreign outlooks and trends and to present US positions. Theirs is principally a world of ministries, departments [government offices], presidential palaces, political parties, and military commands...., and... their analytical work and reporting is, at its core, confidential and carefully guarded. Public diplomats, on the other hand, interact with the host country publics, including—besides officialdom—its media, academic institutions, nonprofits, businesses, and arts entities—among others. These audiences include journalists, educators, professionals, businessmen, environmental and human rights advocates, etc."[14]

### Cultural Curiosity

Public diplomacy officers must be deeply interested in understanding other cultures and how foreigners think. As Thomas Pickering, one of America's most distinguished diplomats, described the ideal press officer: "Someone who is alert to the changing scene, who knows and can spot when troublesome issues come up, who knows what we've done in the past and how to get the ambassador and DCM to formulate how to deal with those issues in the future."[15]

A 2008 survey of more than 200 former senior USIA officials asked what were the most important personal characteristics for success in a

PD career. They agreed that the most important were: cross-cultural understanding and curiosity and respect for foreign cultures; tolerance and empathy; interpersonal oral communication, foreign language skills and writing ability; as well as management, collaborative and networking skills.[16] What the Pentagon calls "situational awareness" for American servicemen is an attitude that PD officers need to acquire and maintain in abundance.

The public diplomacy officer should also have a solid knowledge of American history, politics, economics, society and culture, and be up to date on trends in all these fields back home, although there is no formal requirement for this.

## *Teamwork*

Success as a public diplomacy officer at an American embassy depends on teamwork as much as on individual accomplishment. There are several levels at which teams operate and the officer must be aware of them all and adept in working with them. On the basic level, in the public affairs section, the PAO must provide leadership for other American officers and local staff, and the other American officers must also know how to motivate their local staff as well. On the next level, PAOs must know how to work well with the ambassador and DCM, who write their annual performance evaluation, and also with all the other members of the ambassador's country team. The PAO needs the support of all sections of the mission, including for example the management officer and security officer for internal embassy matters, and the defense attaché and political officer who can be helpful in carrying out public diplomacy programs.

The PAO needs the support in Washington of the regional bureau which the embassy reports to, including not only the PD officers in that bureau, but the deputy assistant secretary (DAS), and also the assistant secretary. And the PAO needs the support of State's bureaus of Education and Cultural Affairs (ECA) and International Information Programs (IIP), as well as of the Undersecretary for Public Diplomacy and Public Affairs. The PAO and the other American PD officers at the embassy must master this complex web of interlocking relationships within the US government in order to accomplish their tasks. The approval for their programs and the money to carry them out, as well as evaluation reports and their "corridor reputation" that affects their career progress as FSOs, comes from others within this system. Success in this environment requires an ability to work well all the time with a variety of different people.

Teamwork is of course a characteristic of the modus operandi of Foreign Service Officers in all of the specialty tracks. In solving problems, developing policy recommendations and carrying out the responsibilities of their assigned tasks, FSOs tend to feel more comfortable consulting with others before making decisions. They find that discussing a problem with others who share the same basic purposes, within an embassy or within the Foreign Service generally, often reveals nuances and options they had not thought of on their own, and leads to better decisions. In addition, FSOs working at an embassy abroad deal with non-Americans on a daily basis and must understand local attitudes and perceptions if they are to succeed in carrying out their tasks. For this reason, they must include Locally Employed Staff as part of their team since they have special insights into local thinking. This is especially true of public diplomacy officers who must understand the nuances of local attitudes by a wide variety of people.

These requirements of FSOs in general and PD officers in particular contrast starkly with many other professions, where the individual operates mostly on a solo basis, or is only dependent on one or two others for success. A university professor, for example, basically operates mostly alone, and is only obliged to work with students but rarely with others. Professors may occasionally work with other academics but on a very temporary basis, and faculty meetings are usually not complex teamwork exercises. Many people thrive on this solo work, while others, such as FSOs, thrive on teamwork.

As one experienced officer puts it,

> PD diplomats operate autonomously from, but on an equal footing with, their traditional colleagues, but the two clearly collaborate on the same basic mission objectives. At any well-run overseas mission, the two strands interweave together all the time, attending meetings together, drafting policy papers together, organizing events together. A good PD officer, for example, can make excellent use of the expertise of an articulate political officer in a media interview or at a program venue, while a Political Section can garner much from a PD officer's knowledge of a journalist's slant or a university's importance... It could be said that, in our overseas missions, public diplomats and their work comprise a different "'culture" than that of traditional diplomats. As "programmers," they facilitate the meeting and dialogue of Americans

and foreigners, and they do this by organizing a whole range of activities, lectures, seminars, institutional visits, entertainments, press events, website content, etc., which allow these encounters to take place.[17]

And one ambassador added: "In the modern world where public and traditional diplomacy are so intertwined, public affairs and political officers should not only work closely together—in many cases their jobs should overlap."[18]

### Impact of the Merger

The 1999 merger of USIA into State had an impact on public diplomacy personnel working at embassies.

When USIA existed, PAOs at embassies were heads of an agency, who reported not only to their ambassadors, but also to the Director of USIA in Washington. A public diplomacy desk officer in a USIA regional bureau was the main contact point for all daily communications with Washington. The head of that regional bureau wrote PAO performance ratings, (the ambassador wrote a separate one) and, at post, the PAO had control of the PD budget, motor pool, and other administrative tools. All of that disappeared with the 1999 merger, as the PAO became a staff member who reported to the ambassador only.[19] The PAO could not appeal to a PD "home office" for support in any dispute with the ambassador, for example, if the ambassador assigned a task that seemed to fall outside the scope of public diplomacy. As one PD officer put it: "The advantage of being on the outside as a [USIA] person, is that you can barge in and say [to the ambassador] 'look, you need to say this.' There is a certain amount of protection from my agency [USIA] if I need to be aggressive about it. Media concerns don't enter into the mindset of the State Department in the same way, so we can understand and complement each other."[20]

The Public Diplomacy Advisory Commission in its 2008 report criticized the State Department for viewing PAOs overseas "more as managers and administrators than as communicators." It also criticized State for "making no special effort to recruit individuals into the public diplomacy career track who would bring into the Foreign Service special experience or skills relevant to the work of communicating with and influencing foreign publics."[21]

State assignment policies since the USIA-State merger in 1999 have blurred distinctions of the PD function. State gave public diplomacy a career track at the time of the merger, and transferred many FSOs from USIA to State positions. State's leadership then stressed that all non-PD track FSOs should know more about public diplomacy work and vice versa. This sounded logical since in the theoretical premise of the merger was to bring public diplomacy closer to "traditional" diplomacy. However it had the consequence in practice of diluting the public diplomacy specialty. Since 1999, State's assignment policy in practice has led to a situation where many public diplomacy positions abroad have been filled by officers who are not in the PD track and who have never done PD work before. In late 2008 for example, there were approximately 600 American public diplomacy positions at our embassies abroad,[22] but State's personnel managers filled many of them with non-PD officers (the Undersecretary for Public Diplomacy is not involved in those assignments). In a careful analysis of PD personnel, veteran public diplomacy professional Mike Canning pointed out that as of January 2008, 226 of the PD track officers serving abroad were not in PD positions, and 127 non-PD track officers were doing PD assignments.[23] State has made some of these cross-track assignments because there were not enough PD track officers at the right level to fill all of the PAO positions. In 2008, the Undersecretary for Public Diplomacy estimated that the shortfall between the number of PD positions and the number of PD officers was 13 percent.[24] Yet many of them have been made for purposes of cross-training, under the general notion that even a political track officer needs to have had experience as a PAO if he or she wants to do a good job as ambassador some day.

While on the surface this may be an appealing argument, it ignores the negative effects of such cross assignments. When officers from non-PD tracks without PD experience are assigned to PD positions, the level of professionalism and effectiveness of that position is diminished, causing resentment among PD officers. The "interchangeability" principle that has prevailed at State has benefited some individuals in the PD track who have received more senior assignments abroad than they probably would have at USIA, but it also has serious drawbacks.

If a non-PD track officer who has never done any PD work is assigned to a PD section of an embassy as a cultural affairs officer, his or her supervisor, the PAO, must devote more time and effort to training and mentoring of a person who may not really be interested in public diplomacy work and may in fact not be happy with the assignment because it seems to be a sidetracking of a career. The PAO would rather have as CAO a PD track officer who is happy to have the assignment, is interested in the work, and has done similar work at another post as an Assistant CAO. To take another example, if a political track officer who has never done PD work is assigned as PAO, his or her subordinates and local staff in the PD section will be in the awkward position of having to teach the boss all about PD work because it is unfamiliar.

In the past few years, the State Department added a requirement that all entry level FSOs must do a consular tour early in their career, in order to qualify for tenure. This new rule applies to PD-track FSOs and further reduces the number of assignments that they will have doing public diplomacy work.

While State now offers a number of specific PD training courses, including in a distance learning format, public diplomacy is a specialization that is best learned mostly on the job working abroad under more experienced officers. Most non-PD officers, even senior ones, usually know very little about PD work. Just as a PD track officer does not need to know all the intricacies of visa adjudications or how to write a report on the local military or economy, a political or economic officer or a defense attaché does not need to know how to process a Fulbright or IVLP application. These are all separate functions, and the PD officer can seek collegial support from the others without being able to do their work.

In addition, as one official report said, the State Department since the 1999 merger has not specifically recruited for PD jobs by focusing on PD skills. Its only recruiting guidelines are racial, ethnic and socioeconomic diversity. It explains that while political and economic track officers need research and writing skills, PD officers need skills in "communication sciences/rhetoric, media relations, public opinion research, marketing, and area and cultural studies, among others." It recommends that State should focus on the importance of PD officers being skilled in "communicating with and influencing foreign publics" and says they need cross-cultural communication skills, media savvy and outreach and persuasive abilities.[25]

## *Specialists or Generalists?*

What has been lost, then, because of the merger, and because of the notion that "every FSO must do PD," is the professionalism and efficiency that came with specialization of the PD officers. Before 1999, when all public diplomacy officers worked for USIA, almost all of them spent their entire careers doing only PD work, starting with an entry level one-year training assignment under an experienced public diplomacy professional. That mentoring system dropped out after the merger as State's human resources bureau took over. Now PD track officers, like all FSOs, are for two tours considered to be in the general category of FAST (First and Second Tour) officers. They must do at least one assignment as a consular officer and it is quite possible they may end up not doing any PD assignments at all during their two FAST tours. State does seek to match up experienced PD officers with new PD officers to provide the new ones with valuable input and guidance from more experienced peers. Though PD mentoring is no longer a formal part of assignments, officers are aware of the importance of mentoring as specified in the precepts of their annual evaluation report. In addition, officers can sign up to mentor others virtually, using online tools to keep in touch remotely when officers move from their initial training assignments in Washington to the field. There is a different view, however, that FSOs should be generally aware of the work of FSOs in other tracks, but it is not necessary, nor is it practical for them to have all the skills required at the embassy. That view says that specialization is vitally important in developing competence and effectiveness, and that some of the best PD officers are those who have come up through the ranks doing increasingly responsible PD assignments under experienced PD professionals.

President George W. Bush's Undersecretary for Public Diplomacy and Public Affairs Karen Hughes recognized during her tenure that public diplomacy professionals were still being discriminated against, despite the USIA-State merger that was supposed to end that. In a message she sent to field posts in March 2006 on employee evaluation reports (EERs), that was specifically addressed to all chiefs of mission, their deputies and all public affairs officers "from Karen Hughes," she tried to address that problem: She said,

> One of the unfortunate consequences of the post-USIA consolidation era is that PD officers have not done well in the overall Foreign Service promotion process. When we looked into this, we discovered that the promotion process in the former USIA did not require a strategic vision of PD's importance and role, and instead focused on how well the officer practiced the PD trade. Many PD evaluations still reflect this philosophy. To help our PD officers advance, I need your help in helping us incorporate the "how this fits in the big picture" element in to PD officers' evaluations. My goal is that this will help ensure that our Public Diplomacy officers receive the recognition they deserve for their hard work and service.... PD professionals,... You should be placing everything

that you do in the context of what the Mission Program Plan is trying to achieve. The bottom line is: Why does what you have done over the past year matter to the Department and to the US Government?[26]

### *Different Cultures*

Because PD officers and other FSO have somewhat different functions they tend to see the Foreign Service through different prisms, and they operate within slightly different "cultures."

It is of course useful for non-PD officers to understand at least some aspects of the public diplomacy function, and this is the basic rationale behind State's policy of cross-assignments into and out of the PD positions at embassies abroad. In the past, when PD and non-PD personnel were strictly separated, the two types of FSO tended not to understand each other's functions as well as they do today because each was so focused on his or her specialty for the purposes of career advancement. They naturally paid less attention to other career tracks.

For example, public diplomacy officers are trained to work closely with foreign media, while political officers often regard media engagements as risky and of little benefit to their careers. As one senior State Department official said, "By and large, the Foreign Service and the foreign relations establishment don't think in public relations terms. Too many people I've seen working with the press at the State Department are fundamentally afraid of them."[27] He added that some political officers, for example, always knew that talking with reporters helped them make policy because they learn valuable information when they do interviews, but most diplomats don't understand that.[28]

The merger of USIA into the State Department in 1999 and subsequent cross-assignments were intended to overcome the cultural divide, and make public diplomacy officers so much a part of the State Department that their work would be appreciated. However, that purpose was not entirely achieved by the merger. Even after the merger, many non-PD officers have continued to regard public diplomacy as a secondary function, not as important as traditional diplomacy, which was the central function of representing the United States officially to the host government by making formal presentations to host country officials. The non-PD officials regarded that as the "real" work of any embassy. Although no one at an American embassy or in Washington ever discussed this distinction, everyone sensed it, and that is to some extent still the case.[29] From a management perspective, it is considered good practice at missions abroad to allow temporary "swaps" of PD personnel, though sometimes this may be one-way, as is the case when a PD FAST officer works temporarily on detail as a staff assistant in the Front Office (a job usually filled by an officer in the political track) and then returns to the PD section, or when he or she spends a number of weeks doing work in another section (but the FSO from that section does not do a "detail" to the public affairs section). This temporary movement of an officer to another section may occur due to a short-term vacancy (e.g., when an FSO is on leave) or a longer term one (e.g., when a position is not filled in that section at the time).

Experienced public diplomacy professionals take considerable pride in their work. They know that, like all FSOs, they have passed the very rigorous written and oral Foreign Service Examination and that staying in this highly competitive profession is an achievement. But PD professionals are not well known outside the diplomatic corps, and they wear no uniforms or medals to show their accomplishments. Political appointees who join the government on a senior level are often pleasantly surprised to find how competent the career service is. For example, when the very successful broadcast journalist Edward R. Murrow became Director of USIA, he became closely acquainted with PD professionals and he remarked, "I could staff any commercial media outfit in the country with people from this agency, and it would be as good or better than any of its competitors."[30] Other political appointees have also found that to be true.

## *Training*

What kind of training should a public diplomacy professional have?

One study recommended that PD officers should have nine-month PD training courses in Washington as economic officers have.[31] Training courses in Washington can be useful if carefully targeted and the Foreign Service Institute offers a range of training courses for FSOs and local staff, including in an on-line format. These include technical training such as how to prepare a budget, how to write grants for educational exchanges and travel, and how to manage specific programs (like the Fulbright and IVLP programs). Languages and area studies, and courses on American history and culture, can be delivered well in Washington, with speakers coming in from the private sector (i.e., NGOs, universities, think tanks) and other government agencies.

However, many of the other skills mentioned above that are necessary to carry out the functions of a public diplomacy officer are developed and solidified far more efficiently at post, on the job, doing the actual work alongside experienced PD officers, rather than solely in a classroom in Washington or through online, self-study instruction.

## Conclusion

Public diplomacy is one aspect of diplomacy, and the professionals who practice it are part of the Foreign Service of the US Department of State. They become FSOs through the same rigorous entry process, and they face the same stiff professional competition during their careers. The 1999 merger of the US Information Agency (USIA) into the State Department has led to some blurring of the lines between the public diplomacy specialty and the other tracks, because of new assignment policies and because all FSOs are now expected to have some knowledge of public diplomacy. Yet the practice of public diplomacy remains a specialty that requires skills and approaches that are in some respects different from those required of other specialties in the Foreign Service. Like all FSOs, they need to be sensitive to cultural differences but their contacts in the local society tend to be broader and more diverse. They all have management responsibilities and tend to supervise more local employees. They do reporting on local public attitudes, but they are not "reporting officers"; rather, they devote their major efforts to communications programs, and using soft power to develop mutual understand and win hearts and minds. And the skills that they need to be effective seem to be best learned on the job, at an embassy, working under an experienced PD officer. These are differences that are still important, despite State's emphasis in recent years on more generalized skills and more use of cross-assignments into and out of public diplomacy positions.

# PART II
## *Field Office Management*

# CHAPTER THREE
## The Public Affairs Officer

The Public Affairs Officer (PAO) at a US mission abroad is the senior public diplomacy official at that mission. He or she is responsible for the overall management of the public diplomacy program in the host country, including determining the issues and target audience to focus on, developing the programs, proposing the programs and budget to Washington, and then managing their implementation.

### Public Diplomacy Staff

The Public Affairs Section (PAS) of the embassy typically includes at least three Americans, a Public Affairs Officer, an Information Officer (IO) and Cultural Affairs Officer (CAO), plus Locally Employed Staff (LES). American positions are filled from Washington, but the embassy is responsible for hiring local employees.

The Public Affairs Section is usually divided into two main subject areas. The Information Officer normally manages all of the "fast media" programs, including the supervision of embassy output via traditional and social media, plus interactions with local media representatives. His or her contacts are mainly local radio, TV, and print media editors and reporters, as well as individuals prominent in social media in the host country. The Cultural Affairs Officer normally manages longer-term efforts such as the educational exchange programs, centers and cultural presentations, so his or her main contacts would be students and faculty at the universities, institution directors, and prominent cultural figures, including authors and artists. (Details of both functions are spelled out in chapters 5–10.) The PAO supervises both the IO and CAO (who at large embassies may in turn supervise other Americans) and is ultimately responsible for overall coordination and the implementation of the post's goals. The PAO handles the higher level contacts in both areas, such as media publishers and university presidents, and senior officials in government ministries dealing with information and culture.

Local employees are crucial to the effective functioning of a Public Affairs Section. They are assigned either to information or cultural work, depending on their expertise, or to the PAO's office, and they maintain their own contacts as well. American officers always depend heavily on local employees for several types of support, since they are bilingual in English and the local language so they serve as translators and interpreters as needed—and they may have proficiency in additional languages. They know in detail about local political, economic and social conditions so they keep the American officers up to date on trends in local policies and thinking. They are bicultural in the sense that they know a great deal about the United States as well as their own country; some have studied in America and many have been sent by their PAOs on orientation and training visits to the United States. Finally, local hires provide vital continuity for the post, since the American officers are normally assigned to a post for only two or three years.

Typical staffing of a public affairs section at a large embassy might look as follows:

*Public Affairs Section*
Public Affairs Officer (PAO)
Executive Secretary (ES)
Information Officer (IO)
Assistant Information Officer (AIO)
Cultural Affairs Officer (CAO)
Assistant Cultural Officer/Exchanges (ACAO)
Assistant Cultural Officer/Centers (ACAO)
Locally Employed Staff (LES)

At a small embassy, the only Americans in the Public Affairs Section might be the PAO, IO and CAO, or at a very small embassy just a PAO. At the other extreme, in a few large countries where the United States has consulates outside the capital city, those consulates might have public affairs sections. Every public affairs section has locally hired staff.

## Determining Post Size

The size of the public diplomacy staff and budget at a given embassy is ultimately decided in Washington with concurrence of the ambassador, but the PAO has input into the decision. The PAO describes and explains his or her program to the ambassador and to Washington in order to justify budget and staffing requests. The PAO is in competition for resources with other posts. Washington's decision is usually based on several factors. These include: the political importance of the country to US interests; its influence on matters of concern to Washington internationally (through the UN or otherwise) or regionally; the degree to which public opinion in the country is hostile to or misunderstands the US relationship; and the ability of the PD effort to reach and influence local public opinion—as affected by political or technical barriers to communication.

The size of the public diplomacy program therefore varies greatly from country to country and this affects its program. Some are relatively large. Indonesia, for example, with a population of nearly 240 million people, is the world's fourth largest country, and very important to the United States because of its strategic position and role in the Muslim world. The US Embassy and the Consulates General in Indonesia have 11 Americans and 51 local staff members doing public diplomacy work in Jakarta, and at the US Consulate Generals in Surabaya, and the American Presence Post (APP) located in Medan. The public diplomacy budget in fiscal 2010 was nearly two million dollars.[1]

India, with 1.2 billion people, is the second most populous country in the world and it is politically important to the United States. Local conditions allow US officials relative freedom to do public diplomacy programming. It has therefore traditionally had the largest public diplomacy staff anywhere, although when budget cuts were imposed on all public diplomacy activities in the mid-1990s after the end of the Cold War, India was included. At that time, the PAO assigned to India was told he would have to reduce by 35 percent the budget and staff. In six months, he cut the Public Affairs Section from 35 foreign services officers and 700 Foreign Service Nationals, diplomacy section in India down to 25 Foreign Services Officers and 400 Foreign Service Nationals. In 2011, the public diplomacy section in India operations still had 25 Foreign Service Officers, but the Foreign Service National staff had been reduced to about 200 people spread across the Embassy in

New Delhi, and the four Consulates in Chennai, Hyderabad, Kolkata, and Mumbai.[2]

China, a major power of great importance to the United States and with the largest population in the world at over 1.3 billion people, has a fairly large public diplomacy staff but the local staff is not as large as in India because Chinese government restrictions constrain the PD program (see further on). The US maintains an embassy in Beijing, plus consulates general in four Chinese cities (Shanghai, Guangzhou, Chengdu, and Shenyang) and one consulate general in Hong Kong. Public diplomacy staffing for China includes 26 US direct-hires and 67 local employees. It currently has one of the three largest US public diplomacy operations in the world. The mission's public diplomacy budget in 2010 was $3.518 million.[3]

In contrast, small countries that are less important strategically to the United States, have far fewer public diplomacy staff. Bahrain, for example, with a population of only 1.2 million people, only half of whom are national citizens, has only one American public diplomacy officer, plus a Regional English Language Officer.

## *Exceptions*

There are however, special cases where Washington approves extra resources. Since 9/11, for example, Iraq and Afghanistan have received very large public diplomacy budgets because of the ongoing conflicts there and Washington's priorities in dealing with them (see details in chapters 11 and 12).

For a few countries, the rationale may not always be obvious but the PAO has made a persuasive case for substantial reasons. One example is Germany. Germany has had the largest US public diplomacy program in all of Europe, despite the fact that US-German bilateral relations have been excellent, the German public has generally been well disposed to the United States, and many American commercial products, movies and TV shows are available there. When he was the PAO in Germany, Bruce Armstrong successfully argued that public diplomacy is still needed there, because many Germans have misperceptions about America. He said that was especially important in East Germany where the people are critical of America even twenty years after German reunification because they had been fed unfavorable views of the US during decades of communist propaganda and socialist anti-capitalist indoctrination. They remain rather skeptical of America's role in the world, and they also have very little contact with the United States.

In the East, after reunification, high school teachers of Russian suddenly had to teach English, a language which many of them had to learn from scratch. Often teachers would be just one lesson ahead of their students.[4]

Brazil is another example of a large PD program where a justification is not immediately obvious. One recent study pointed out that although US-Brazilian official relations are excellent and Brazilian public opinion generally has very positive views of America, our embassy there has one of the biggest public diplomacy programs in all of the Americas and one of the highest levels of funding. The PAO has sustained this high level of activity by making several points to Washington. First, the Brazilian government finances a large portion of the PD program and to sustain that beneficial partnership the United States must demonstrate its serious interest in the program. Moreover, the United States and Brazil represent the two largest populations and two biggest economies in the Western Hemisphere and it is vital to maintain the existing relationship, that will not necessarily thrive without careful tending; Brazil has for example shown that on some issues of concern to the United States, such as policy towards Iran, it can follow a different line. These arguments have been persuasive in Washington.[5]

## Public Diplomacy Strategic Planning

In planning a public diplomacy strategy, the PAO must set reasonable goals while maintaining flexibility to alter course as circumstances change. The PAO must understand US priorities in that country and globally, as well as local concerns relating to US interests. The PAO must also ensure that the strategy has the support of the ambassador and the country team, and the approval of Washington.[6]

To develop the PD strategy, the PAO might follow four sequential steps:

1. Assess and evaluate local public concerns on issues of importance to the United States, to determine the most appropriate programs to deal with those issues,
2. Identify the target audience,
3. Take into account any local obstacles to programming, and
4. Gain approval of programs and the budget from the ambassador and Washington.

## Assessing Local Concerns

A careful analysis of local attitudes toward the United States and perceptions about issues of importance to the US national interest should be the first step in strategic planning. This does not mean that the PAO ignores Washington's policies. On the contrary, the task of the PAO is to take into account the US government's global and regional priorities, as well as its bi-national policies, and seek to match them as much as possible against local concerns. A unilateral monologue that ignores local views would be ineffective, and a focus exclusively on local priorities that ignores American interests would also fail. But the local perspective always differs from the Washington one in at least some respects and the PAO must try to bridge that gap. As one experienced PD professional noted, "Washington does wholesale, posts do retail."[7] Massachusetts Congressman Tip O'Neill famously said, "All politics is local," and for the PAO the same general concept applies: effective PD programs must take local realities into account. Since each country is different, an effective public diplomacy program must start with such an assessment and not simply present a standard program as developed in Washington for worldwide use.

Assessing local public opinion, as the first step in the PAO's strategic planning process, will naturally lead to a determination of the issues the post should give its priority attention to. Those local priorities tend to vary a great deal from country to country. Here are three examples. In South Korea, for example, the two issues causing most problems for public diplomacy have been trade (e.g., the importation of US beef) and the presence of US troops (who sometimes antagonize the local population).[8] In contrast, a study of US public diplomacy in Turkey found that the issues that most concerned the Turkish public when looking at the United States were totally different: (1) The Kurdish question as related to the US invasion of Iraq; (2) The US position on Armenia's genocide claim, and (3) Feelings of betrayal on Cyprus—issues that were not naturally high on Washington's agenda with Turkey.[9] In Egypt the public's priority issues in 2011 were however closer to Washington's: Iraq, the Arab/Israeli conflict, and American attitudes toward the Arab and Muslim worlds.[10]

In Afghanistan, according to the PAO, his public diplomacy strategy in that country in 2011 had "four broad goals of countering extremist voices, strengthening people-to-people ties, helping build Afghan communications capacities, both human and infrastructure, and expanding media outreach and getting our message out to a broader audience." He admitted that "helping the Afghan government develop its capacity to better communicate with the Afghan people" such as "training spokespersons, training people how to be effective communicators, training people within the government how to get a message out, how to explain themselves to their people" was not a traditional public diplomacy function but it was "a key goal of ours... (to) help the Afghan government at all levels... better connect with its own citizens and explain their own policies."[11]

## Washington's Impact

Public opinion toward the United States is of course everywhere affected not only by local issues but also by America's global policies and by the public's opinion of American policy that may differ from their view of the American people. Polls showed that around the world, foreign public respect for the United States declined during the administration of George W. Bush and his policies, even where there was high regard for the American people. Poll numbers improved when Barack Obama was elected, although in some regions like the Arab world, they declined after an initial improvement.

For example, in Germany, a poll in 2003 found 57 percent of Germans held the opinion that the "United States is a nation of warmongers" and only 6 percent said they believed President Bush was concerned with "preserving the peace."[12] The disclosure of the human rights problems related to the Bush administration's "War on Terrorism," in particular the Abu Ghraib scandal in 2004 and Guantanamo Bay helped undermine transatlantic trust.[13] When asked who the Germans would vote for if they were allowed to cast their votes in the 2008 American presidential elections, an overwhelming 69 percent would have chosen Barack Obama over John McCain, and only 26 percent of Germans would have voted for the Republican candidate.[14] Two years after his election, Obama remained generally popular with Germans, and 63 percent of Germans had a favorable view of the United States.[15] One public diplomacy official who served in Germany says Germans became much more receptive to outreach by American public diplomacy officials once Obama was elected, and it has been much easier to engage German media as well as German citizens in a dialogue. Obama's election has moreover attracted more people to programs offered by the public diplomacy section of the US Embassy in Berlin and has in particular facilitated the outreach towards youth.[16]

In Lebanon, as in all Arab countries, public opinion has been very critical of Washington for its policy on the Arab-Israeli conflict. When President Obama was elected, approval ratings went up to 45 percent but they declined again in 2010 because their high hopes for him were not met, and only about 20 percent of the population viewed him positively. Furthermore, as Obama's ratings fell, the Lebanese public's approval of Iranian President Ahmadinejad and Venezuelan President Chavez, both of whom are staunchly anti-American, improved. Also problematic for the US is the belief on the part of large numbers of Lebanese that Iran's nuclear program is peaceful: 92 percent believe that Iran has a right to pursue the program, and of those that believe the program is aimed at attaining weapons, 31 percent still advocate Iran's right to pursue it.[17]

## Public Opinion versus Official Relations

PAOs know that a good bilateral political relationship does not necessarily translate into positive public opinion toward the US, and vice versa. The reality is usually much more complicated. During the presidency of George W. Bush, for example, he had excellent relations with British Prime Minister Tony Blair, who supported his American foreign policies including the war in Iraq, but the British public was very critical of those policies, a fact that required close attention by the American public diplomacy staff working in the UK. During that period, British favorability ratings toward the United States showed a steady decline from 83 percent in early 2002, to a dramatic low of 48 percent in March 2003. Public opposition to the Iraq War was at 52 percent before the invasion.[18]

Conversely, despite the ongoing confrontational bilateral relations between Washington and countries like China and Iran, it is striking that public opinion in those countries tends to be more favorable toward the United States than unfavorable. According to a 2006 Chinese opinion poll developed and conducted by Horizon Research Consultancy Group, one of the most prominent Chinese local management consulting and market research companies, 73 percent of the Chinese people had a positive view of the United States and 83 percent had a positive view of US culture; they also ranked the United States behind Russia as the second most important country that China should keep a close relationship with.[19] As for Iran, a World Public Opinion poll of Iranians in 2011 found that 60 percent favored the restoration of diplomatic relations between Iran and the United States, and a similar percentage favored direct talks between the two states.[20]

Nor does American economic assistance guarantee local public support. For example, since 2001, the United States has provided $500 million annually on nonmilitary assistance to Pakistan, and President Obama increased that level to $1.5 billion annually for five years. In spite of this significant assistance, the approval rating of the United States in Pakistan has remained very low. According to an August 2009 Pew Global Attitudes Project survey, 64 percent of the people of Pakistan consider the United States to be an enemy while only 9 percent described it as a partner.[21] The numbers have gotten worse since President Obama was elected. In June 2012, according to a Pew Research poll in Pakistan, 74 percent of the Pakistani public regarded the United States as an enemy and only 8 percent as a partner. Fully 80 percent regarded the United States unfavorably while only 12 percent had a favorable view, and only 7 percent had confidence in President Obama while 60 percent had no confidence.[22]

A similar situation prevails in Afghanistan, where the US has spent over $38 billion on reconstruction since 2001 and President Obama in 2009 agreed to raise American troop levels from 70,000 to 100,000 to support the government, yet public opinion of the United States is quite low.[23]

## How PAOs Evaluate Public Opinion

Years ago, Walter Lippmann described public opinion as "pictures inside the heads of these human beings, the pictures of themselves, of others, of their needs, purposes and relationship, are public opinions." He added: "The picture inside so often misleads men in their dealings with the world outside.... [because] the factors which limit their access to the facts.... are the artificial censorships, the limitations of social contact, the comparatively meager time available in each day for paying attention to public affairs, the distortion arising because events have to be compressed into very short messages, the difficulty of making a small vocabulary express a complicated world, and finally the fear of facing those facts which would seem to threaten the established routine of men's lives."[24] It is the task of the public diplomacy professional working at an embassy abroad, to try to understand the pictures inside the heads of the local public he is dealing with, and to devise ways and means of communicating with that public as an American.

In order to evaluate local public opinion, the PAO asks: what are the issues the local public cares about that are of concern to US national interests, and what are their positive and negative views of America relating to those issues? Some of those issues may not be on Washington's priority list but nevertheless important for the PAO to focus on.

In analyzing local public opinion, opinion polls are usually of limited use. A few Western countries allow unrestricted polling of political attitudes, but most countries do not. The State Department's Intelligence and Research bureau does an annual survey of polls that assess attitudes toward America in a general way, and these are of some limited use to field posts.[25] Polling by reputable firms such as Gallup has only been permitted in a few countries, and in those, only for the past decade.[26] Many governments simply ban objective polling. Even if polling is allowed, results may not be reliable if the public is fearful of giving honest answers. In any case, PAOs need more intensive and more frequent assessment of local opinion than polls even in the best circumstances can provide. For that they depend on several sources.

First, the Americans consult on a daily basis with their Foreign Service Nationals who can interpret opinion trends for them. Second, they and their local staff members meet frequently with a wide range of citizens, who reflect opinion on issues of interest. Third, they undertake a through and systematic reading of the local media, including newspapers, radio, and television, with emphasis on commentary and the way news stories are presented.

In assessing local opinion by monitoring the media, the PAOs must be sure not to follow only the local media that are in English—which often are edited for foreigners—but also to monitor the vernacular media that are usually a much better mirror of local concerns. For example when he was PAO in Pakistan in 2011, Walter Douglas discovered that his staff was not paying much attention to the Pakistani media in local languages but relying instead on the Pakistani newspapers in English for local opinion. He assigned several members of his local staff to review the Urdu newspapers and evening TV talk shows and found that their content was far different from that of the English papers (and much more hostile to the United States), so he set up a regular monitoring and reporting system for them that he used to base his programs on and he also reported on local opinion to the ambassador and to Washington.[27]

In this monitoring of local opinion, special attention is paid to local criticism of the United States whether based on misunderstandings or deliberate distortions. This is an ongoing task, in which the PAO constantly updates and revises the analysis as circumstances change.

A public diplomacy officer who served in Indonesia put it this way in 2011: "Each embassy does much of its work on its own because only it knows best what the local situation is. It knows the host-country people. It knows the culture. Hopefully it speaks the local language. So it is not that Washington tells Jakarta in detail what to do with public diplomacy. Washington sets broad policies and authorizes the budget. But they leave day-to-day decisions and programs and implementation to the Ambassador and the Public Affairs Section. And decisions are based on what is relevant to Indonesians."[28]

Taking into account those local concerns as well as Washington's priorities, the PAO, in consultation with his or her American and local staff, will select the issues the post should focus its main efforts on during the coming year. This list can change, as circumstances change, but the exercise of identifying priorities helps the PD team develop its programs in a coordinated fashion.

### Identifying the Target Audience

The next step in planning after analyzing local opinion and determining the basic program priorities is to identify the priority and secondary target audiences. This is done by analyzing local communication and influence patterns to identify the people who are opinion leaders or "influentials" who have a significant impact on the thinking of officials and of the public at large. It should include people who are "movers and shakers" in society, who are important in shaping the local discussion and setting agendas for discussion. They are people who may be multipliers of the message, because they are credible spokespeople who are listened to. As a practical matter, no public diplomacy program can possibly reach everyone in the country directly, so the focus is on those people who are most respected locally for their opinions about matters relating to US interests. As one USIA director noted, a PAO's budget would not allow him to send everyone in his country a postcard, even if it were entirely devoted to that.[29]

In the past, the public affairs section of each embassy compiled an "institutional profile" analyzing the target audience in the country. This formal document largely disappeared with the merger in 1999, although many PAOs use this approach informally, since it is very helpful in audience identification. The audience selection includes an evaluation of the role of the media in conveying information and opinion. It looks at political parties if they exist, and at the educational institutions, including university faculty and student leaders, cultural associations, nongovernmental organizations and civic groups, individual cultural personalities in arts and letters, and others who play influential roles in the local society and who are opinion leaders. It includes selected government officials, such as the ministers of information and culture, although most government officials are more the concern of the ambassador and other embassy sections. The target audience list generally does not include Americans—some are contacts of the commercial or consular section or of the ambassador—because they usually do not have significant influence over local public opinion.

The target audience must include not only people who are basically friendly toward the United States, but also those who are highly critical or even adamantly opposed to American policies and values, so long as they are accessible, and not entirely irreconcilable. It must also include the silent majority of people in between, who have no strong opinions but who may passively accept and not question the attacks of the critics, however misinformed.

Since 9/11, the US government has focused more on two specific groups—youth and Muslims—for special attention.

### Focus on Youth

The target audience analysis has always identified those younger individuals who have potential to be future leaders and who are therefore important targets for public diplomacy programs. But in the past, the focus was primarily on elites, on the assumption that they were the people who led public opinion in the country so influencing them had a multiplier effect. Casting the net more widely was considered to be too expensive. Recently, however, focus has shifted more to youth, as future leaders whose opinions are not yet firmly set.[30] After 9/11, the State Department created the Office of Global Youth Issues that seeks to support field post attempts to reach youth abroad.[31] But each post tailors that effort in its own way.

For example, in France, PAOs have shifted to focus on youth after shifting away from them earlier. One 2011 study quotes an American diplomat in Paris, saying: "Targeting the young population was abandoned during the [19]90s because mostly of budget cuts and it has undermined US public diplomacy. The diplomats came to the realization that it was a bad idea and that it was time to rebuild" this outreach.[32]

In Lebanon, the post has "an emphasis on targeting youth." According to the Cultural Affairs Officer Jennifer Williams, the post does so because the embassy can therefore "reach people before they become entrenched in a political party or mindset."[33] One study of Kenya quoted a US official saying that "the younger a person is, the easier it is to introduce them to new ideas." As a target audience in Kenya, youth are a significant segment of the population, making up 65 percent of the population under age twenty-five.[34] A State Department report on Thailand says about the post targeting opinion leaders: "Among these opinion leaders, much of the Public Affairs Section outreach is youth-oriented, intended to engage the successor generation."[35]

Some posts have specific local reasons to focus on youth. In India, according to a former CAO there, "elites were influenced for so long by their friendship with the Soviet Union and many were in power at that time. Elites looked on US with mistrust, and it is tough to change those opinions. Post the opening of the economy, US public diplomacy officers began trying to develop a counterweight to this with the younger crowd who are more open and do not accept the ways of the past. While public diplomacy officers continue to invite elites to functions and engage with them on a government-to-government level, public diplomacy officers are not counting on them to move the ball forward in people-to-people discussion."[36]

Some posts, like the one in Egypt, have been engaging with youth for some time. But when the Egyptian street uprising ousted President Mubarak in 2011 it was led by youth, and the post's effort to engage with youth was redoubled. According to one study, youth and "new audiences" are the primary target audiences today for public diplomacy efforts in Egypt. "So much of the revolution was led by tech savvy young people," states a US official. While "these are not traditional targets of U.S. public diplomacy," they are central to American relationships in Egypt. It has been a US priority to engage these populations in the past, "that is not as well known in Washington. So we needed to reemphasize it." One official said, "We've been reaching out effectively" to these populations for a decade. "That's why our alumni were in the square.... We have, for years, been teaching people about how to make peaceful change in government and how to be a responsible citizen. All of these messages we have been delivering to young people for the last 10 years." He went on to say, "I partially see the revolution as a manifestation of our message successfully getting to people." However, the US is "ramping up" its efforts to more comprehensively and effectively address these populations.[37]

In Sierra Leone, one study of public diplomacy said:

> The median age is seventeen and the host government as well as the U.S. Embassy focuses heavily on youth. Many of these young people are unemployed, ex-soldiers from the civil war, or are still in school. Most of them are very vocal and participate actively in politics and public activities. Because of their political activism, and because they seem receptive and willing to listen, change, or learn, they are interesting for PD purposes. The primary target audience for U.S. public diplomacy programs in Sierra Leone is therefore teenagers and young adults, people thirteen to thirty-five years in age.... The public diplomacy program targets young people also because youth were main players in the civil war in Sierra Leone.[38]

### *Engaging Muslims*

After 9/11, the State Department created a new position of Special Representative to Muslim Communities that reported to the secretary of state, which was intended to coordinate outreach to Muslim groups.[39] Circumstances however varied considerably by country.

Countries with Muslim majorities all made Muslims a special focus. For example, the public diplomacy staff in Indonesia, where 86 percent of its nearly 240 million people are Muslim—the world's largest Islamic population—undertook several measures to reach them. They intensified efforts to reach Muslim leaders, opened a dialogue with students in Islamic schools around the country and talked to Muslim women's groups, including the subject of terrorism in the discussions. The PAO brought Imam Yahya al Hindi, Georgetown University's Muslim chaplain, to Jakarta to give talks and meet with religious leaders. He also arranged a town hall meeting between religious leaders in Washington DC and Jakarta by digital video conference. The post also selected Indonesian Muslim leaders for three-week visits to the United States under the International Visitor Leader Program, and students doing religious studies to the US on Fulbright grants.[40]

In Egypt, during the 30 years of the Mubarak presidency, the embassy had had very limited contact with members of the Muslim Brotherhood in deference to the government that demonized them.

That changed when Mubarak was ousted in 2011. In November 2011, Deputy Assistant Secretary of State Jacob Walles was the first senior US official from Washington to meet with the leaders of the Muslim Brotherhood's newly formed Freedom and Justice Party at its new headquarters in Cairo.[41] This opened opportunities for public diplomacy professionals in Egypt to engage Muslim leaders also, and they have done so. It was made easier in 2012 when the Muslim Brotherhood's Freedom and Justice Party won a plurality in the parliamentary elections and then its candidate Muhammad Mursi won the presidency. However, the effort became more complicated in 2013 when widespread criticism of Mursi grew and the United States was blamed for supporting him. The coup that overthrew him in July 2013 was then blamed on the US—so the embassy had to deal with false accusations coming from both sides.

Even outside the Arab and Islamic world, notably in Europe, American public diplomacy professionals moved from priority targeting of leading elites to focus more on the minority Muslim communities.[42] This focus was continued by the Obama administration for example in France whose Muslim communities is the largest in Europe. As several reports have confirmed, "American embassies have been instructed to court second and third generations of immigrants from North Africa, Turkey or Pakistan." One aim of this change of target is to de-legitimize "the appeal of terrorist recruiters," but another is to get to know as well the "future leaders of Europe. " As the former Paris Information Officer put it, "Until 1989, the priority of our policy was the cold war. Since September 11th 2011, it is oriented towards the Muslim world. We would like to build links."[43]

In countries that have large Muslim populations, posts have always tried to engage with them. One study of Sierra Leone says: "Religion also plays a role in how Sierra Leoneans view the United States and the American people." Since nearly 60 percent of the population is Muslim, this affects their perception. One Sierra Leonean, who knows his country well, put it this way: "A lot of the Muslims in the country see the U.S. as against their religion and judge it based on that."[44]

In Thailand, PAO Kenneth Foster said that the post right after 9/11 had responded to Washington's instruction to all US embassies abroad to establish and/or strengthen relationship with the Muslims in the host countries as well. He said the embassy then sought to engage with the Muslim communities in Thailand's three southern provinces of Yala, Pattani, and Narathiwat, explaining that the wars in Afghanistan and Iraq were not wars against Islam, and presenting a balanced picture of

American culture and society where Muslims live in peace with freedom of religion. According to Foster, this function of public diplomacy is important because some Thai Muslims are not aware of the fact that there are a large number of Muslims in the United States. Therefore, sharing experiences among Muslim from the two countries are deemed indispensable for Muslim outreach programs.[45]

In Kenya, although the Islamic community constitutes only 10 percent of the population, after 9/11 the PAS developed a communications campaign that reached out to moderate Muslims and stressed religious tolerance, interfaith cooperation, and the origins of Islam. It uses the full range of PD materials—lectures, printed materials, visits—to communicate these messages. It also started English lessons for madrassa teachers, support for Muslim vocational training schools; speaker programs featuring a number of American-Muslim scholars; US military projects to rehabilitate schools and clinics and to dig wells in Muslim communities; and support for Muslim nongovernmental organizations. But as an official explained, "Many moderate Muslims might not appreciate being singled out as moderate by the United States. Some may fear that being seen as 'moderate' and in solidarity with the U.S[.] suggests a lack of commitment to Islam. That's why we have to take extra care in crafting our messages so they are well received by the majority of Muslims."[46]

### Identifying Obstacles

Program planning must of course also take account of any local restrictions and obstacles that specific programs and efforts might face, whether they exist because of local cultural, social or technical reasons, or because of governmental restrictions.

Social and cultural limitations might include, for example, the inadvisability of sponsoring an American ballet performance in a very conservative location such as Saudi Arabia, or putting on a play in English in a city where few people speak English. In Afghanistan, for example, the literacy rate is very low so post officers could not depend on traditional means of working with newspapers and they therefore sought to reach a broad audience by depending a lot on radio and television.[47] Technical restrictions might include the difficulty of mounting a social media campaign in countries where few people have access to this medium, as in Sierra Leone, for example (see details in the pages that follow).

Security problems can be more serious obstacles to overcome, although they vary from country to country. A study of public diplomacy in Lebanon in 2010, for example, noted: "American diplomats' movements are restricted to the confines of the Embassy and areas deemed safe by the Embassy security officer. Movement in Hezbollah controlled territories in the Bekaa valley and in the South are especially problematic. This causes the most hindrance to public diplomacy efforts, since most of the anti-American sentiment, coupled with poverty and lack of education, makes these regions particularly eligible for Embassy programs." According to the CAO in Beirut, "The Embassy's Foreign Service Officers are restricted in their travel throughout the country for fear that they may be targeted for their nationality and high governmental status.... However, through the participation of Foreign Service Nationals and Lebanese volunteers, who are generally free to travel, the programs do have a chance of success."[48]

Afghanistan is a more extreme case, because the country is a war zone. When General Stanley McChrystal was the US commander there, he described the inherent difficulty of conducting information public diplomacy programs in competition with the Taliban as follows: "Information operations drive many insurgent operations as they work to shape the cultural and religious narrative. They have carefully analyzed their audience and target populations accordingly. They use their Pashtun identity, physical proximity to the population, and violent intimidation to deliver immediate and enduring messages."[49] The PAO in Afghanistan in 2011 said that the security situation prevented diplomats from engaging with the people as they do elsewhere, in "receptions, dinners, having coffee or going out to a restaurant with people. That was more difficult if not impossible, but the key element of getting outside the wire, outside the embassy, in Afghan institutions and ministries and universities and schools and NGOs, we could do and—with some risk, more risk than, you know, many other places, but... you can't do public diplomacy if you are unable to do that."[50]

Equally problematic are the constraints on programming that some PAOs face due to restrictions imposed by the host government. In Cuba, for example, public diplomacy professionals work under very significant handicaps. The Cuban authorities prohibit direct access to local government officials, and they limit the scope of US officials to a 25-mile radius from the Interests Section. Moreover, the usual PD instruments of people-to-people contact, student exchanges, democracy promotion via working with local organizations, and working with the media, are simply impossible because of official restrictions and surveillance.[51]

The most extreme cases are in Iran and North Korea, and in 2012 in Syria, where the US does not have any diplomatic presence so all of the public diplomacy activity must be conducted from outside, mostly by broadcasting and social media (see following chapters.) China also imposes restrictions that hamper the PD program there.

## Coordinating with the Ambassador and with Washington

The final step in the strategic planning process for the PAO is to develop a specific program and budget and seek approvals from the ambassador and Washington. (The different types of *program* will be discussed in subsequent chapters.) The following are the steps the PAO must take to gain approvals.

As the chief of one of the embassy sections, the PAO reports directly to the ambassador who must approve all public diplomacy projects. The PAO is also a member of the ambassador's country team and must work with its members. The country team includes all section chiefs, some of whom are State Department officials, and some who represent different Washington agencies. The number of sections varies depending on the size and local circumstances, including the importance of the country. The following is a typical staffing pattern for a large embassy, showing the section heads, the bureaucratic abbreviations of their positions, and the Washington agencies that they represent, although the actual personnel configuration depends largely on the details of bilateral relations.[52]

*Large Embassy Country Team*

Ambassador or Chief of Mission (COM)—State
Deputy Chief of Mission (DCM)—State
Consular Officer—State
Political Officer (Poloff)—State
Economic Officer (Econoff)—State
Management Officer—State
Regional Security Officer (RSO)—State
Public Affairs Officer (PAO)—State (formerly USIA)
Foreign Commercial Service Officer (FCS)—USDOC
Defense Attaché (Defatt)—DOD
Military Assistance Officer (Milatt)—DOD
USAID Mission Director—USAID

Homeland Security Officer—HHS
Labor Attaché (Labatt)—Department of Labor
Legal Attaché (Legatt)—Department of Justice
Agricultural Attaché (Agatt)—Department of Agriculture

In a small embassy, the country team might include only an ambassador, DCM, political/econ officer, consular officer, administrative officer, and PAO.

The PAO works with the ambassador and the country team in two respects. First, the PAO is required to integrate the public diplomacy plan into the mission's strategic plan (MSP) as developed by the country team and approved by the ambassador and Washington. It outlines US national objectives and analyzes the major obstacles to the achievement of those objectives. In the past, when USIA existed (1953–1999), the PD plan was an unclassified document developed by the PAO and the ambassador was consulted but approval was given by USIA Washington. Since the merger with State in 1999, the PD plan is an integral part of the classified MSP that covers all sections of the embassy and is approved by the ambassador and State's regional bureau in Washington.

The PAO should also seek the support of other members of the country team, as appropriate, to help carry out the public diplomacy program. Some can be recruited as speakers, others can open doors for contacts, or help arrange local program venues.

The public diplomacy program proposals in the MSP serve as a general guideline but efficient PAOs know how to be flexible to take advantage of unanticipated opportunities. As the PAO in Hungary, Michael Hurley, put it, despite the MSP,

> quite a bit of the work that we do here in Hungary is necessarily unplanned. Since we have a fairly small budget, we don't invite big groups or performers over the way we used to. But they show up on our doorstep here. We had the New York Philharmonic come in, the Pittsburgh Symphony recently... these are not projects that are funded by the embassy, but we work with them to bring some publicity to them and also perhaps do a reception, so we get them together with people they might not meet... a big part of what we do is facilitating those kinds of meetings.... Recently, the Harlem Globetrotters were in Hungary.

When they performed, the PAO gave a speech to a crowd of 10,000 people at halftime, and presented a "Sports Diplomacy Award" to each of the players, while explaining to the audience how much they had contributed to American culture as African Americans.[53]

Public diplomacy goals tend to evolve slowly and incrementally so plans generally do not change radically from year, but occasionally a major event may cause new objectives to be added.[54] The best example of that is the impact of the 9/11 terrorist attack on the United States and the Bush government's decision to make the Global War on Terrorism a top priority. For public diplomacy posts around the world, Washington signaled this meant a new focus on Muslim audiences and youth. First the State department organized a conference on engaging Islam that took place in Cairo in October 2002 for US officials working in countries with significant Muslim populations. This led to the creation of a television program, "Muslim Life in America," that was produced and sent to posts to place on local television, but the program was not as successful as hoped because it was seen as a transparent attempt to present a positive picture of Muslims in America at a time when some of them were being harassed.[55] But as noted above, individual public diplomacy posts did their evaluations based on local conditions and many of them focused on Muslim audiences.

In addition to the MSP, the PAO to be effective must work closely with the ambassador and other embassy officers to enlist them to support and participate in public diplomacy programs. The PAO can help the ambassador and other officers deal with the press, by briefing them on local reporters and editors, and recommending talking points. Beyond that, the PAO can enlist the ambassador and other officers to participate in public events, where they can add prestige and expertise to the occasion. As an American public diplomacy official in Indonesia explained:

> Public diplomacy is not only done narrowly by the Public Affairs Office. The Ambassador does it. USAID does it. Peace Corps does it. Public Health does it. Public diplomacy is widely accepted as major tool for all operations of the Embassy, and people-to-people activities are not only conducted by the Public Affairs Section but other parts of the Embassy and the Ambassador. For example, USAID funds several university linkage programs between the U.S. and Indonesian institutions of higher education as a new initiative, and the newly returned Peace Corps English teaching program certainly promotes education and people-to-people exchanges in a broad sense.[56]

In short, it is the task of the Public Affairs Officer to manage the building of communication bridges between the United States and the local public. To do so, he or she must start by understanding the local culture and local attitudes towards matters of interest to the United States, then identify target audiences and obstacles to communication, and orchestrate programs that address areas of concern and misunderstanding between the two countries. In the following chapters we will examine some of the means by which this is done.

CHAPTER FOUR

# Contacts and Personal Networking Techniques

Public diplomacy practitioners regard direct, face-to-face oral communication as one of the most powerful techniques for communication across cultural borders. Edward R. Murrow, who was President Kennedy's USIA director, famously said, "It has always seemed to me the real art in this business is not so much moving information or guidance or policy five or 10,000 miles. That is an electronic problem. The real art is to move it the last three feet in face to face conversation."[1] He meant that face-to-face engagement with the audience is a very effective public diplomacy tool that can facilitate almost everything the public affairs section wants to accomplish. Experienced practitioners agree, and they often cite Murrow's "last three feet" rule.[2] A veteran PD officer and scholar, with tongue in cheek, calls face-to-face communication a "Killer App." He says: "Far more effectively than Twitter, Facebook, or other social media, it brings people together, leading to significant exchanges of ideas and in-depth relationships."[3] Although Murrow made his career in broadcasting, he knew that the best way to conduct public diplomacy was in face-to-face encounters. The reason is that in such encounters, the American diplomat can engage in an interactive dialogue, during which he or she can develop a nuanced understanding of the perceptions and concerns of the target individual, and speak directly to those concerns in trying to dispel misconceptions and achieve better understanding.

In addition, a major task of the public diplomacy professional is to build a picture of local thinking on issues of relevance to the United States, and a good way to do that is through a conversation with local individuals who are representatives of segments of the population.

Especially in countries where the media are not entirely free, talking to people one-on-one reveals attitudes that are not publicly expressed but are important. This contributes to the embassy's overall understanding of how the bilateral relationship is going. Moreover, such conversations help the public diplomacy professionals think about programs that might be useful in that country.

Direct communication for public diplomacy purposes takes place when an American official meets with one or more foreign nationals. It also occurs however when American private citizens are sent abroad by the State Department to lecture on their specialties, or when foreign nationals visit the United States in the educational exchange program. Also useful, but less so, are the long-distance interactive discussions by videoconference, webcasts, or remote podcasts between American officials in the United States and individuals abroad. All of these encounters can serve public diplomacy purposes because they allow listening, response and dialogue in direct encounters allowing give and take.

### Basic Approaches

#### Contacts and Networking

Successful face-to-face encounters depend on, and in turn reinforce, the careful development of personal contacts. Personal contacts are created by repeated office calls, and in social functions. American diplomats usually find that they must not only put a full eight-hour work day (which they must do by law) or longer, but they also have many social obligations in the evening and on weekends, including receptions, national days and dinners. These are all regarded as working functions, whose primary purpose is not frivolous, but is intended, rather, to develop and deepen personal contacts in a purposeful way.

An ongoing effort must be made to expand the list of contacts through networking. Ideally, American diplomats who are newly arrived at post should be introduced by their predecessors to their most important contacts and they should find files with details about past embassy associations with target audience members, but this does not always happen. However, once established at post, they should always be looking for opportunities to expand the reach of the embassy to new people who are important to US interests, rather than depending on old invitation lists.

One rule of thumb for an effective public diplomacy officer is to get out of the office as much as possible every day, relegating paperwork, the inbox and the Internet and the computer screen to a lower priority. This is more difficult to do today than in the past, because email messages requiring attention accumulate now 24/7, unlike the past when telegrams exchanged with Washington moved messages more slowly. But getting out of the office is also more important today than ever before because of the security requirements that have steadily increased since the terrorist incidents of the 1990s and especially since 9/11. At many embassies, visitors are now discouraged from entering our embassies to meet with Americans today because they must now be carefully registered, pass through security screening, leave cell phones and identification at the gate, and be escorted inside the compound. Visits to embassy public affairs sections have declined as a result, making it more important than ever for the Americans to leave the embassy to seek contact.

*Dialogue*

Another important rule of thumb is that communication with a foreign audience works best when the American begins by listening and ensures that the conversation is a genuine dialogue rather than a monologue. Contrary to popular belief that American public diplomacy is a monologue, effective practitioners know that they can achieve a great deal by listening first. Doing so shows respect for the other person and his or her views, and a willingness to listen to complaints or criticisms. It also allows American diplomat a chance to tailor a response to the other's views that is relevant. Third, it allows the American also to gain a deeper understanding of local opinion, and empathy for the other's views. That provides food for thought for the next encounter—plus possible material for a reporting cable to Washington on local opinion. The creative part of the American's participation in the exchange is to find ways to present American views in the context of a discussion, and a topic, that the other person has raised. Of course there is usually time to bring up new subjects as well, but the conversation goes best when the American listens first.

Public diplomacy officers know that in order to carry out an effective dialogue with a non-American who does not share their culture, they must be careful to remain as open-minded as possible—or at least appear to be—seeking to understand the other's point of view as best they can. They must listen carefully, and not be overly dogmatic in asserting their own opinions, allowing for the fact that their views might in some respects be incorrect, without conceding points they know to be untrue. Their task is to help others understand American foreign policies, society and culture, and they must do that honestly, but in discussions with people who may have a very different opinion of America, they cannot be too dogmatic but must show a willingness to listen. The philosopher John Stewart Mill argued that "truth can only emerge best from the clash of contrary opinions" and that "He who knows only his own side of the case, knows little of that."[4] The public diplomacy officer who appreciates that attitude, and at the same time politely defends the ideas and facts he or she is certain are correct, usually does well. That officer can usually develop effective communication skills by engaging in an open-minded discourse.

The Eisenhower administration's mission statement for USIA said that its purpose was "to submit evidence to peoples of other nations by means of communication techniques that the objectives and policies of the United States are in harmony with and will advance their legitimate aspirations for freedom, progress and peace."[5] This modest mission, to "submit evidence," is in tune with the attitude of many public diplomacy practitioners, especially in today's world, where the advances in technology have led to a 24/7 flood of information, misinformation and opinion about America and issues that involve the United States, and American diplomats know they can only hope to participate in the discussion, not to control it.

### *Followup*

Effective management of contacts requires the maintenance of useable records. In the past, American public diplomacy officers wrote memoranda of their conversations ("memcons") with local contacts, and some still do. The memcons contained quotes from their interlocutors, some analysis of the importance of those quotes and any significant biographical information learned, and some were classified. In any case, information obtained by PD officers may end up in reporting messages to Washington, either written on single conversations or, more likely, collected with others into a report on current thinking about an issue of importance to the United States.

Record keeping is very useful for contact management. In the USIA era, an unclassified "Distribution Records System" (DRS) was developed that contained lists of target audience members, divided into priority and secondary groups, with their complete contact information and relevant biographical data, including their engagements with Americans, plus their special interests that might be met by public diplomacy programs. Although this formal system fell into disuse, many PD officers today keep updated rolodexes or more elaborate contact files.

### Other Embassy Officers

In January 2006, Undersecretary for Public Diplomacy and Public Affairs Karen Hughes sent out a telegram to all embassies entitled "speaking on the record." She specifically addressed it to ambassadors and deputy chiefs of mission as well as public affairs officers, and the main point of the message was to encourage all of them to think of themselves "as advocates for America's story each day." She said she wanted to change the State Department culture about the press from risk avoidance to advocacy, and said they and their staffs should get out "frequently in front of the cameras" and in the columns of the local newspapers, and mobilize their staffs to "wake up every morning with media in mind." She listed what she called "Karen's Rules" for dealing with the press (see details in chapter five).[6] Hughes followed this telegram ten months later with another one repeating her rules and again specifically urging ambassadors to "get out on the media and to support their staff who do appear on the media."[7] It was clear that Washington wanted ambassadors and other embassy officers outside of the public affairs section to participate in public diplomacy.

This was new. Most PD cone officers did not need any such encouragement, but they welcomed the Hughes instruction because it made easier their efforts to get non-PD officers out speaking in public. With the advent of American Centers and later American Spaces, a convenient venue appeared within which officers could conduct people-to-people diplomacy (see chapter 9).

## A Variety of Contacts

### Diplomats or Private Americans?

It is important for public diplomacy practitioners to have as broad a range of contacts as possible. Are there any important contacts out of reach? Private Americans or diplomats?

Some commentators who have written on public diplomacy assume, incorrectly, that private Americans have better access to the public in foreign countries than diplomats do. Some think, also, that US diplomats intentionally spend all their time only with foreign government officials[8] but this is not true of public diplomacy professionals. Others claim that American businesses working abroad are more culturally sensitive than diplomats, have better marketing skills that make them better at public diplomacy, that diplomats live in isolated compounds, and are shunned because US policies are disliked.[9] Some argue that the US government should make extensive use of the expertise of private companies who understand foreign audiences better.[10] It is true that, as several observers have pointed out, in today's world there are many private sector Americans who have contacts abroad, and some of them do understand foreign attitudes and how to communicate across cultures.[11]

But much of this criticism underestimates the fact that American public diplomacy professionals are in fact engaging, on a daily basis, with broad sectors of the foreign society that they are working in, and thereby they are serving the national interest. Private American citizens living and working abroad can play a helpful role in our discussions in foreign countries but they often have a narrow mandate—such as selling a product or service—and they may not be interested in trying to represent America in all its aspects, as US officials are paid to do.

What about access? In fact, American diplomats usually do have access to a wide spectrum of the local society and they can meet with all, or almost all, sectors of that society. Living there, they learn that very few people they want to engage with are out of reach if they make the effort to engage. This is so for several reasons. First, because the US status as a powerful country whose policies affect lives around the world, anyone interested in finding out more about US intentions would likely welcome the chance to talk with an American ambassador or other embassy official. It is clear that what US diplomats say is a much more authoritative version of official government policy, which is often what the local public wants to know. Private citizens may have comments on America but they are not authoritative because they lack the access to official information that diplomats enjoy. Second, diplomats are also much better at explaining US policy since they know the nuances of the policy. If they have been in the country for any length of time, they have developed a good understanding of local views of the United States that they can take into account in their discussions. Thus foreign journalists, media commentators, politicians, officials, professors and students and others interested in international affairs, typically welcome a chance to talk to an American diplomat.

Moreover, even harsh critics of US foreign policy or other aspects of Americans society, are also likely to want to engage with an American diplomat, not only to hear what he or she has to say but also to convey their views to Washington, through the diplomat. Except for the very small number of extreme critics of the United States in some countries who do not want to be seen with an American official, almost everyone of interest to the American official is accessible, if the official makes an effort. In fact, the critics are often flattered when the American official pays attention to them and listens to what they have to say.

Experience has shown, therefore, that US diplomats based abroad have several advantages over private Americans in communicating with the local public. Private citizens on the other hand often speak from the perspective of the private interests they represent, whether commercial or otherwise and thus do not necessarily represent America as a whole, as US diplomats do.

## Government Restrictions on Contacts

What if the host government objects to contacts with the opposition? In those cases, public diplomacy officers should push against those restrictions as much as possible because it is important to stay in touch with the views of opposition elements, and to try to ensure that they know and understand American views. In pushing against those barriers, the PAO must consult with the ambassador, since violating host government rules can risk expulsion (being declared "persona non grata") or otherwise do harm to the official relationship. Yet PAOs should not automatically be intimidated by government displeasure, but should push the envelope to engage with opposition elements insofar as possible.

In some cases the ambassador may comply with the government's concerns and ban contacts with opposition elements. The classic case of this occurred when the American ambassador to Iran in 1979, at the request of the shah, ordered all embassy staff to avoid contact with dissidents, depriving the US government of vital information about the Khomeini revolution.

In other cases, the ambassador has encouraged public diplomacy officers to extend their circle of acquaintances as far as possible, in order to enhance the embassy's dialogue with all elements of society. They may in fact have more opportunities than some other embassy officers, because they carry the title "cultural attaché" or "information officer" rather than "political officer" who may be suspected of being CIA. Moreover, if the CAO manages a library and the exchange program, this may make the function look benign so people are more willing to be in touch with them.

For example, in Yemen in the 1980s, the political officer had great difficulty making contacts with Yemenis, although he was talented and spoke fluent Arabic, because they thought he was CIA. But when he ended his tour, he switched jobs and stayed on as public affairs officer. He suddenly had access to a wide spectrum of Yemenis who considered him to be the cultural attaché and therefore "safe" to meet with. Labels are important. It is also important for the PAO to have the support of his ambassador in reaching out to new contacts. For example, as PAO in Cairo in the 1980s I had extensive contacts with Marxist critics of the government, and when the prime minister called my ambassador and asked him to order me to stop, the ambassador responded to him that I was just doing my job, and told me to continue to reach out. PAOs appreciate that kind of support from the ambassador. It should be noted that some opposition figures or individuals, on their own accord, may avoid or limit contacts with embassy officers when they deem contact is detrimental to them for political reasons. Nevertheless PD officers should engage with whoever is willing to be contacted and is worth engaging.

### PAO as Intermediary

It is not always possible of course for every American public diplomacy officer or every American at the embassy to follow personally the "last three feet" rule of face-to-face engagement. Not only time constraints but distance from remote areas limits the amount of personal contact. If there are important contacts in rural areas, public diplomacy officers may only rarely have time to visit them. The last three feet however are often bridged by others including other embassy officers, visiting American speakers, English teachers, librarians, Fulbright professors and other Americans (see later chapters), and here the PAO can play the role of intermediary, bringing people together.

In addition, some members of the local community may not be only part of the target audience, but they can also be useful surrogates for American officers if they are reasonably well disposed to the United States. Local voices tend to be more credible than American voices, and to the extent they are willing to explain the United States in reasonable terms, they can be very helpful. It would be a tactical error to make them too obviously part of a public diplomacy plan, so this must be handled with sensitivity. Recent returnees from visits to the United States and alumni with whom embassies retain relationships are often good candidates for this role, especially because they are free to travel anywhere in America and talk to anyone so they are usually convinced that they came home with a true and unbiased picture. This technique follows an old principle of communications that was expressed as early as 1965, when Paul Lazarsfeld and Elihu Katz proposed the "two-step flow" of communication. Their theory stressed the importance of the credible human factor in effective communication, meaning that a message transmitted by electronic means (radio or television) was far more credible and had a much greater impact if it was relayed to the audience by human beings, especially "key opinion leaders."[12] Experienced public diplomacy officers know that very well.

There are some occasions when public diplomacy is not appropriate or is counter-productive, and quiet, traditional diplomacy is the preferred course. This might be the case, for example, when the US government believes that an authoritarian government with which it has excellent relations, should become more democratic, both for its own sake, and for the sake of the bilateral relationship, but the host government would strongly object to our public advocacy of democracy locally. Rather than make the case for democracy loudly in public, it might be more effective, depending on circumstances, to make the case privately to senior officials.

### Contact with Officials

Although host government officials are usually not high on the priority target audience list for public diplomacy officers, some of them such as officials in the ministries of information and culture can be appropriate contacts for the PAO, for several reasons. In much of the world, ministries of information have considerable influence over most or all of the local media. It is common for them to have monopoly control at least over radio and television, so they can authorize or deny permission for TV or radio reporters to interview Americans. They may also influence what is written in the newspapers. The minister of culture may have influence over the universities, and might be able to approve or deny access to university professors. They may also have control over programming venues that the public affairs section wants to use for a performance or lecture. Therefore it is important to cultivate these officials to facilitate various public diplomacy programs.

The ambassador and other embassy officers of course have extensive contacts with senior government officials in all other ministries. The political officer will cultivate contacts at the foreign ministry, the military attaché at the defense ministry and so on. But most of them are of little direct interest to the PAO, who, if necessary, can work with these other ministries through other embassy officers.

### Contact with Foreign Diplomats

At each post, US diplomats are according to protocol expected to have friendly relations with diplomats from other countries, and some of these contacts are useful. The American diplomats tend generally to be better informed than the other diplomats assigned to the same country because they represent the United States and because of US influence worldwide, they tend to have better access to host country officials. American embassies also have the benefit of very good intelligence about world events from other US embassies and from Washington. Other diplomats therefore seek out the Americans, so the relationship can be uneven.

Maintaining regular contact with the entire diplomatic corps would not be useful, but some diplomats can be helpful to the public diplomacy staff, if they for example have very good access locally. For example, for an American embassy in an Arab country, the diplomats from other Arab countries tend to have good local contacts and information about what is going on, and they stay in touch with each other. So diplomats in this group tend to be useful to the American embassy.

### Sustaining Contacts

Contact work must be sustained and contacts assiduously maintained over time because only in that way can trust be developed. In particular, when it is necessary to ask a contact for help of some kind, the chance of that request being successful usually depends on the closeness of the relationship. As one experienced diplomat put it, "Whether you have friends when you need them depends to a large extent whether you have made friends when you didn't need them."[13] Diplomats should therefore make a point of seeing contacts regularly to build up the relationship, and not just contacting them when you need something from them (such as to complain to a journalist about a hostile editorial).

Developing trust in contacts, so that the discussions and conversations are candid and therefore more useful, takes time. Tours at an embassy are usually only two or three years—and more and more even one-year tours in so called "unaccompanied" tours and in dangerous locations—which is a short time to develop deep relationships, so longer tours tend to be more productive in that sense.

For example, as a junior officer at the American embassy in Cairo in the 1960s, I developed contacts with several junior university professors and newspaper columnists some of whom who were in more important and interesting positions when I returned a decade later as PAO at the embassy. One of the professors, for example, became deputy foreign minister and another became prime minister, and I was able to reconnect with them.

Local employees can of course accompany American public diplomacy officers to meetings to do the necessary interpreting. They help sustain engagement with audience members over the years. Yet, in some cases, an interpreter (who is usually either a local person or a third country national) can inhibit the conversation when one or both sides want it to be kept confidential. For example, when I was ambassador to Yemen, a very senior official who spoke no English insisted that I not bring an interpreter with me because he wanted to hear directly from me and he wanted to keep the discussion strictly confidential.

### *American Citizens as Partners*

Most Americans resident in the country tend to be lower priority contacts for public diplomacy purposes, unless they have unusually good insights into the local society and culture. The embassy's commercial attaché will usually have a wide range of contacts in the resident American business community, but few of them can offer much help or advice to the PAO because their interests tend to be focused rather narrowly on business.

On the other hand, American private sector companies have in certain circumstances been excellent partners in specific public diplomacy programs. For example, when Kenton Keith was Public Affairs Officer at the US embassy in Cairo, he worked with Ambassador Frank Wisner to bring a major cultural presentation to Egypt at very little cost to the US government. Ambassador Wisner persuaded American companies that were doing business in Egypt to sponsor the visit of an American opera company, an event that furthered public diplomacy goals and gave the sponsoring companies some credit as good corporate citizens. This approach has been duplicated in other countries where there is a significant American commercial presence.

Other public-private partnerships can result in high-quality cultural programs as well. For example, PAO Bridget Gersten and her public affairs team partnered with the Long Island Youth Orchestra in New York to bring them to Vladivostok, Russia, while local Russian partners pitched in on costs to lodge the more than 80 members of the musical entourage. Similarly, Gersten brought a group of mariachi musicians from California for a project that involved a partnership with local Sister Cities in the San Diego area and US community college. The event thrilled the local population, with standing ovations, as many Russians experienced this genre for the first time in their lives. The group returned for a second visit in 2012, back by popular demand.[14]

For information operations of the public affairs section, editors and journalists of local media are their main focus of attention. But they must also consider whether any American or other foreign journalists need attention. American reporters are a special case. In the past, there were many American journalists working abroad as foreign correspondents; that number has dwindled down to only a few today, but if a crisis occurs abroad, they show up to cover the story. Up until 2013, the Smith-Mundt Act had prohibited the use of public diplomacy materials to influence American citizens, yet it did not otherwise inhibit American officials from having professional contact with American media professionals, in Washington or abroad.

In the United States, the relationship between an American officials and an American reporter is often an adversarial one. As a veteran reporter says, "Reporters have a right and a duty to suspect the motives of officials."[15] The official's goal on the other hand is to further the interests of the government, so he or she is careful in answering the reporter's probing questions, to be truthful but not reveal classified information. In fact, however, most reporters are not working to embarrass the government, and most officials are not working to hide mistakes.[16]

When an American diplomat based at an embassy abroad deals with an American journalist, this same adversarial relationship carries over, with some modification. American diplomats know that American reporters based abroad are often excellent sources of information for the embassy. But diplomats know that they should be cautious with reporters who come through on a brief visit, because they might not play by the ground rules. The interplay between diplomats and reporters is both cooperative and adversarial. Sometimes their agendas coincide, and sometimes they collide. Usually they coexist warily. Yet diplomats who ignore reporters are shortsighted because they often have excellent contacts and useful information. When veteran diplomat Philip Habib was ambassador to South Korea, for example, he always asked to see visiting reporters as soon as they arrived in country and again before they left because he wanted to have them ask questions useful to him, and he wanted to know what they found out.[17]

A diplomat who gives a journalist information that he does not want to be attributed to the source will carefully spell out the ground rules at the beginning of the interview. If the diplomat trusts the reporter, either because the reporter works for a very reputable media outlet, or because they know each other well from an extended relationship, the diplomat can be relatively certain that the reporter will respect the ground rules. But a diplomat working in a foreign country often is not so sure the reporter will respect the ground rules unless they have worked together and established trust. Trust may also not exist between diplomats and American reporters from lesser known media outlets who make a short visit to the country where the diplomat is posted and visit the embassy for a briefing, in which case the diplomat may tend to be more cautious. To build up positive relations and trust within the journalist community, embassies have included foreign journalists on IVLP programs or worked with Washington to put together special programs dedicated to issues in journalism so that reporters and editors learn first-hand about ethnics in journalism and related topics, meeting US counterparts face to face.

## Truth and Loyalty

Contrary to popular belief, American diplomats should never lie. Trust is very important in any relationship between an American diplomat and local contacts, especially in the media. Edward R. Murrow, as Director of USIA, said: "To be persuasive we must be believable; to be believable we must be credible; to be credible we must be truthful. It is as simple as that."[18] Public diplomacy professionals follow that rule. They know if they lie, their contacts will be undermined and perhaps ruined. In practice, the basic rule to be truthful is not difficult to follow. Occasionally tension might arise when the diplomat is asked for a personal opinion about an aspect of US policy that he or she as an American official should defend but personally disagrees with. In that case, the solution is neither to express personal criticism of the policy (which would be disloyal) or to lie and endorse it personally, but rather to decline to express a personal opinion. Instead, the diplomat should try to explain, objectively, the reasons that the US government has chosen that policy and why it has support from the American public.

## Conclusion

American FSOs understand the importance of personal contacts but those who have experience in public diplomacy abroad know that networking is an absolutely essential part of their work. They regularly try to get out of the office, escaping the inbox and computer messages from Washington in order to practice Murrow's dictum on the "last three feet." They know that face-to-face engagement with a variety of members of the local public helps them understand local attitudes and respond to criticisms and misperceptions. They may include selected officials, diplomats and American journalists among their contacts, but they especially seek out opinion leaders in the local society, including any of our harshest critics who will talk to them. They may need to cope with local government restrictions on contacts but they find ways to do that. They know that dialogue rather than monologue works best, and that truthfulness is important because the ultimate purpose is an honest discussion on topics of mutual interest.

# PART III
## *Information Programs*

CHAPTER FIVE

# Traditional Information Channels

American public diplomacy (PD) professionals working at US diplomatic missions abroad use a variety of communication methods to accomplish their objectives. Broadly speaking, they can be divided into (a) information activities carried out primarily by the information officer (IO), and (b) educational and cultural activities carried out primarily by the cultural affairs officer (CAO), both under the general supervision of the public affairs officer (PAO). These two functions are quite different in purpose, means, and effects. Three chapters will describe and analyze the information functions; this chapter will focus on the traditional information channels and chapters six and seven on the electronic social networking media, new in the twenty-first century.

The traditional types of PD communication activities supervised by the IO can be differentiated into six main types: (1) talking to reporters and editors, (2) media placement, (3) local television and radio access, (4) printed materials, (5) ambassadorial interviews, and (6) mediating other communicators.

## Talking to Reporters and Editors

Typically, the IO is the key person at an embassy designated to talk to media representatives, although on especially sensitive issues the PAO or even the ambassador may want to handle that task. Both the IO and the PAO cultivate media contacts and they come to know whom to trust among reporters and editors. Any American embassy official who speaks to the press must know interview ground rules and make clear at the start of the interview which rules are to be followed. Not all officials do that, and some non-PD diplomats are unsure what the different rules mean. The basic ones are these:

1. "On the record" means the information is attributed to the source by name and title;
2. "On background" means attribution hides the actual identity of the source with a euphemism that is agreed to in advance; it could for example be attributed to "an American" or "a State Department official," or a "knowledgeable source," not further identified;
3. "On deep background" provides no attribution and no direct quotes, implying the information is based on "the wisdom of the reporter";
4. "Off the record" means the information may not be published in any form, and technically not even taken down in notes or recorded.

Veteran diplomat Chip Bohlen added some of his own guidelines for dealing with reporters: Take them seriously; never tell them an untruth, but you don't need to tell them everything; never deal with an iffy proposition; never discuss something that is being decided; never denigrate a fellow worker; and if you don't know the answer, say so.[1]

Bohlen's admonition about an untruth is a key point. Trust is very important in any relationship between an American diplomat and the media. A diplomat who gives a journalist information that should not be attributed to the source will carefully spell out the ground rules at the beginning of the interview. If the diplomat trusts the reporter, either because the reporter works for a very reputable media outlet or because they have an established relationship, the diplomat can be relatively certain that the reporter will respect the ground rules. But a diplomat working in a foreign country is often unsure the reporter will respect the ground rules if they have not worked together and established trust. Trust may also not exist between diplomats and American reporters from lesser known media outlets who make a short visit to the country where the diplomat is posted and visit the embassy for a briefing. In this case the diplomat may tend to be more cautious.

Occasionally a foreign journalist who is a critic of US policy may ask the American official about his or her personal view of the policy. If the official agrees with the policy he or she can say so. If the official happens to disagree with the policy, the best response is to decline to comment, saying his personal view is not important. If the critic insists on knowing, the American can repeat his or her refusal to comment. In that way the official has not been disloyal or dishonest, but at the same time the interlocutor may have taken the hint that the official is not entirely behind the policy, which does no real harm. In any case, the American official should not confide his or her personal disagreement with policy because that might end up as a quote in the local press, doing harm to US interests—not to mention to his or her own career. If the reporter breaks the attribution rules, or misquotes the diplomat, the reporter will be reminded of the agreed rules after the fact and will find that he or she is less trusted with information in the future.

For example, during the George W. Bush administration, an Arab newspaper editor who engaged in a conversation with an American PAO and criticized the US invasion of Iraq might ask the PAO's personal opinion about that policy. If the PAO believed the invasion was wrong, he should decline to answer the question, but instead explain why the president had decided to invade and point out that the Congress and most Americans had supported the policy, facts that are important in our democratic system. In this way, the American provides useful information without being disloyal.

### Media Placement

Another information task of the public affairs section at any US diplomatic mission is to persuade local media to print material helpful to American interests. The PD staff provides articles and other materials to editors of local newspapers and magazines and encourages them to print them in whole or in part. The International Information Programs bureau (IIP) at the State Department in Washington provides materials electronically and the IO selects and adapts them for local dissemination, although some are acquired directly by local media. When a local newspaper or other media outlet uses these materials, this not only achieves widespread distribution but also adds credibility to the material.

There are two basic rules to follow when placing material. First, depending on circumstances, the embassy does not need to require attribution of the source of the material because the point is not to claim credit for the material but rather to ensure that it reaches a wide audience. The IO (or PAO) also does not request that the editor hide the source but leaves it up to him or her. Secondly, it is very important that the transaction with the local media editor be based on persuasion rather than financial compensation or a quid pro quo arrangement. The PD staff should never pay for placement because it degrades the quality of the information presented and creates an expectation that all placements will be paid. Nor should the transaction be clandestine or deliberately hidden if there is a danger that revealing the source of the information would damage the relationship. The relationship should be based on trust and honest cooperation, and the placement based on persuading the editor that the information is accurate and beneficial. So placement must be an open arrangement, in which the editor sees the value of the material offered. The American officer must carefully balance these two requirements. This principle is central but has sometimes been misunderstood.[2]

Whether or not a local editor will publish material supplied by the US embassy depends on several factors, including the nature of the local political system, the attitude of the host government and the disposition of the individual editor. If the editor or the media outlet tend to be hostile to the United States—or if the host government is hostile and controls the media—it will be very unlikely that this media outlet will be willing or able to publish anything favorable to the United States. On the contrary, this media outlet will be likely to print material provided by its own government and other sources that is harmful to American interests. China is a good example of a media environment hostile to the United States. On the other hand, if the host government is friendly to the United States or allows press freedom, and if the editor personally has a friendly attitude toward the United States, chances are much better that the editor would be willing to print materials supplied by the embassy. Brazil and the United Kingdom are good examples of this.

The problem for public diplomacy in hostile media environments is not only that the local editors and publishers are under orders not to publish anything helpful to the United States, but also the government has the ability to control the public narrative through the media outlets it controls or owns directly. In China, for example, the government influences public perceptions through biased reporting and news coverage by the state-controlled Xinhua News Agency, and the Chinese Communist Party's *People's Daily*. The constant flood of news and opinion from these official outlets shapes the communication environment, and it also encourages self-censorship by media personnel who usually tend to be especially careful not to cross the line, which may be somewhat vague, so they err on the side of caution.[3]

A foreign newspaper editor may be suspicious of materials an American diplomat supplies and rely more on his or her own sources, whether from the wire services or from the host country government. Conversely, the editor may not trust his or her own government to supply accurate information and might even trust US embassy sources more. The IO in any case must make an estimate of the editor's attitude and of how best to approach him or her under the circumstances. That estimate is done by reading the newspaper's editorials, talking to the editor himself and asking the advice of the embassy's local employees.

In countries where the United States provides economic assistance or disaster relief, the embassy's IO has often undertaken a special effort to publicize that assistance and relief. For example the IO in Cairo has for years worked to help the Egyptian media carry stories about USAID projects, even to the extent of providing transportation and special background handouts to the journalists to report on project openings. However, since 9/11, USAID has increased its own effort to publicize what it is doing abroad.[4]

What if a local newspaper or magazine prints a story or other material that is harmful to the interests of the United States? Can the PAO get a retraction or correction placed in order to minimize the damage? In many circumstances, a retraction or correction is difficult to achieve. If the original harmful story was deliberately and knowingly selected to do harm to the United States, there is little chance it can be undone. Syria is an example of that kind of environment. On the other hand, if the editor is generally well disposed to the United States and not restricted by his government, but merely printed the original story thinking it was accurate; he or she might be amenable to a follow-up correction as a result of a phone call from the PAO or the ambassador. This might happen, for example, in the United Kingdom or France. That phone call would carry special weight if the American officer had cultivated a personal relationship with the editor that resulted in some mutual trust. Ambassadors themselves occasionally get involved in such cases.

## Local Television and Radio Access

For decades, IOs and PAOs around the world have sought to gain access to local radio and television programs for American officials and others who can explain US policies and aspects of American society and culture. Embassy websites sometimes carry Voice of America material, but it is far more effective to have local radio and TV broadcast material that PAOs provide. Public diplomacy officers know that these local media, especially radio, reach the largest foreign audiences. Local television is usually also far-reaching, but the vast majority of the world's population uses radio. By 2010, 75 percent or more of households even in developing nations for example had access to a radio, while only 20.5 percent of those households had access to the Internet.[5]

Access to foreign radio and television for American officials is usually not easy. The same challenges apply as to local print media, but in many countries, even where there are independent newspapers, radio and television might be controlled directly by the government, making access rules more difficult. Yet the benefits of gaining access for PD purposes are considerable. As a rule, American public diplomacy officers seek to arrange for themselves, their ambassadors or other US officials to participate in interviews and talk shows, even when the interviewer or the talk show host and guests are strongly critical of the United States. The idea is that it is better to participate than to leave the stage to critics.

### The al-Jazeera Boycott

The longstanding belief that PD professionals should make every effort to have US officials appear on local radio and television whenever possible was tested when the George W. Bush administration decided to boycott one major Arab satellite TV station, al-Jazeera.

Al-Jazeera was established by Qatar in 1996 and it quickly became the leading TV channel in the Arab world because of its new approach. It was the first Arab television channel to send reporters into Israel. It was the only TV channel to open a bureau in Afghanistan in the 1990s, which gave it privileged access to the Afghan government and al Qaida when the United States invaded that country after the 9/11 attack. Washington had paid little attention to al-Jazeera, but when Afghanistan suddenly became the source of breaking news worldwide, and al-Jazeera broadcast exclusive statements by Usama bin Ladin, al-Jazeera quickly attracted the Bush administration's attention. The administration decided that al-Jazeera was deliberately being anti-American. Some even suspected bin Ladin was using it to send secret messages to his agents and followers. They said, "By broadcasting the words of a terrorist, al-Jazeera is supporting terrorism."[6]

US officials formally complained to the Qatari government. In October 2001, when then Secretary of State Colin Powell met in Washington with the Ruler of Qatar, Hamad bin Khalifa, Powell complained about al-Jazeera, saying it was "helping Usama bin Laden by uncritically broadcasting his messages." The Ruler rejected the complaint, saying his government in fact had "no responsibility for al-Jazeera program content."[7] Although the Qatari government funded it, the channel was established as an independent company, so technically the Ruler was correct. The Bush administration then imposed an unofficial and unspoken ban on contact with al-Jazeera, so no US officials appeared on the channel.

But after Karen Hughes took over as Bush's undersecretary of state for public diplomacy and public affairs, she lifted the ban on al-Jazeera and encouraged officials proactively to engage with foreign media outlets. Moreover, Hughes instructed ambassadors and PAOs to seek to appear regularly on al-Jazeera to explain American views. She then broadened the policy to encourage proactive involvement with all media. A former television reporter in Texas, and a close advisor to President Bush, she understood the importance to American public diplomacy of engaging with foreign media. In her instruction, she said,

> When I arrived at the State Department, there was an unofficial policy that our ambassadors had to get pre-clearance from Washington before they could engage with the media...I have totally changed that policy, and not only encouraged [engagement] but also tried to provide information to help our ambassadors get out and be America's face and voice and presence in the countries where they serve our country. We have now made public diplomacy a criteria [sic] in the evaluation of every single Foreign Service officer and every ambassador. That's a major change because we went through a period in 2003 and 2004, we were involved in very difficult policy decisions and no one was out describing them on the airwaves. We have dramatically increased our presence in Arabic, on Arabic stations. We have set up regional hub operations to recognize the increasingly regional nature of the media today. We have two fulltime Arabic speakers now in Dubai whose job it is to get on Arab media and explain America's policies and values and communicate our position on issues of importance to the Middle East.[8]

Between September 2006 and April 2007, the American presence on Arab media increased by 30 percent.⁹

As Professor Marc Lynch correctly wrote in defense of Hughes's decision:

> al-Jazeera is still by far the most watched and most politically influential Arab television network. Its programs are the most important place where Arab views of the United States and American policy are formulated... All America's absence from those debates accomplishes is to cede the field to its enemies, to allow hostile arguments or allegations to go unchecked, and to give speakers on those programs no incentive to take American perspectives into account. Over the last year and a half, the American government—from Undersecretary Hughes and the State Department to the Pentagon—have largely come to understand that reality and have begun re-engaging with al-Jazeera for pragmatic reasons.¹⁰

## Following Guidance

In January 2006, Karen Hughes issued important guidelines for dealing with the press that she sent to embassies around the world, addressed directly to PAOs, ambassadors, and deputy chiefs of mission. She said she did so because there was a climate of risk avoidance at the State Department in dealing with the media that she wanted to change, and her first point was to "think advocacy," encouraging diplomats strongly to speak out and engage with the media. She said American diplomats did not need clearance if they quoted from what senior US officials had said on the record and she promised to provide more such statements. She included qualifiers, however, warning diplomats not to "get out in front of" policymakers on any issue and also not to commit the United States to providing resources when commenting on local disasters. She also said that if an embassy official gave an interview to a US-based journalist, or to an outlet with widespread international distribution, State should be notified—showing special sensitivity to what might appear in the American media. At the end of 2006, Hughes issued these same "Karen's Rules" again in a telegram to all embassies, this time adding a special pitch for ambassadors and other embassy officers to get out and do television interviews.¹¹

One example of the delicate balance between candor and policy advocacy occurred in 2006 when Alberto Fernandez, the director of the public diplomacy office in the State Department's Near East bureau made a statement to al-Jazeera in Arabic that caught the attention of the American press. Fernandez is a very talented Arabic-speaking officer and he had been doing several interviews every day with Arab media in Arabic. On one occasion while defending US policy in Iraq, he argued that there had been mistakes by many countries in that situation, and added that there had been "arrogance and stupidity" by the United States in Iraq. When it became a news story, he was admonished by senior State Department officials that this was an inappropriate comment by an official. He apologized, saying he had misspoken and added: "This represents neither my views nor those of the State Department." Undersecretary Karen Hughes defended him as did others. Professor Marc Lynch said the sentence was taken out of context in which Fernandez was correctly showing laudable self-criticism to establish "credibility and a reputation for candor."[12] Fernandez did not suffer any negative career consequences; he was later appointed as ambassador to the Republic of Equatorial Guinea and other senior positions.

Occasionally diplomats make mistakes and issue public statements that are not fully authorized. In September 2012, for example, a public diplomacy officer at the US embassy in Cairo issued a statement on Twitter that tried to prevent criticism of an anti-Muslim American private film that was being discussed in the Egyptian media. Although he cleared the statement with the charge d'affaires (the ambassador was away), Washington instructed him not to use it but he did anyway and was reportedly criticized by State Department officials for using it and repeating it. The US presidential campaign was going on at the time and the issue was picked up by Republicans as a gaffe by appearing to take sides with the protesters, but President Obama said, "It came from people on the ground who are potentially in danger. And my tendency is to cut folks a little bit of slack when they're in that circumstance, rather than try to question their judgment from the comfort of a campaign office."[13]

The State Department has an internal dissent channel that is intended to be used by American diplomats who want to express their disagreement with specific policies. Ultimately a diplomat who finds Washington policies impossible to defend in good conscience can resign, although this does not happen often. In February 2003, for example, FSO John Brady Kiesling resigned from the Foreign Service in protest against President Bush's decision to go to war against Iraq. Two weeks later, FSO John H. Brown resigned from the Foreign Service for the same reason. They had each been FSOs for more than twenty years. Kiesling had served at US missions in Athens, Tel Aviv, Yerevan, and Casablanca.

Brown had served as a PD officer at US missions in London, Prague, Krakow, Kiev, Belgrade, and Moscow.[14] They could not in good conscience continue to defend Bush's policies so they left the Service.

## Disseminating Printed Publications

In the twentieth century, USIA field officers distributed a variety of printed publications in hard copy to foreign audiences, as described in chapter one. In the twenty-first century, field officers still distribute printed material and the types of content are very similar, as are the PD purposes. But the delivery technique has changed considerably. The IIP at the State Department produces pamphlets, brochures, press kits, paper shows (small travelling exhibits), photo galleries, and posters. Each publication is written with a different and specific PD audience in mind, and IIP consults with posts on content. The materials are produced in several languages in addition to English. State's Foreign Affairs Handbook says, "Embassies and missions abroad are encouraged to download and disseminate to key audiences complete journals as well as individual articles, in print and electronic form...Journals are also marketed directly to international audiences via the World Wide Web, and the daily Washington File carries journal articles."[15]

This means of delivery takes advantage of modern electronic technology, but at embassies, the embassy's public affairs section has several options. It can print the material locally, which is particularly useful for translated texts to ensure accuracy. Or, because the publications are unclassified and available worldwide, the PAS can retransmit the material to local audiences electronically or inform local audiences of its availability online so they can print it out themselves. Washington also sends some publications to its overseas printing facilities where hard copies are produced and sent on to posts. Each post receives printing allocations as part of its annual budget approval. Some printing is done in the Manila, Philippines, printing plant that has been operating for years.[16]

The publications are available not only in English, but also other languages. As of 2014, they were being published in French, Spanish, Russian, Arabic, Farsi, Urdu, Chinese, and Portuguese, and in six thematic categories:[17]

1. Democracy, civil society, and education. Examples of titles are: overcoming barriers to equal education, the constitutional convention of 1787, Supreme Court, community service, NGOs;

2. Peace and security. Examples of titles are: the United Nations, NATO, Western Hemisphere partnership;
3. Environment, science and technology, and health. Examples of titles are: global warming, combating wildlife trafficking, new frontiers in science;
4. Economic growth and development. Examples of titles are: corporate social responsibility, social entrepreneurship;
5. All about America. Examples of titles are Thanksgiving, pop culture, summer jobs, and on major cities; and
6. Events. Examples of titles are: a NASA mission, a visiting Congolese delegation.

### Ambassadorial Interviews

Local media editors and reporters are more likely to want to interview the American ambassador than the PAO or IO, so the public affairs section typically works to facilitate such interviews. They sometimes may need to persuade the editor or reporter to do it and they sometimes also need to persuade the ambassador to do it. A few of them also need coaching, but some ambassadors are very good at press engagement and even are active in reaching out themselves. This helps the PD program considerably.

For example, as the PAO in Kenya John Haynes said about his boss: "With a proactive Ambassador, we are in the newspapers, radio and TV almost every day and frequently in the headlines. While this does provide a high profile for our presence and positions, one could argue that our other programs—education, cultural and information—affect people more directly and allow them to have a personal experience with a representative of the USG, which probably influences their opinions and thoughts more significantly."[18]

One ambassador summed up the skill set that PD officers have when he said:

> Hopefully, the State Department will learn what USIA forgot: that its most important asset is its people in the field. Any time the United States needed to speak to the Croatian public, my PAOs used their contacts and expertise to arrange the most effective way for me to communicate: an exclusive interview with an opposition newspaper, a guest appearance on state-run television, a speech at a university, or an extensively covered ride on a

refugee tractor. This low-tech, relatively low-cost approach gave us far more coverage than all the expensive programs coming out of Washington. The State Department must adequately support these officers in the field. Their work is the substance of public diplomacy. The department would make an excellent start by reversing the trend that favors marginal Washington-based programs to people in overseas posts. The department should also ensure that consolidation increases the opportunities for USIA personnel. In the modern world where public and traditional diplomacy are so intertwined, public affairs and political officers should not only work closely together—in many cases their jobs should overlap.[19]

## Mediating Other Communicators

One of the most effective ways to communicate with a foreign audience is through others who are trusted sources of information. If a PAO or IO can identify a local personality who is well informed about the United States and reasonably open minded in his or her judgments of America, this person might be well worth supporting. This support might include providing factual materials and background on US policies, or on American society and culture, or talking points that the local personality might not have considered. If the ideas and information are used in the local press, the fact that they are presented by a trusted compatriot can give them credibility. The added advantage is that the presentation would be in the local language, using terms and references the audience would clearly understand.

This support must be offered carefully, on a friendly basis, without giving the impression that the local spokesperson is being hired or asked to do anything unpatriotic. The information is offered simply to help inform rather than to set the person up as an unpaid surrogate. Also, the American officer must be reasonably certain that on balance, what the person would say would be accurate and generally helpful to the United States, even if it includes some criticism.

Among the best candidates for this kind of support are returnees from US-sponsored visits to the United States, including Fulbright students and professionals, or recipients of International Visitor Leader grants (see details of these programs in chapter ten). Returnees from these programs often have had positive experiences they are willing to share with others, and can be encouraged to do so.

For example, one PAO in Cairo was asked by an Egyptian television station to appear in a program on American politics, but instead of simply accepting the invitation, the PAO suggested that the TV station invite an Egyptian scholar who had recently returned from the United States where he had studied the American political system. The PAO explained that the returnee would be a better interview subject since he was fluent in Arabic. The TV station agreed, and the interview successfully presented information and opinions that advanced American interests.

## Washington Support

As President Bush's undersecretary of state for public diplomacy and public affairs, Karen Hughes took several steps to improve State's effort with the foreign press, in addition to the ones mentioned above. First she set up a "rapid response" team of PD specialists in the State Department who had bilingual language skills (first Arabic, then other languages) to monitor foreign media for news and commentary about the United States, and put out a daily bulletin that summarized these foreign media clips and included guidance from US officials on the daily topics. The guidance was brief, unclassified and taken from previous public statements, so they did not need to be cleared and could be distributed quickly. These bulletins go to all embassies and consulates, as well as to government officials in Washington.[20] PAOs and ambassadors found them extremely valuable as up-to-date talking point material that could be used right away.

Hughes also established a small unit at State called the Digital Outreach Team that monitored Internet traffic in Arabic and other languages. The bilingual staff selected key bloggers and others for response, engaging these individuals in an ongoing online conversation. Third, Hughes set up what she called "media hubs" in Dubai, London, and Brussels, created to enable a quick response to Arab and European media news items and editorials. Placing these hubs in the time zones where Arabic media were appearing, and staffing them with PD professionals fluent in Arabic, allowed a much faster response and quicker engagement with those media than had been possible from Washington. By 2014 State had expanded the concept so that there were media hubs in London, Brussels, Dubai, Tokyo, and Johannesburg for those geographic regions, and in Miami for Latin America.[21] The stated purpose was to connect foreign publics with US spokespersons who could discuss American policy.[22]

## Conclusion

Although the PD information environment has changed considerably in the twenty-first century with the growth and adoption of new electronic media channels (discussed in the next chapter), the "traditional" media of newspapers, magazines, radio, and television still reach many more people and have a powerful impact on foreign opinion on matters of interest to the United States. Moreover, many of the techniques that were used throughout the second half of the twentieth century to connect with those traditional media are still used in 2014, although the sources of information and means of delivery have changed.

CHAPTER SIX

# Social Networking Media: Use by Field Posts

This chapter will describe how social networking media are being used currently to advance public diplomacy at American missions abroad. The following chapter will analyze their benefits as well as the costs and constraints that such channels present to the practice of public diplomacy.

Today these tools are quite widely used by public diplomacy practitioners around the world. Yet PD practitioners at field posts know that social media are not a panacea, and not a substitute for other more traditional means of communication, but rather as a very important supplement. They are most effective in reaching younger audiences, and the younger American diplomats tend to be more adept and skillful in their use. But not everyone is reachable by social media, because of personal habits, local restrictions or simply inadequate local technology. Moreover, field officers know that devoting budget and staff time to social media usually means doing less of something else, so the choice is a tradeoff because State's resources are limited.

## The Adoption of New Media

Electronic and social networking media are relatively new tools in public diplomacy. The Internet and the World Wide Web became available in the early 1990s, and SMS (short messaging service) started a decade before that. Public diplomacy professionals at USIA made some use of them before the agency's demise in 1999 but only in very limited fashion. First, they tried the electronic media that allowed rapid dissemination of information unilaterally. In the 1990s they created websites and began to use SMS to reach their audiences. It was not until after the middle of the first decade of the twenty-first century when the more advanced social networking tools were created that American diplomats started using them for public diplomacy purposes.[1]

Delays in the use by public diplomacy professionals of the Internet and the new social networking tools were due in part to the decline in funding and staffing of public diplomacy under USIA at the end of the twentieth century and under State in the early years of the twenty-first century, as discussed in chapter one. For almost a decade public diplomacy missed opportunities to develop a vigorous global internet programming capability to reach millions due to insufficient funding and a lack of trained career personnel.[2]

Even in the early days of Facebook and Twitter (2004–6), some PD practitioners—particularly the older generation—were skeptical about their value and continued to argue that "the last three feet" rule was more important. This attitude reflected an initial skepticism about the new tools that existed also outside of the diplomatic corps. For example, while some observers argued that the Arab Spring, which began in early 2011, could not have happened without social media, others such as popular writer Malcolm Gladwell dismissed the idea that social media were so powerful.[3] One expert says USIA recognized the value of the Internet and attributes the slow adoption of social media to risk-averse State Department bureaucrats after the merger.[4] However, in the State Department, as in American society generally, social media were gradually recognized as important communication tools.

Also, when social media first became available, some diplomats were skeptical that they would warrant the significant resources required to maintain the accounts.[5] This is still a concern. Posts increasingly must divert resources to new media and recruit a new, younger staff, and they must shift priorities and budgets if they are to take advantage of new media.[6] It is, moreover, more difficult for governments to control social networking media than it is for private citizens to do so, therefore diplomats must deal with these newer media in ways that are different from the traditional media. Public diplomacy officers did, however, gradually make some limited use of new electronic communication devices after they became available. By 2013, public diplomacy professionals were using the major social networking tools.

By then, Facebook, Twitter, and YouTube were the social networking media most commonly used for PD purposes. In addition, PD professionals were also using Google Plus, Tumblr, Flikr, Pinterest, and Instagram. Social media accounts managed by the International

Information Programs bureau (IIP) at State in Washington reached more than six million people, while US embassies abroad reached another 15 million. State's PA bureau also has separate Facebook and Twitter feeds in English that deal with US policy matters but tend to have a short-term focus.[7]

Public diplomacy officers at field posts realized that the new media are tools not only for communication but also for planning and evaluation. According to one study of public diplomacy:

> The nature of new media allows for improved accounting and evaluation of public diplomacy programs. By using new media technology, public diplomats can provide more quantitative evidence for evaluation and funding purposes. With online media such as Twitter, Facebook, YouTube, and mobile phone technology, more information about the number of "followers," "fans," and subscribers to the State Department pages can be recorded. With blogging and text postings, the State Department can use mapping techniques to follow message penetration to foreign audiences. By mapping the key words and phrases mentioned in messages from U.S. government officials with the key words and phrases used by foreign responders, we can get a better picture about whether U.S. policy messages are being internalized abroad.[8]

This may or may not be true, but face-to-face communication is almost certainly more likely than electronic communication to reveal what ideas are getting through to the interlocutor. Communicating is not necessarily the same as persuading or influencing, which is more likely to take place face-to-face.

A senior official at State gave this example: "I need to know what a college student in Cairo does when he goes on the internet. What sites does he visit? Who does he talk to? Does he IM [use instant messaging]? Because I want to get into those conversations, if I know the top five places that young people in Cairo go when they're on the internet then I can be there, I can pre-position myself. If I don't know that I just put stuff up on the internet and hope people come."[9]

The new tools are different also because they offer instantaneous communication. Yet they serve basically the same purposes that the traditional media have always served, namely to communicate with foreign audiences in the most efficient way. The new media are especially important tools to reach younger audiences, which are both more likely to use them and more proficient in them. The technologies that became available in the twenty-first century simply offered new channels to supplement the older ones. Telephonic conference calls and Electronic Dialogues used in the twentieth century by PD professionals in Washington and field posts were therefore antecedents and precursors to the social networking media that were increasingly adopted in the twenty-first century in many countries.

At US missions abroad, the public affairs section is responsible for the use of these new media, although some ambassadors also manage their own sites (see the paragraphs that follow). In Washington, the entities at the State Department that manage these media are the IIP and the Bureau of Public Affairs (PA), both under the direct supervision of the Undersecretary for Public Diplomacy and Public Affairs.

When Dawn McCall became the head of IIP in 2010, she reviewed its work and decided the bureau was not responding sufficiently to the needs of field posts. She restructured the bureau, asking IIP staff to listen more to field posts and circulating analyses of best practices, which acknowledged that posts should be the drivers of PD efforts since they know their working environments best. McCall established regional groups and thematic packages to correspond to PAO needs. (This concept fit well with the thinking of professional PD field officers who know every country is different.) She structured the major themes into a formal thematic calendar with a menu of information products that posts could choose from, which allowed IIP to show posts what they offered so the posts could plan ahead. Before that, posts might make requests for support IIP could not comply with because of lack of time. Each of the 12 packages was based on previous post requests and included print materials, social media, and Power Point materials that could be edited locally, plus speakers and videos. They were available in several languages. IIP also created a Social Media Hub[10] that contained user manuals to help field posts manage their Facebook, Twitter and blogging sites.[11]

In 2012, McCall encouraged field posts to expand their reach to new audiences through social networking media, asking 20 selected posts to double their Facebook and Twitter numbers by a deadline, in what she called the "20/100/100 program." The posts essentially did so and she added another twenty posts to that challenge.[12] As of summer 2013, the program was in its fourth cycle and had proven extremely successful for countless posts in every region looking to expand their social media audiences.

State's Public Affairs bureau (PA) traditionally has focused its attention on the domestic American audience, including the management of the daily briefings by State's spokesperson who communicates with the press corps based in Washington, DC. However, PA also communicates to some extent with foreign audiences. According to US officials, in 2012 PA became much more active in reaching out to audiences abroad, including by using social networking media. PA developed Twitter feeds in eight languages and became active on Facebook. It uses these tools to conduct question-and-answer sessions with US officials on a regular basis. PA's effort is in parallel with that of the IIP bureau, and officials work together to prevent duplication.[13]

It is useful to think of communication tools for public diplomacy in two categories: primarily unilateral or essentially interactive. The first type of tools (Washington File, websites, YouTube, Rapid Reaction) allows Washington to provide information to public diplomacy officers and other embassy officials that they can use with foreign audiences unilaterally. The interactive tools (Facebook, Twitter, and others), allow audience response and dialogue. Note that many of the PD tools used in the twentieth century were unilateral; only some, like educational exchanges, speaker programs, and personal contacts, were interactive.

## Unilateral Electronic Communication

### Early Transitions to Digital

One of the first major efforts to use unilateral electronic means for public diplomacy was the "Washington File," the digital successor to the Wireless File that had been a PD mainstay throughout the twentieth century. It began to transmit in 1995 on the Internet, to comply with the digital age. Then a new digital platform called "America.gov" was created in 2008 to disseminate policy information and other matters in English and other languages. But in 2011, given the upsurge of such social networking tools as Facebook and Twitter, the State Department suspended America.gov and only kept it as an archived site for previous postings. In making the announcement, State said, "We've Gone Social" and recommended that users follow US government-sponsored social networking platforms.[14] This shift symbolized public diplomacy's greater emphasis on dialogue and interactive engagement. PD professionals had always known that dialogue was better than monologue, but now this carried into the new media. The Washington File continues in archived form.

A senior official in State's IIP bureau, Duncan MacInnes, said the decision to move on from America.gov was meant to be a shift to a "more proactive" web engagement strategy that would use Facebook, Twitter and YouTube more. MacInnes said that a six-month review had led to the shift in strategy: "The new paradigm, particularly for reaching youth, is you have to go to where people already are on the web. People don't visit you, you have to go to them. The material we produced for the America.gov centralized site is now pushed out to the embassy sites." MacInnes added that the role of social media in the uprising in Egypt had "validated" the shift. "It was a moment of revelation for many people," he noted. MacInnes admitted that the US government is not particularly entrepreneurial as an organization, generally, "but we need to be because things change every year, every six months. We will continually look for new ways to get things out." He added, "We're teaching people to write shorter.... We'll produce an article, we'll reduce that to a 200-word piece that can be used for a Facebook page and three or four Tweets that can be used on a Twitter feed and instant messaging." MacInnes also stressed that State was working hard to use these new media in foreign languages. He said, "We've also discovered... that the web has gone from 75 percent English three or four years ago to 70 percent foreign languages now." The content sent out to embassies is now translated into major languages, including Arabic, French, Spanish, Russian, and Chinese.[15]

### *Websites*

The World Wide Web, created in the 1990s, soon led to the creation of websites sponsored by the US government. By the twenty-first century, essentially every American embassy and consulate abroad had a webpage designed to reach foreign audiences with information in the form of text, photographs and sometimes video and audio material. Before the advent of two-way interactive social networking media, US PD professionals at each diplomatic mission depended on websites to provide information on a variety of subjects to their audiences. Washington provides the material but PD professionals at posts select and shape the material to fit the interests of their host countries. The embassy website carries basic policy information relevant to the host nation, plus details about the various sections of the embassy and the services it provides. The websites also contain a great deal of practical information such as names of responsible officials, data on specific countries, travel and visa information and at embassies, information on consular matters such as how to obtain a visa and hours of operation. The State Department also maintains its own website (http://state.gov) that contains policy statements, information about the Secretary of State and other Department personnel, and practical information relating to visas and travel restrictions.

However, these websites are not central tools for public diplomacy.[16] For PD purposes, as one US official says, in the twenty-first century "websites are not too useful because they are static."[17] With a variety of new media now available, even websites are regarded as insufficiently fast to keep up with PD needs. Moreover, they are usually only in English, although some embassies do include a version of their website in the host country's language.

The State Department also created CO.NX (http://co-nx.state.gov), a public website that integrates video, audio, and print into a flexible platform, that delivers content to facilitate dialogue. State also has its own Facebook page. This makes possible the widespread transmission of speeches or town hall meetings by senior officials, as well as online chats with foreign audiences about US foreign policy by Washington and by embassies. It can offer an interactive conversation by video, audio or just text, depending on the bandwidth available to the foreign participant.

State's Education and Cultural bureau (ECA) has an interactive website for foreigners who participated in its education exchange programs, so that they can keep in touch with each other and with Americans they met while in the United States. That bureau also has a website that is intended to engage English language learners.[18]

Some embassies have produced specialized new media products. For example the public diplomacy section of the US embassy in Russia also distributes an electronic quarterly magazine *Otkroy Ameriku* (Discover America).[19] The magazine publishes the ambassador's speeches, announces upcoming cultural events and provides readers with stories about life and politics in the United States.[20] However, the magazine leaves something to be desired in quality and layout and struggles to attract a significant audience. The embassy's website also links to a Russian-language page with extensive reference information about the United States. However, all the information provided at that website can be easily found in other online sources, where it is usually better organized.[21]

## The Rapid Response Bulletin

In 2004, the Undersecretary of State for Public Diplomacy and Public Affairs, Karen Hughes, created the "Rapid Response Unit" (RRU) in the State Department. When she established the RRU, it focused on the Middle East but eventually its scope was expanded to cover the world. The task of this small group is to monitor worldwide public opinion as expressed in foreign media around the clock and to identify major issues of importance to the United States. The RRU team compiles a daily bulletin that summarizes one or two major issues in a brief paragraph, followed by a presentation of brief US policy statements that related to those issues. The policy statements are already in the public domain so the RRU team does not need to clear them. These bulletins are sent to all US diplomatic missions around the world five times each week, where they provide PAOs, ambassadors and other US diplomats with a handy reference tool of cleared US policy statements to use with local audiences. The RRU bulletin is also distributed around Washington, DC, for US officials' use. PAOs and other US diplomats abroad find these RRU bulletins very valuable as supplements to the longer policy statements they receive in telegrams, and on RSS feeds from IIP. Because they are condensed, they save time and for sensitive issues, they offer a check on the exact language that Washington wants to be used. State's Inspector General declared it "useful in supporting public diplomacy overseas."[22]

## Videos

Videos, either on YouTube or on other social media, have been useful PD tools in many countries. By 2013, State's YouTube account had more than 40,000 subscribers. The most active embassy accounts are in Thailand, Brazil, Russia, Israel, and the United Kingdom.[23]

South Korea, for example, is one of the most "wired" countries in the world, with an estimated 37 million Internet users out of a population of 48.5 million. But not all channels work well for public diplomacy. The Facebook and Twitter pages at the US embassy in Seoul, which mainly have content already on the embassy's website, have very few users, but when Patrick Linehan was the PAO in South Korea, he made excellent use of YouTube. He asked a group of students to advise him on the best way to reach out and sustain a dialogue with young people about issues that matter to them. They recommended videos posted on the web. Linehan made arrangements for panels of young people to ask questions of US officials on various topics suggested by students such as trade, immigration, and educational exchanges and posted the videos on the embassy website. This "Embassy Youth Forum" expanded when students used flip cameras at different campuses to film their peers who could not attend the forum.[24]

In Thailand, the PAO produced, either locally or with the help of the IIP bureau, video clips that support his public diplomacy themes. He not only posted them on YouTube and other outlets but he also offered them to local television stations. As one study of public diplomacy in Thailand concluded, this service "creates reciprocal relationship between the Embassy and the local media" because, while the Embassy creates programs addressing its own purposes, they posit themselves as self-funded producers that offer "free of charge" programs to Thai TV stations. Hence, Thai TV stations like Channel 3 and 7 find this term of cooperation convincing. This helps the Embassy to reach out to Thai audiences that do not have access to new media.[25]

In France, according to a PAO who recently served there, the US embassy in Paris is increasingly working with social media because the Internet is widely used. The PAO launched a YouTube channel in 2009. She said: "Social media are also good for conveying information to a large number of youth audiences [and] YouTube provides a good medium for conveying messages in a form that people find accessible."[26] In India, the embassy in New Delhi, the American Center Kolkata, the US Consulate General Chennai, and American Center Mumbai each have their own channels on YouTube with regular video updates both especially made for the channel as well as recordings of cultural activities.[27]

In Chile, the American PD staff manages "santiagopress," a YouTube channel that is updated approximately every two weeks. It has carried, for example, Spanish-language videos of interviews with then-Ambassador Wolf, American art exhibits, musical performances, conferences, and even a video showcasing the experiences of a Chilean high school student who attended science camp at the University of San Diego. The YouTube channel in 2013 had 269 subscribers and slightly more than 4,000 channel views. Total upload views however, reach more than 42,000. The embassy also maintains a Flickr page, which includes photos of various events, including, for example, a Thanksgiving luncheon for Fulbrighters in Chile.[28]

The IIP bureau has facilitated and promoted the production of introductory videos of ambassadors when they first arrive at their posts.

The short clips feature the ambassador speaking to the local public about the bilateral relationship and providing some biographical material. The embassy then posts it on its media outlets and sometimes gets it placed on local television. For example in India, when Ambassador Nancy J. Powell arrived in India in April 2012, the post had her introductory video subtitled in 14 local languages and arranged to have it shown on Indian TV as well as social media.[29]

Finally, several years ago the IIP created a "contest" under the name "Democracy Video Challenge" in which audience members could express their views on topics of mutual interest. Although not interactive because it does not involve an ongoing exchange, it did make use of the new technology to reach new participants.[30]

## Interactive Electronic Communications

During the first decade of the twenty-first century, the State Department dramatically expanded the number of different interactive electronic tools for its public diplomacy professionals. By 2013, public affairs sections at nearly all embassies were using Twitter and Facebook. And by that time, many of them were also using several other new tools: SMS, Google Plus, and Tumblr, which allows users to post multimedia content as short blogs; as well as the photo-sharing devices Flikr, Pinterest, Vimeo, and Instagram.[31]

All of these electronic tools allow responses from recipients and therefore they can be used for interactive communication. The following are the major ones that American diplomats are currently employing for public diplomacy purposes.

### *Short Messaging Service*

Many PAOs have found short messaging service (SMS) especially useful for public diplomacy. SMS, a system that allows communication between fixed line or mobile devices, was first established in the 1980s, and it is an excellent PD tool because today it is the world's most widely used data application in the world, with an estimated 3.6 billion active users, or three-quarters of all mobile phone subscribers. PAOs in some embassies use SMS as a means to alert their contacts to fast-breaking news or provide other information directly in a speedy manner. PAOs often use SMS simply for outgoing messages carrying simply policy alerts, but since it is has two-way capabilities it also has interactive characteristics and can help US officials engage with selective small audiences.

For example, a 2011 study of public diplomacy in India reports that the country

> boasts a massive community of mobile phone users [so] SMS or texts are a major source of communication and information, as many mobile phones are not Internet-enabled. The current PAO stated: "One of benefits of the job being in Delhi is that, with Twitter and SMSing—one can actually really be in touch with a large number of people. You can follow Indian journalists who are good friends and contacts by following their Tweets. You can send and receive SMSs all day long. It is a lot easier to have contact with people that a lot of people thought we left out after merger between USIA and the Department of State. For example, I may see a journalist only once every two to three months, but I may be in touch two to three times a week with SMSs.[32]

A study of public diplomacy in Egypt reported that the US embassy website there "offers a link for journalists to join the embassy SMS service. SMS messages are used quite frequently to alert journalists, media, and academic contacts about speeches, and [they] constitute a key tool for public diplomacy staff." It reported that Embassy Cairo's Facebook site, on the other hand, had few fans, and said: "Public diplomacy professionals in Egypt know that SMS is the best new technology for their purposes in Egypt. The large number of cell phone users and the infrastructure make this one of the most effective ways to reach people.... The public diplomacy staff uses the link on the embassy website to notify journalists quickly of news items, and to communicate directly with their contacts."[33]

One PD study made the following recommendation: "Utilize SMS as much as possible. SMS is a great tool for public diplomacy for the following reasons. First, it can reach the remotest audience who may lack Internet infrastructure. Second, because it does not create any permanent cyberspace locations, SMS enables one-time or ad hoc activities. As seen in China and Africa, SMS conferencing allows for town-hall meetings in which the State Department can preselect the questions they would prefer to answer. This effectively taps into local voices without committing to an unmanageable scale of communication."[34]

It has been found that SMS is especially useful for public diplomacy in Africa, where one study pointed out: "According to March 2009 statistics gathered through a Gallup poll, only one percent of Africans have Internet access in their homes, therefore most people in Africa use Internet cafés.... Mobile phone use however, is different. By the end of 2008, Africa had the highest mobile growth rate in the world. There are currently over 246 million mobile phone subscriptions in Africa. The cost of having a mobile phone has been decreasing over the years, making it a fairly common possession. Because of the decreasing costs, mobile phones have done a better job in reaching people that live in rural villages and towns in Africa. For these reasons, SMS usually far outpaces any other form of new media in Africa." The study concluded: "For outreach to nontraditional audiences in Africa, SMS and podcasts were excellent ways of communicating to the general African population, especially those living in rural areas. The accessibility of mobile phones places U.S. policy messages at the fingertips of Africans from all walks of life and podcasts blend very well with traditional radio broadcasts. Online social networks were not as effective as SMS, primarily because of obstacles in Internet access and because there was not enough two-way communication. By working with private organizations such as Afrigator, MXit, and Safaricom, U.S. policy messages reached a greater audience."[35]

In July 2009, when President Obama made speeches in Cairo and Ghana, the State Department PD staff, in coordination with the White House, conducted a worldwide SMS-based event. People from across the African continent and around the world texted more than 17,000 questions and 50,000 instant messages to the White House in three languages. President Obama produced a podcast in which he answered some of the questions from Africa, and PD officers in Africa took the podcast to radio stations, which broadcast it locally.[36]

### Digital Outreach Team

In November 2006, Karen Hughes established a "Digital Outreach Team" (DOT), a small group of public diplomacy professionals who engaged foreign bloggers in ongoing discussions about U.S. policy. State said: "The Digital Outreach Team contributes to selected Arabic, Persian and Urdu-language web forums and blogs in order to provide accurate statements of United States policy and values and counter misinformation."[37] The Digital Outreach Team then expanded to connect with online audiences in Chinese. Each of these teams writes blogs and contacts existing bloggers in the relevant countries to engage with them on matters of importance to the United States. In this way they are "inserting the government's voice into conversations on prominent blogs and forums and engaging an often skeptical audience on their own ground." As a senior State Department official said, "The blogging team's willingness to address hard issues in an open and transparent way mitigates rancor and helps get our message heard, copied and amplified."[38] The Chinese language team, for example, writes a blog they call "Wild Geese From Foggy Bottom," which gained syndication inside China in Chinese media outlets in both digital and traditional media formats.[39] By 2014 the Digital Outreach Team under the Center for Strategic Counterterrorism Communications was operating in Arabic, Urdu, Punjabi and Somali to counter hostile propaganda and misinformation about the United States.[40] DOTs were also very active on YouTube.[41]

By 2010, some outside researchers had evaluated DOT's effectiveness in countering misinformation. Some studies found it had mixed results, not always dispelling misinformation and in some cases being unpersuasive. One DOT director, however, argued that the system was useful even if it occasionally had shortcomings, saying, "We can't guarantee that by going online and engaging we're gonna change [or] influence anybody, but I can guarantee you if we're not there we won't influence a single soul."[42]

### Facebook, Twitter, and Other Tools

The social networking channels most used by the US government for public diplomacy are Facebook and Twitter.

State's PD Facebook platforms had over 19 million followers as of February 2013. The top ten most-followed US government Facebook accounts include four global accounts managed by IIP Washington that have more than 2.4 million each: "eJournal," "Democracy Challenge," "Our Planet," and "Innovation Generation." Each of these accounts is in English. IIP Washington also manages Facebook pages in five foreign languages: "Amreekani" in Arabic, "Iniciativa Emprende" in Spanish, "Vision of America" in Persian, "American Diary in Russian," and "Generation Innovation" in French. "Vision of America" and "Innovation Generation" are among the top 10 of State's most popular Facebook pages. The latter page hosts a "global conversation about innovation and entrepreneurship" that seeks to "spark a discussion amongst community members about innovative thinking and practical advice for starting a business, helping each other achieve success."[43]

At embassies abroad, in 2013 the most followed embassy Facebook pages were at the US embassies in Pakistan, Indonesia, Egypt, India, Bangladesh, the Dominican Republic, Argentina, Thailand, and Serbia. In that year, State's Twitter accounts had over 1.9 million followers of the 500 million worldwide. The embassies in Indonesia, Colombia, Egypt, and the consulate in Guangzhou were among State's top 10 Twitter accounts.[44]

The social networking environment varies considerably from country to country, and the unique circumstances of each country must be taken into account when evaluating social media's potential as a PD tool.

In Indonesia, at the embassy a team of four staff in the public affairs section, headed by an American officer and including three local employees, manages the Facebook site. It promotes cultural events, offers tourist promotional videos of US states subtitled in Indonesian and pictures of the Embassy's batik collection. It encourages discussion and redirects questions that are beyond the expertise of the team. The posting that announced President Obama's visit to Indonesia boosted interest in the site because it appeared several hours before the regular press release was issued by the embassy. That particular page quickly gathered more than 1,000 posts, "likes," and comments, including invitations to President Obama to come to dinner in private homes.[45]

The US embassy in Paris also maintained Twitter accounts for Ambassador Charles Rivkin and for the embassy.[46] The embassy also maintains a blog.[47]

In India, the PD staff in New Delhi and in four other major cities work diligently on their Facebook sites that are updated multiple times daily.[48] The posts on New Delhi's Facebook page are mostly informational about upcoming events while Mumbai's page featured some specific posts that were signed by individual Foreign Service Officers and Foreign Service Nationals in addition to the generic "American Center Mumbai." The PD staff also uploads photos to its Facebook photo space, as well as to its Flickr site. As the PAO at the time [2011] stated, "We are really, really pleased with our online presence. Over the last two years, we have made a big effort with our Facebook presence. You get a real sense of community and community involvement with Facebook. I feel like our Facebook identity has a real identity;

our Facebook members are really active and engaged in answers. For example, we had a hip hop band perform in Delhi, then the group went to Chandigarh and we posted the upcoming event online. Someone had posted on our Facebook page a question about whether you need tickets, and others in [the] Facebook community had said this is free. A group from Delhi posted saying they are going up and renting cars together. This provides a real sense of cooperation, and we see it as a success in using Facebook: we have created an Indo-US community online."

In Thailand, American PD professionals have more opportunities to use social media than their counterparts elsewhere in the region such as in Myanmar, where the embassy must depend on traditional media such as cultural centers and on "old school programs," which are people-to-people interactions[49] Embassy Bangkok has an official website and a Twitter account, but its primary social media tool is a Facebook account with a wide range of news and information on US policies and embassy events. In 2013, the embassy in Bangkok had more than 150,000 Facebook likes and over 50,000 Twitter followers.[50]

In Chile, because bilateral relations with America are excellent, the US PD staff can use multiple social networking channels to reach its audiences, as a 2010 study shows. That staff manages a Facebook page, posts almost daily updates on embassy news, cultural activities, program announcements, and current events related to the United States and Chile. The public affairs section maintains a Twitter account (EmbajadaEEUUcl) that is by far the most active of its social media outreach programs, with nearly hourly tweets in Spanish on everything from the English language student of the year, Thanksgiving traditions, and the US response to North Korean attacks on South Korea, to a Voice of America program reviewing the latest mobile tablet. The embassy also maintains a Flickr page, which includes photos of various events, including a recent Thanksgiving luncheon for Fulbrighters in Chile.[51]

### *Ambassadorial Involvement*

The use of social media is not confined to the public diplomacy staff. In fact some of the most effective efforts are made by chiefs of mission who use these media and identify themselves in doing so.

When John Beyrle was ambassador to Russia, he said: "I have a blog now that we spend a lot of time putting together. When I travel out to the regions, I find that to be a very good way to reach the Russian people directly with the sorts of messages that we want to get out to them about what really unites the United States and Russia these days. What's interesting about the blog is, in addition to being transmitted, it's also an opportunity for me to be on receive, because I spend a lot of time in the evenings reading through the reactions to the blog. When I do a blog posting sometimes I'll get between 15 and 150 responses. I can't respond to them all, obviously, and some of them are kind of wacky, but a lot of them just give me a sense of what the average Russian thinks and how he or she responds to what the American Ambassador has to say. And that really helps me a lot—helps us a lot here—to kind of hone the message a little bit better."[52]

When Kristie Kenney was appointed as US ambassador in Thailand in 2010, following her tours as ambassador to Ecuador and the Philippines, she made full use of social media. Upon arrival at post, she found the local press had been highly critical of her predecessor, Ambassador Ralph Boyce, after Wikileaks revealed his 2007 cable criticizing the king, because the king is highly respected.[53] Ambassador Kenney promptly sought to convey a better American image by using YouTube messages to give assurances that she would not become involved in domestic political disputes, which had been the source of many criticisms of Ambassador Boyce. She then gave TV interviews on Thai PBS (free-to-air station) and Viewpoint (a cable TV political program), stating that "my goal here in Thailand will be to be a good friend but to leave issues that are for Thailand to solve to Thailand."[54] These gestures made a positive impact on the Thai public.[55]

Ambassador Kenney also recorded two introductory videos that the embassy in Bangkok posted on YouTube, with links to the embassy's Facebook page. They were immediately picked up by local social and traditional media outlets. She maintained a Twitter account that by 2013 had more than 41,000 followers and a blog that has helped her connect with the Thai public. As she says: "For me, it's a connection and it's a way to connect people...and it allows people to feel that they can reach out to the ambassador, who is not just a figure hidden in a big building." They have been especially positive about her because Wikileaks published her predecessor's negative comments about the future of the monarchy released a month prior to her arrival in Thailand. She has carefully avoided such controversy and always explains that everything that she puts on Twitter is "personal and not official." One report said: "Kenney is popular in Thailand because her updates are personal, written by her and she is often responsive, taking time to respond to messages she receives on the service. This personal approach feeds into many Thais' interest in reading snippets from famous people's lives, as well as the chance to reach out and contact them."[56]

There are many other examples of ambassadors making use of social media, although the content varies considerably in accordance with local conditions.

When Kathleen Stephens was the US ambassador to South Korea (2008–11), she wrote a blog about political and non-political issues ranging from the non-proliferation treaty to her experience visiting temples and with Korean food.[57] And when Daniel Clune arrived in Laos as ambassador in 2012 he promptly started his own blog that provided his personal thoughts about his new assignment.[58]

In Kenya, when Michael Ranneberger was US ambassador there (2006–11), he frequently used social media to publicly speak out against corruption by politicians. His own Twitter posts made both general comments on the reform agenda and criticized or commended the Kenyan government's efforts on specific aspects of the agenda. The Kenyan government and politicians complained loudly that he overstepped his diplomatic mandate.[59] But he responded: "Despite warnings by some, I will still speak out supporting reforms in Kenya. President Obama and the Kenyan people demand nothing less!" For example, one post that commended the removal of a police chief and in others he called for the removal of Aaron Ringera, the head of the Kenya Anti-Corruption Commission, who was reappointed despite a perceived poor performance by his organization in fighting corruption. One Tweet said he was "Outraged by Ringera's reappointment.... What to do? Suggestions?"[60]

As the US ambassador to Serbia from 2007 to 2009, Cameron Munter made extensive use of YouTube to make positive comments about Serbia and bilateral cooperation, as well as to mention such sensitive issues as Kosovo to send a signal to the government and the public. On one occasion he posted a YouTube interview in which he said, "We think that the trauma of the last 20 years is very difficult and we want to make sure that we focus with our Serbian friends on the future. Except for the disagreement about Kosovo, I am optimistic we can do that."[61] In Japan, when he was Deputy Chief of Mission (DCM), James Zumwalt, wrote a regular blog in Japanese and English that attracted considerable attention for his views and experiences.[62]

In New Zealand, after David Huebner, a lawyer and political appointee, arrived at his post in December 2010, he attracted the attention of State Department officials for significantly building up his embassy's social media capabilities.[63] Huebner started his own "Ambassador's blog" and supported the launch of embassy Facebook, Twitter, Google Plus, Pintarest, Istagram and Flickr accounts, as well as a Sports Diplomacy blog. He regards social media as complementary to traditional media rather than a substitute, and sought to combine the two and cross-promote them rather than view social media as a stand-alone function. Like PD professionals, he believes in interacting with audiences rather than just disseminating information.[64]

In yet another example, the former US ambassador to Germany, Philip Murphy, used the internet to offer virtual town hall meetings, with each session focusing on one topic of relevance for Germans and Americans, such as Afghanistan, soccer, or green technology.[65] And in January 2014, the newly arrived US ambassador to Japan, Caroline Kennedy, Tweeted that she was "deeply concerned" by the "inhumaneness" of a Japanese commercial dolphin hunt that had taken place. The Japanese response was that the hunt was perfectly legal, but the ambassador's tweet received global media coverage because of her celebrity status as the former president's daughter.[66]

## Conclusion

American diplomats were at first slow to adopt social networking tools for public diplomacy, but now they make full use of those new tools. PAOs devote time and staff hours to these new media. They use unilateral social media such as websites, videos, the new Rapid Response bulletin. They also manage the embassy's interactive tools such as Facebook and Twitter, and many US ambassadors have accounts on both. State's Digital Outreach Teams carries out dialogues in several languages with key bloggers in selected countries. In several ways, therefore, the public affairs sections of American embassies around the world have made use of the latest communication technology to communicate with the local public, often with the direct participation of the American ambassador.

CHAPTER SEVEN

# Social Networking Media: Factors to Consider in Their Use

There is no question that social media can be of great benefit to US public diplomacy, as discussed in the previous chapter. This chapter analyzes the various factors that PD professionals who work at embassies abroad must consider when they use those media, and the choices and the constraints they face in selecting one or the other type.

Social networking media do not by any means provide a panacea or a complete substitute for other PD instruments. Local conditions, including government restrictions or technical limits on their use, may constrain their effectiveness. They also require substantial staff time to manage them properly. Therefore depending on circumstances, social networking media can and should be used to supplement other means of communication.

## Government Restrictions

US embassy public diplomacy personnel in a number of countries must cope with various forms of restrictions on their communication with the local public. In China, the government blocks Facebook, Twitter, and YouTube.[1] In 2013, the state had two million people working as online media monitors, which is more than the 1.5 million than the country had in its active military.[2] One extensive survey in 2005 by Harvard Law School's Berkman Center for Internet and Society found nearly 19,000 of the roughly 204,000 distinct websites it tested from within China were blocked—including all the top ten sites produced by using the search keywords "Tibet," "Taiwan," and "equality." China's state censors thus take a very broad view of what poses a threat to the country's territorial integrity and unity.[3] Another study found that China's censors, operating under the Law Guarding State Secrets, has prevented reporting on such topics as corruption and the lifestyles of government officials, and that because of the vagueness of the rules, many Chinese exercise self-censorship, adding to the problem.[4]

Nevertheless, PD officers working in China have found ways to get around the restrictions. They created an electronic outreach section to develop and use new media, including blogs, web chats, and the Chinese social networking service Weibo (the Chinese equivalent of Twitter), to reach the almost 470 million Chinese with access to the Internet. The Beijing Embassy's Weibo account has over 360,000 Chinese followers. Its Weibo postings offer basic knowledge about the US political system and bilateral relations as well as the ambassador's meetings and travels in China and have been very popular among Chinese netizens. The Weibo postings cover topics from the introduction of basic knowledge about the US political system to the latest developments in US-China relations, ranging from the activities of important cultural and political figures in China to the US Ambassador's meetings and trips in China. These posts, which occasionally have come close to criticizing the authorities, have been very popular. The embassy established a group of 50 Chinese bloggers, chosen from 50,000 influential bloggers in China's cyberspace, and assigned them to use the US Embassy's electronic media programs.[5]

According to a US official in China, US diplomats are pleased that they "reach millions of ordinary Chinese through our blogs, websites and even Twitter, despite the fact that it is officially blocked in China.... Programs in China usually need official government approval and are subject to Chinese government objections, cancellations and misinformation. Nevertheless, we manage to do a lot within this restricted environment and are reaching millions of Chinese online. Over the last year [2011], our U.S. mission in China has built a significant online presence in China's large, carefully monitored blogosphere. The embassy and five consulates together maintain more than 50 Chinese language blogs and microblogs with roughly two million followers."[6]

Cuba is an even more extreme case of government restrictions. The authorities control all traditional media and less than 2 percent of the population has access to the Internet. American official representation in Havana is through an American Interests Section of the Swiss Embassy since diplomatic relations were broken in 1961, and the Cuban government severely limits US diplomats' abilities to act. In the past, the post undertook a very unusual approach, mounting a large news ticker on the top of a building in Havana, but the Cuban government retaliated by erecting dozens of black flags to block it from view, and the former US Chief of Mission Michael Parmly discontinued the project in 2007.[7] One PAO found social media to be an outlet even though it too is very limited. She reported that she carried out "a number of programs despite the constrained environment. . . . We run on-site information resource centers, which provide free Internet access to the Cuban public—uncensored access; . . . [with] a variety of distance learning programs; a couple of examples: on independent journalism, journalistic practices, on information technology, on leadership programs. We offer courses on blogging, on basic computer technology, English teaching. We work with new media to the extent that we can. Again, the connectivity issues in Cuba make it difficult because most Cubans aren't connected to the Internet. But we run a Facebook page, we have websites, we use SMS and Twitter to a certain extent."[8]

In the few countries where the United States has no embassies or consulates, State has undertaken special measures, using social media tools, to do public diplomacy long distance by creating "virtual embassy" websites managed from Washington. Such sites were created for Syria in 2012 by State's Near East and North Africa Bureau (NEA) and for Iran, two countries where the United States in 2014 has no normal diplomatic presence. In Iran, public diplomacy officials have for several years used that digital outreach and electronic media as the best way to reach Iranian audiences, particularly since the 2009 Iranian elections.[9] Now a more elaborate "Virtual Embassy Tehran" has versions in English and Farsi.[10] The Syria platform has versions in English and Arabic. Both include links to social media sites managed by the IIP and PA bureaus and both look like websites managed by normal embassies abroad.

## Limited Local Capabilities

PAOs have found that not every country has sufficient local technical capabilities making it possible to reach audiences via social media. As one study noted, "[Traditional media] in Africa are not being replaced by new media tools. It is best to think of new media as a complement (not a replacement or even a supplement) to traditional media and public diplomacy work; in many cases, the traditional and new are blended. When it comes to the widespread culture of communication in Africa, the 'last three feet'—as Edward R. Murrow called face-to-face communication—are irreplaceable." The same study found that the problem was compounded by lack of staff: "In the situation where nine PAO positions were vacant, and four others were being covered by individuals who were managing another cone, PAOs stationed at African posts often have little time to dedicate to new media."[11]

As noted above, many PAOs in Africa have found SMS may be more useful than Facebook because of very limited local technology. According to one American PD official, African countries are tending to "leapfrog the need for a PC and moving directly into mobile media" and by 2012 it was becoming the most "mobile continent on the planet," and developing new apps for mobile phones and smart phones as well as "pipeline" cables going into the ground around the continent. Many Africans use SMS and increasingly they are accessing Facebook and Twitter on their phones.[12]

Another example comes from Sierra Leone, which missed the social media revolution because of its civil war. Most Sierra Leoneans are not Internet users and most do not even have electricity at home. One PAO started a Facebook page for the Freetown Embassy but it has had very few fans. Former PAO Danna Van Brandt commented: "We've had some success, communicating with journalists via SMS, burning podcasts to CD and getting them translated to local languages for radio stations around the country, but the tools that work here are certainly not the same tools that work in Tokyo, or even in Nairobi." So in 2008 and 2009 the post used unusual methods to promote the election of President Obama, because of widespread interest in him. They erected giant screens around the country for election night in 2008 and for the Obama speeches in Cairo and Accra in the summer of 2009. The post also partnered with local cinema centers to broadcast the US presidential debates, the inauguration, and Obama's Cairo and Accra public speeches. They gave micro-grants to dozens of cinema centers throughout Freetown that showed the speech live, free of charge, to all comers, reaching thousands. Because of very limited electronic capabilities, the big screens turned out to be the most effective means of communication.[13]

## Security

Another type of constraint that social media have overcome arises from security concerns. For example, in south Thailand, because of unrest involving daily bombings and shootings between Muslim insurgents and the Thai military, embassy personnel can only visit the area with the permission of the embassy security officer and the DCM. The PAO conducts programs for audiences in that area via digital video conferences. This allows them to include audiences in this high-risk zone for programs originating in Bangkok or in the United States.[14]

In the Arab world, the upheavals that began at the beginning of 2011 and spread throughout the region made this an area of more intense social media activity. Field offices worked harder than ever to keep up with local events as security threats to US interests increased and stayed at an unusually high level. Some posts closed temporarily, others required nonessential personnel to leave or did not allow officers to be accompanied by dependents. All of that made it much more important for American diplomats to keep track of unfolding developments and a major source of their information turned out to be social media.

## The Right Messenger

As noted in the previous chapter, some ambassadors have enthusiastically adopted social media as an effective means to communicate, and in many cases this has been a great benefit to public diplomacy. However, not all chiefs of mission are adept at using these tools. In some cases the ambassador may not come across well in the local cultural context. Moreover, saying the ambassador's words are "purely personal" is a difficult distinction to make, and may lead to misunderstandings. In any case, the ambassador's use of social media usually takes the time of the public affairs staff to support the ambassador and this means time away from other duties, so PAOs may regard it as a mixed blessing. Moreover, it may require a special staff attached to the front office just to handle the new chores. For example, when John Roos was ambassador to Japan, his Twitter was second in popularity only to that of Susan Rice with 50,000 followers. But his output of two or three Tweets daily required four people to help him: one special assistant to clear content, two staffers to prepare the English and Japanese versions, and a fourth as webmaster. So the effort is not without a cost.[15]

The effective practitioner of public diplomacy is however often the mediator rather than the originator of useful ideas, and this mediation works when he or she engages in social media exchanges, moving the discussion in useful directions.

## Meeting Raised Expectations with Limited Staff Time

US PD practitioners seek to expand the number of interlocutors by using social networking sites, but any site started by the US government raises expectations that anyone who poses questions will receive answers and engage in a conversation. If those expectations are not met, the person seeking the engagement is likely to become disappointed, frustrated, and critical. As Professor Joseph Nye has pointed out, "plenty of information leads to scarcity of attention."[16]

One complaint about CO.NX is that users receive no reply from US officials to their comments. The best PD tool in these circumstances can be SMS, because it is a one-time and ad hoc communication and the US official can choose which messages to answer; also it overcomes infrastructure hurdles.[17] This was illustrated by a situation in 2009 in Pakistan, when an angry dispute arose on the US embassy's CO.NX discussion board. On September 5, 2009, a Pakistani man named Mushtaq Sethi asked about the Blackwater company that provided security to US personnel. When he received no reply, he said: "Will the Co.Nx Moderator or someone from the State Deptt [sic] kindly oblige by responding." Another Pakistani man Mohammad Mansoor Ali Ansari joined in, saying: "The issue is quite volcanic. I believe the State Department has chosen to glue its lips to speak further on this topic." Then Seema Raja commented: "Mr. Ansari if [sic] seems you are quite right! In fact it isnt [sic] only this issue but all the Topics posted here have never recieved [sic] any officials response from them." Mushtaq Sethi commented on September 19: "It sure is disappointing." On October 9, Seema Raja wrote again: "Hello, Hello anyone here from the Co.Nx or the State Department without having ears stuffed with cotton sound proofing? Please respond?" One report on this exchange said that after ten days of silence from the State Department, "the users seem to have determined that they would never receive a response from a U.S. officer, [so they] began conversing with each other on the possible involvement of private military companies in training terrorists in Pakistan, offering skewed opinions not necessarily based on solid facts. By providing a venue for such discussion and failing to provide facts, new media in this specific case does more harm than good to U.S. public diplomacy."[18] This example shows how posts can raise expectations that they are unable to meet, a danger with all new social media. Unless the post is prepared to devote resources, including staff time and money to the exercise, the PAO must consider whether it is worth doing.

Another example comes from Kenya, where one study found that although Facebook invited the public to post comments and requests responses, "these responses do not come fast enough for some eager readers, and some readers have expressed frustration at the lack of response from the embassy." It said that by not responding to posts in a timely manner, the embassy runs the risk of frustrating users and consequently losing this audience's attention. It seems that the embassy is quicker to respond to posts that mention the reform agenda, but then do not address comments that are critical of the United States. In one post, a reader stated, "Mr. Ambassador. You know these people who have ruled Kenya since 1963 don't take you seriously! You will talk, but at the end of the day, they know you and all the western foreign missions are mere talkers, and irritants at best. So they will ignore you, and business will go on as usual." This post went unanswered, although it was in response to a question the embassy posed to all users in a discussion forum. According to an embassy official in Nairobi, they have removed several messages that were considered offensive but generally the give and take has been positive.[19] One analyst noted: "Although the ambassador asks for suggestions in that post, there is no place on the Twitter page where the Kenyan public can answer his posts and suggest what should be done. The Twitter page is a one-sided conversation that captures the American point of view on the reform agenda but doesn't present any Kenyan voices."[20]

In Bahrain, the embassy found itself in a sensitive position when in 2011 the opposition mounted serious street demonstrations against the local government. As the argument grew heated, both sides used all available media to make their case. The embassy issued numerous statements to local media expressing concern for violence about the protests and calling for respect for universal human rights. But the PAO found that each side selectively reported US statements to fit its own agenda, so the embassy began posting full, unedited versions of its policy statements on its Facebook page. It also created a new Twitter account with recorded content for its YouTube channel for the first time, to cope with the plethora of misinformation. But, according to the PAO, opposing sides used the embassy's Facebook page "to conduct a proxy war of words, posting poisonous sectarian commentary. And we eventually had to post a strongly worded terms of use statement and had to block a handful of users for violating those terms. We tried to be a part of the conversation to the largest extent possible. But our message was sometimes buried in the avalanche of responses that we received." The PAO concluded: "We need to examine how and to what degree we participate in those conversations, consider our rules of engagement with our online interlocutors, and consider what that potential blowback might be.... In a small place like Bahrain, it might be more effective in certain instances to have one-to-one conversations as opposed to trying to broadcast to the many."[21]

In some cases, participants in an electronic discussion simply use the channels to vent their anger. One Egyptian posted an angry comment on Embassy Cairo's YouTube education page: "I can't understand you! You are killing our people in Iraq, stealing our treasures in Kuwait and Saudi Arabia and the gulf generally, you treat us like animals here in Cairo, and you arrest our guys at your 'stupid country.' If you hate us...then why do you attract us? What is your problem with us? WHEN WILL YOU LEAVE US ALONE?"[22]

Even where the embassy finds its social media seem to be effective generally, sometimes it is overwhelmed by the challenge. The embassy in South Korea has great potential for using social media because that country has the fifth largest number of Internet subscribers in the world despite its small population (approximately 50 million), and almost 100 percent of those subscribers use broadband, not dial-up, allowing for much faster connection speeds. More than 80 percent of households have computer access at home.[23] The embassy in South Korea partners with Daum Communication to offer "Café USA," an online chat room in which Ambassador Kathleen Stephens and other embassy officials regularly engage, and which was linked to her blog where she writes not only on policy but also about hiking, temple visits, and Korean food. One report said that these were "efforts to build trust, to make friends, to engage, so that they will be accessible when the Americans need friends to listen to them." However, the repost admitted that even the fast social networking media cannot always keep up with events, as the embassy learned when large anti-American protest demonstrations broke out in 2008 and misinformation circulated so rapidly in all media that there was an emotional popular outburst. The embassy tried to respond quickly but because of the plethora of new media this was difficult.[24]

The difficulty of providing a timely response has caused frustrations among Americans as well. One study quotes an official in the IIP bureau in Washington saying: "It's a matter of engagement and dialogue; is it working or is it just giving people a chance to yell?... you picked up maybe 2000 Facebook users, but now what? Do you have a way to stay in touch?"[25]

The complaints from frustrated people, whose expectations have been raised that the embassy will engage with them in give-and-take, and respond promptly to their comments, put a great deal of pressure on the staff of the public affairs section. The staff time that social networking consumes can be considerable, and the PAO must be willing to devote resources to it. Public diplomacy officials have found that in some posts it is the last add-on responsibility, usually assigned to a staff member of the information section, to do after the more traditional duties are completed. Many posts have been forced to delegate responsibility to locally employed staff members to handle the traffic, especially if the exchanges are in the local language. That in turn raises clearance and authenticity questions. By its nature, social media use requires fast responses, and the post must be prepared to handle that. One senior official at State encourages posts to assign at least one person full time to keep up with social media "because it requires constant monitoring."[26] At some posts, one person is not enough and several are required to keep up with the dialogue.

## Clearances

PAOs also face clearance questions: should he or she seek clearance from the ambassador or DCM for a statement relating to policy when a quick response is desired? The PAO can use previously cleared guidance but may get questions or comments outside the scope of available instructions. Clearance policies may in fact vary from embassy to embassy, since some ambassadors and DCMs tend to be more risk averse and keep their PAOs on a tighter leash. For some topics, especially non-political factual discussions, embassies can use local employees to manage the conversations online. To some extent, they can also handle policy questions, provided they have sufficient guidance and stick to it. In a few cases, FSOs have sufficient local languages to engage in discussions in local languages. For example, in Cairo, an FSO who is a native speaker of Arabic recently was assigned to handle many of the online discussions on policy issues.[27]

Ambassadors and DCMs usually keep an eye on this issue but sometimes there are glitches caused by the need to react quickly. For example, in September 2012, when an Egyptian mob scaled the wall of the US embassy in Cairo and burned the US flag to protest a film critical of Islam that had been made by a private American in California, the embassy released a statement that appeared to apologize for the film, saying: "The Embassy of the United States in Cairo condemns the continuing efforts by misguided individuals to hurt the religious feelings of Muslims—as we condemn efforts to offend believers of all religions." The next day the White House disavowed that statement, saying, "The statement by Embassy Cairo was not cleared by Washington and does not reflect the views of the United States government." The embassy's Twitter feed quickly issued a new statement condemning both the film and the violence of the protest.[28]

Moreover, PD officials have indicated that there are American diplomats who continue to believe that some questions or comments by the public should not be "dignified with a response" because they are stupid or deliberately provocative. PD practitioners, however, tend to believe that ignoring even those comments is a mistake because it risks losing credibility and influence in the conversation.[29]

One PD study made this sensible recommendation to PAOs: "Limit the channels to the ones you are sure to use for a long time. It would leave a bad impression to close a channel that once functioned as a window for communication between a foreign audience and U.S. officials. For the same reason, the 'discussion' function or its equivalent on these platforms should not be provided unless the State Department can respond in a timely manner. Alternatively, there should be a clear disclaimer that not all feedback or comments will receive a response."[30]

## Deciding Which Language to Use

In most countries, using social networking media in the local language is more effective than using only English, although a combination of English and the vernacular seems to work best.[31] The US embassy in South Korea, for example, has a website in English and Korean that includes links to Facebook, Twitter, and YouTube, and to two blogs, Café USA and Cafe IRC, which are both in Korean.[32] US Embassy Riyadh shifted to the use of Arabic on its social media in 2011 to engage users in their native language, resulting in an upsurge in user numbers and an increase in followers on Twitter and Facebook.[33]

In Cairo, the embassy's website is in English and Arabic, with a link to a full Arabic version. The embassy in Tokyo has a Facebook page in Japanese and English. A study by a Japanese researcher says: "In Japan Japanese generally do not feel comfortable using English for research and communication. It is thus wise that the U.S. Embassy employs primarily the Japanese language for conversations on Mixi (Japan's most popular social networking service) and Facebook."[34] This embassy also issues a *U.S. Information Alert*, an email service that delivers periodic information bulletins in Japanese to subscribers, customized to each subscriber's indicated areas of interest, and *American View*, a quarterly online Japanese-language magazine that provides readers with articles about the United States and its relationship with Japan.[35]

According to a report on PD in India, the embassy in New Delhi sends messages out on Twitter in both English and Hindi and re-tweets in regional languages such as Malayalam, Tamil, and Urdu. It concludes: "As traditional elites and many urban middle class Indians speak English, communicating in regional languages supports the effort to reach out to Indians in secondary and tertiary cities."[36]

## Conclusion

In 2013 the State Department's Inspector General undertook a review of social networking media and reported that the International Information Policy bureau (IIP) had made "effective use of technology" and "has made a significant contribution to the Department of State's digital diplomacy outreach effort, increased the reach of its publications, and expanded the use of video in public diplomacy (PD) work." But the report added that IIP's digital outreach should "focus more on PD goals rather than raw numbers of social media fans." The Inspector also said the IIP leadership "failed to convey its strategic vision to staff members" and said that McCall's 2011 reorganization of the bureau "did not resolve structural problems and caused new organizational difficulties."[37]

It is true that mere numbers do not tell the whole story of effectiveness. As one PAO has said, "Counting the likes on Facebook or the number of tweets doesn't necessarily mean that people are agreeing with us. And we need to know who we're talking to."[38] The use of social networking tools must be based on deliberate and thoughtful employment of resources. It is also true that they cannot replace, but only supplement, face-to-face communication. But social media are likely to remain a fixture of American public diplomacy because they are now widely used by our diplomats, including ambassadors, and because they have the support of the highest levels of the State Department. When she was secretary of state, Hillary Clinton spoke out several times in favor of internet freedom, devoting speeches to the subject in January 2010 and February 2011. In the latter speech she said the Internet had "become the public space of the 21st century—the world's town square, classroom, marketplace, coffeehouse, and nightclub." She said Internet freedom was a "foreign policy priority" for the United States, and that it had "become part of the daily work of our diplomats... on the ground at our embassies and missions around the world."[39] Secretary of State John Kerry also is a supporter of social media; as senator he had his own Twitter account (@JohnKerry) and when he became Secretary he joined the State Department's Twitter account, signing it simply "—JK."

American officials experience some frustrations in trying to use social media, but they realize they must try to find ways to do so. Ambassador John Beyrle, who was the American ambassador to Russia, 2008–12, puts it this way: "[One] challenge is just how dynamic the media environment is here and especially social and new media, which we spend a lot of time trying to track, and just trying to keep track of what the best inputs and outlets for us are. It's just a constantly shifting scene and I think we need to stay light on our feet to make sure that we're finding the best avenues for getting our message out." He added: "There's a kind of false perception out there that the young generation understands what America is about. Some of the biggest misperceptions we have come from young people, so reaching out through social media is really important. We've got two or three people on staff here who spend their time doing nothing but social media, both in terms of monitoring what's happening out there, and also finding ways for us to insert ourselves."[40]

Social media are here to stay as a PD tool. It is clear that PD professionals and other diplomats—not just young ones—are increasingly persuaded of the importance of using social networking media in their work because these media are being used by millions around the world and as one experienced diplomat says, all PD practitioners need to find ways get into that discussion.[41] The more traditional means of communication such as radio and television reach more people, but the social media usually reach the more influential people in the society and they are faster. The practitioners know that these new tools need to be employed wisely, therefore, in conjunction with other tools and also face-to-face encounters, and depending on local conditions.

# PART IV

*Cultural and Educational Programs*

CHAPTER EIGHT

# American Cultural Programs

The word "culture" has different meanings. It can mean the conceptual patterns that a society shares, or the way its members make sense of the world around them. It can also mean a society's knowledge, beliefs, attitudes, values, morals, customs, laws, capabilities and the habits that they have acquired from being a member of a group. It is very important for a public diplomacy professional to have a good understanding of his or her own culture, and also of the culture in which he or she is working when posted to an American embassy abroad (see chapters three and four). Public diplomacy professionals also use the word culture to mean the tangible manifestations of a society, as seen in literature, art, music, theater, the educational system and political behavior, that in some ways reflect those underlying beliefs. They use these manifestations to communicate to foreigners the essence of American culture, in what they call "cultural programs" that are discussed in this chapter. Those programs present various aspects of American society and culture directly to audiences in foreign countries.

To make these presentations, the US government sends private American experts, specialists and artists and artwork abroad, as tangible demonstrations of American cultural, social and intellectual manifestations. Unlike the educational exchange programs (discussed in chapter ten on exchanges), these activities all take place in foreign countries.

The purpose of these programs is to help foreign audiences understand fundamental aspects of America in an honest way, by presenting examples of American society, culture and thinking that demonstrate its complexities and true characteristics. The purpose is usually not directly related to foreign policy advocacy, although an understanding of aspects of American society and culture may help indirectly provide insight into our foreign policies as well.[1]

The PAO and CAO, in consultation with their local employees, plan the local cultural program and submit requests to Washington for any parts of it that require funding and other support. They decide what types of program would be most effective in presenting an accurate picture of American society and culture, given the local environment. They may consult with local institutions, such as universities, nongovernmental organizations (NGOs), government agencies, and private entrepreneurs to determine what kinds of American programs would be interesting locally, and they may partner with them to share costs and administrative duties. The American side might provide American speakers, athletes, or special envoys, musical or theatrical presentations, libraries and translated books, English lessons, teacher training, student counseling, or exhibits. The host country side might provide program space, promotional advertising and logistical support, media promotion, and in some cases the necessary official permission to put on a public event.

The embassy must of course be careful not to undertake programs that might offend local sensitivities, or present aspects of American culture that are so unfamiliar locally as to communicate unhelpful messages. For example, a performance by an American ballet company that might be very effective in Paris could well cause negative reactions in Riyadh. Moreover, if American speakers or performers of some types regularly appear locally under private sponsorship, it may not be necessary to duplicate the private effort but more efficient to organize programs that would not otherwise be available.

During the second half of the twentieth century, Washington provided posts with a variety of cultural presentations, performers and speakers, and the budgets were generous for this function. During the past two or three decades, however, funding for cultural programs and presentations has declined. The causes of this decline have been that public diplomacy budgets generally have been diminished, and meanwhile some private sector commercial funding abroad has become available. Moreover, since the USIA merger into State and the recent ascendance of the Pentagon in communicating with foreign audiences, Washington has tended to focus more on the short term information side of public diplomacy rather than on cultural programming that has a long term impact.

One of the best arguments for cultural and educational programs can be made in countries where there are serious bilateral political differences with the United States and the host government restricts what the embassy can do to communicate with the local public. The cultural or educational programming can at least appear to be nonpolitical and be carried out despite political hostility. In Venezuela, for example, the US government has had to rely on these public diplomacy instruments because the Venezuelan government refuses to cooperate with the US Embassy in many ways, and even refuses to allow regular contact with local officials. As a result the public affairs section finds ways to communicate directly with the people that appear politically innocuous. According to Benjamin Ziff, former PAO (2006–9) the post has regularly emphasized person-to-person public diplomacy strategies, even in today's highly technologically advanced world. American officials go into rural cities, to community centers, and work with different private organizations to host non-political events where they can speak and interact with Venezuelans. As instruments, the post emphasizes focuses American speakers, cultural events, English teaching and also educational exchanges.[2]

Following are analyses of each of the main types of cultural and educational program.

## American Speakers

Bringing American experts in specific subjects of interest to the local audience, to give lectures and hold other forms of discussions, is a very important public diplomacy tool. Originally called the "American Participant" (Ampart) program, and later called the "US Speakers" program, it has been a feature of PD efforts for many decades. Washington recruited American private sector experts on various subjects, determined by PAOs to be of local interest, to travel abroad on lecture tours to several countries. In 2003 and 2004, respectively, Washington sent out 700 and 872 American speakers worldwide.[3] The speakers are not told what to say, and they are free to criticize policy if they wish, but in they are usually selected for their relative balance and objectivity.

An expansion of this type of program took place starting years ago with the inauguration of interactive discussions by long distance telephone, involving either private sector experts or American officials. Often conference calls were arranged so that journalists or others in several countries could be connected at the same time with an American expert or official in the United States. Then when the technology allowed it, the technique of videoconferencing ("Digital Video

Conferences" or DVCs) was added to the program, with a dedicated office in Washington assisting posts with them. The use of DVCs continues today, with posts often setting up these events with Washington's assistance or independently.[4]

For example, each year, the embassy in Tokyo invites fifty to sixty American speakers to Japan and arranges up to two hundred programs for them, to speak on different topics ranging from security and politics to economics, to US society and culture, and music. The PAO in Japan also mobilizes embassy officers to talk about their fields of expertise. Starting in 2004, this embassy has sponsored a series of talks under the label "Basic Course on Contemporary America" (Gendai America Kiso Koza), which makes use of both visiting experts and embassy officials. The PAO attempts to present more than one point of view on controversial subjects. The embassy in Tokyo also recruits "targets of opportunity" speakers who happen to be passing through Japan and have worked with the embassy in the past.[5]

Other posts have also arranged speaker programs ad hoc when a person qualified to give a presentation happens to visit the country. This occurs in France, where because of its limited budget, the post relies heavily on such targets of opportunity. For example, when Jodie Foster was in France to make a movie, the embassy arranged for her come to a meeting with French artists to answer their questions. And because of his personal relations with show business, Ambassador Charles Rivkin was able to invite as well Woody Allen, Samuel L. Jackson, Warner Brothers CEO Barry Mayer, and Sylvester Stallone to meet with French audiences.[6] As the CAO in Paris put it, "Our ambassador has been very successful in getting U.S. star power...to help us with our outreach efforts to the French public in general, and French youth and diversity communities in particular. It has been very impactful for French youth to get to meet such legends, to get to hear about their careers and the hardships that they have had to endure and overcome in order to reach the very top of their industries and get life and career advice from such international figures."[7] In addition, for programming the US embassy works closely with, and provides grants to, networks of associations like the Franco-American foundation "who are carrying out work in support of the public diplomacy's mission goals."[8]

Nonpolitical topics tend to be the focus for American speakers in countries where the public is highly critical of United States policy, since American speakers in that way can provide a means to keep communication channels open. Such presentations help remind audiences that there is more to America than just our foreign policy. In Syria, for example, even before the 2011 uprising the government was so hostile to the United States that officials were inaccessible and its security apparatus intimidated private citizens from meetings, but the PAO was able to arrange for American experts to come to Damascus to give talks on their specialties. In 2010, for example, the PAO recognized that the Syrian authorities were interested in teaching children with disabilities, so she arranged for the State Department to send to Damascus an expert in that subject, Professor Jill Williams of Kennesaw State University. Professor Williams spent two weeks speaking to teachers and education administrators and working with the Syrian NGO Amaal, an organization that was part of the First Lady's "Trust for Development." This was the first time in five years that the post had been able to work with the education ministry. Professor William's husband, a journalist, conducted specialized training programs for Syrian journalists, an effort that won praise from the Syrian president.[9]

Embassies can also amplify their outreach to larger audiences by arranging media interviews or recording their presentations and posting them on YouTube or via other channels on social media. And the Bush administration added a "Strategic Speakers" program that focused on State Department priorities. For example in 2007 it sent speakers to Muslim countries to talk about Muslim life in America, and by 2007 they had visited 14 countries.

## Sports and Special Envoys

For decades, the US government has sent American professional athletes abroad as part of a public diplomacy program intended primarily to reach youth. Basketball coaches for example were sent to countries where the sport was popular, to work with young people in sports camps and in special sessions with local coaches. These programs were effective partly because they were clearly non-political and provided a service that was in demand locally. This "Sports Diplomacy" by 2007 had a budget of five million dollars. In that year the State Department sent baseball star Cal Ripken to China, and in 2012 the Obama administration sent basketball star Kareem Abduljabbar, an American Muslim, abroad for a similar task.[10]

In 2006, State expanded the idea. President George W. Bush selected Michelle Kwan, a very successful American figure skater, to go abroad not as an athlete to train foreigners in a sport but rather as a Public Diplomacy Envoy. This was a new concept. It built on Michelle Kwan's international fame from her skating successes—she is the most decorated American figure skater ever, having won five world championships. But her success in a sport was only a door-opener that made use of her global name recognition. As a Chinese-American she was especially well suited to talk about American social and cultural diversity. She was born in the United States of parents who emigrated from Hong Kong and she speaks Cantonese at home. Since 2006 she has travelled for the US government to China, Korea, Argentina, Russia, Ukraine, and Singapore. She explained her role in this way:

> as a public diplomacy envoy, I have a couple of goals. First is to have a positive influence, to be able to share my story, the things that I have learned through sports like hard work, dedication, focus—falling, sometimes, on the ice...and getting back up. And these are universal concepts—and I hope that these students can apply into their own lives. And...second is, by that interaction, by having a dialogue—a conversation, not a monologue—that we can learn about each other. Hopefully they can learn about America—the U.S.—and sometimes they have misconceptions about the United States. Sometimes they think of the U.S. and they think of Hollywood or they think of New York...and sometimes even bad misconceptions that I might be able to answer some of the questions that they might have.[11]

### Cultural Presentations

Organizing "cultural presentations," that is arranging for performances abroad by American musicians, actors, dancers and other such professionals, is an important public diplomacy instrument. The PAO must carefully consider which type of performer would be most effective for the local audience. Are there certain types of cultural expression that America is good at that are popular locally, so that a live performance would attract an audience that would appreciate it? Conversely are there some types that are so foreign or unknown that presenting them would be counterproductive? Also, does the American private sector already supply a sufficient number of performers on a commercial basis so that the embassy does not need to duplicate that effort, such as sending an American ballet company to London or Paris?

Cultural presentations offer the advantage of being nonpolitical. That is, in a situation where there are serious bilateral political tensions between the United States and the host country, these events can present a positive and benign face of America to the audience. The local population might stay away from a speech by a US official but might attend a concert by an American musical group. The event therefore provides balance to the view of America and it also provides an opportunity for American officials to come into contact with local audiences who they otherwise would not see.

A prestigious cultural presentation may however involve the US ambassador, depending on the circumstances. The ambassador to Russia 2008–12 John Beyrle put it this way in 2011: "[If] you ask, what's the role of an Ambassador in terms of public diplomacy, it's something that's almost very personal for me. Here in Moscow, what we try to do—[my wife] Jocelyn and I try to do in particular together—is host a lot of events at our residence, Spaso House. We do a lot of cultural concerts, both with American artists who are visiting, but also with Russian artists as well who have some sort of connection to America—either they play jazz, or they've just recently returned from a tour of the United States, and we find that's a very good way to reach an audience that's right there in the house to show how much we value culture as part of public diplomacy outreach." He added: "We've brought bluegrass to Russia; we had the first ever hip hop concert at Spaso House a few months ago with tremendous turnout of people that I'd never seen in the American Ambassador's residence before. We are bringing contemporary theater here, doing exchanges between theater students in the United States and Russia." He said the embassy "has been able to sponsor a lot of musical, theater, and dance groups here, starting with Alvin Ailey just a few months ago, which played to sold out audiences, and culminating with the Chicago Symphony Orchestra, which is going to do a tour in Russia next year, and that will be the first time we've had a major American symphony orchestra in about 10 or 15 years, I think."[12]

In countries where public opinion toward the United States is highly critical because of American policies, PAOs may find that cultural presentations are ways to communicate with target audiences that would otherwise be inaccessible. For example, a 2009 opinion poll found that public opinion in Serbia and Pakistan was the most negative toward the United States among forty-two nations. PAOs in those two countries knew that it was very difficult to present American views on policy issues to them. They therefore sought ways to bring non-political cultural presentations to that audience. The PAO in Serbia on one occasion arranged for the US Navy band to perform at the Guca summer music festival. A State Department official concluded: "the people who attend this festival are often people who love to hate America and the West. The last thing they would expect was for Americans to come to Guca." Despite this, the US Navy band was generally well received, and the press was eager to cover the event. The program was a big success because it provided a means of reaching an audience that might otherwise be written off.[13] In Pakistan, the PAO said this in 2011: "[W]e found that the cultural programming had a tremendous impact. Because of the danger it had been deemphasized. But this fall we were bringing back all of the musical performances and all those other things that go with it. But in a country that's got such a difficult media environment, we felt that it's really important to put a lot of resources behind this. And we think it's having a very good impact."[14]

In Syria, even before the 2011 uprising, the government had shut down almost all of the US embassy's public diplomacy programs and prevented the PAO from meeting with any of the usual public diplomacy contacts, such as newspaper editors and university professors and officials. The PAO therefore focused on cultural presentations as a way to keep engaged with the audience. In 2010, the PAO arranged the following: four American musicians gave a hip-hop and break dancing show, Syrian-American pianist Malek Jandali played before a packed audience in the St. Elian's Cultural Festival in Homs; three documentary film makers including Egyptian-American Jihane Noujaim spent ten days in Syria screening their films in Damascus and provincial cities; the Chris Byers Jazz Quartet played in Damascus and three provincial cities.[15]

In 2006 the State Department started a Global Cultural Initiative in partnership with the Kennedy Center, the American Film Institute and others. For example it sent the pop music band Ozomatli on a tour to Jordan, Egypt, Tunisia, India, and Nepal. They carried out their Middle Eastern cultural presentation tour was noteworthy because it was undertaken despite the fact that it was known to be highly critical of the Bush administration and the war in Iraq and having played at that political demonstrations.[16]

## English Teaching

Public diplomacy professionals know that English teaching is a valuable tool. English, like any language, carries cultural freight with it. Learning English from an American teacher helps students learn about the United States and American teaching materials can convey a great deal about all aspects of America. Teachers are highly respected in most societies, and they tend to be credible sources of information to their students, and because foreign students studying English with an American usually leads to discussions of issues well beyond grammar and vocabulary. The teachers have many opportunities to convey information and nuances about many aspects of American society and culture. For English classes to enhance an understanding of America in this way, American teachers are best, although non-Americans, who know the United States and its society and culture well, can also be effective.

An additional benefit is that foreigners who know English have better access to American information materials, including print media (books, magazines), and electronic media (radio, television, and the Internet) as well as films. Moreover, English is also required of foreigners who study in the United States, on any level. The Bureau of Educational and Cultural Affairs (ECA) that oversees the English Language Programs office views English language education support as a means of increasing participating in US exchange programs since English proficiency is a criterion in the selection process.

Secretary of State John Kerry has expressed strong support for State's English language programs because, as he says, English has become "the language of business, the language of exchange, the language of diplomacy and of the world in many ways."[17]

In the past, many public diplomacy operations abroad included direct English teaching programs, for these reasons. But because of the shrinking of public diplomacy budgets after the end of the Cold War, many of those programs were shut down, or outsourced to private companies. Ten USIA posts in the Arab world, for example, conducted English teaching programs but by the twenty-first century all were closed or outsourced to NGOs.[18] For example, the American NGO Amideast took over responsibility from the embassy for English language teaching programs in Bahrain, Tunisia, Yemen, and Syria. In Latin America, however, US embassies still work in partnership with the popular bi-national centers that operate independently and generate revenue through classroom instruction.

In a 2009 report, the US Senate Foreign Relations Committee stressed the important contribution that English teaching programs have made to the success of American public diplomacy and encouraged that they be strengthened. The Committee expressed regret that in many cases the teaching programs had been discontinued or outsourced to private organizations, because it felt that they should be done directly by the public diplomacy section of the embassy to be most effective.[19]

In some cases, it could be argued that teaching English is not a priority. That is not only true in English-speaking countries such as the United Kingdom and Australia, but it is also true in France where a study of public diplomacy found that there is no significant demand for it.[20] In China, already more than two hundred million people are studying English, so demand is very high, but the embassy has decided that teaching English is not a high priority because there are so many private language schools. The embassy does provide a list of recommended teachers, and its website maintains a link to a chat room for Chinese-English language exchange.[21]

The State Department has a program of "Regional English Language Officers" (RELOs), professional teachers of English as a Foreign Language English (TEFL) who are posted abroad to support English teaching to foreigners. There are some 30 RELOs abroad, each one responsible either for a single country or for a group of countries in a specific region, where they organize seminars and workshops on teaching methods, and support the PAO's efforts to promote the teaching of English. State also has a program of English Teaching Fellows who are assigned to teach English and provide teacher training in designated foreign institutions, usually for one year. For the year 2013–14, there were 86 English Teaching Fellows assigned abroad in all regions of the world.[22] The English Language Specialist program recruits academics in the field of teaching English as a Foreign Language (TESOL) for short-term assignments abroad advising foreign teachers, ministries of education, language program directors, and many other organizations that support English language education.[23]

In Thailand, for example, the RELO, located in the public affairs section, promotes effective English language learning, fostering the use of the language as a medium of communication in Southeast Asia including Cambodia, Laos, Taiwan, Thailand, and Vietnam.[24]

### *Access Microscholarships*

In 2004, the State Department started a program it called "Access Microscholarships" for young, underserved people between the ages of 14 and 18 in Muslim countries, providing them with scholarships to study English locally. This program was intended to raise the level of English of a target audience group that the Bush administration was especially interested in. It was conceptually linked with exchange programs because it was hoped that some of the graduates would gain sufficient English language skills to allow them to go to the United States to study, and it was more cost-effective than sending them to the United States simply for language instruction. It was especially hoped that it would support the YES student exchange program (described in chapter ten) by helping teenagers prepare for study in the United States: posts had difficulty finding Muslim youth with sufficient English to enter American high schools, and the Access Microscholarship program was expected to help remedy that.

In its first four years, 44,000 students in 55 countries participated, and the numbers grew rapidly. It expanded to a total of 32,000 teenagers from underserved communities in 44 Muslim countries by 2007, and by 2014 approximately 95,000 students in more than 85 countries have participated in the Access Program.[25] The only criticism of the Access program has come from one Senate report that expressed concern that the YES program was not large enough to take in all of the eligible Access graduates.

Public diplomacy professionals have praised the Access program. The former CAO in India said: "We are able to reach a lot of folks and get them interested in English as medium to get them interested in the U.S., democracy and themes that were important to us. It also gave students hope that if they mastered English, they could do better in the job market and in their careers. At their schools, English language teaching is mediocre if taught at all."[26] An evaluation by State's Education and Culture Bureau gave the program high marks, saying that in addition to learning English, students "gain an appreciation for American and wider world culture and values" through summer camp activities, movie nights, and materials used in the classroom that discuss American culture, and concluded that "the overall changes in views and knowledge of the United States, sharing new knowledge, and growth of leadership skills and professional development were at extremely high levels."[27]

The English Language Programs office and individual posts are utilizing social media in innovative and creative ways to connect with their audiences and to network English teachers from around the world. This includes the launch of a new video game, "Trace Effects" and Facebook pages, including for the Access program. It also includes a new website "American English" that provides teachers and learners of English with fresh, relevant content for their classroom use and own professional development.[28]

## American Books and Periodicals

PAOs have found ways to promote American books. One is through libraries (see next chapter) and another is by sponsoring translations into the local language.

During the heyday of public diplomacy under USIA, the Agency started several programs that continue to this day, to translate and publish American books in foreign languages. Washington, in collaboration with the posts, selects titles for translation, secures the rights, and arranges for publication. Posts hire translators, arrange printing, and usually distribute a certain number of copies free to target audience members, allowing the publisher to sell the rest. Classic nonfiction works such as DeToqueville's *Democracy in America* or James McPhearson's *Abraham Lincoln and the Second American Revolution*, and fiction such as *The Adventures of Huckleberry Finn* have been translated for years.[29] Often contracts are made with local publishers to obtain the rights and buy back a certain number of the books and set a price. Translations into Spanish and Portuguese have been especially effective tools in Latin America, and French translations are effective in French-speaking Africa. Translations are less effective in Western Europe because commercial publishers are able to make a profit with translations there.[30]

The Arabic translation program, for example, started in Cairo in the 1950s and a parallel program began in Amman after that. Despite the IT revolution, both programs are still going, but their output is limited. For about $50,000 each, Cairo is able to produce only 3,000 copies each of ten books annually and Amman somewhat fewer. The post keeps 1,000–1,500 for free distribution while Amman publishes 2,500 and keeps 750, while the publishers sell the rest. The process of title selection, copyright acquisition, printing and distribution takes 8–18 months. In 2009 a Senate report praised the program but found it much too small.[31] In 2003, an independent study group had already proposed that the program for book translations into local languages be increased.[32] As of 2013 that has not happened.

A new way to promote American books has recently been devised with the advent of the Kindle and other electronic reading devices. In Senegal, the PAO, Sharon Hudson-Dean, hosted a reading club for which she provided Kindles and books from a list provided by the Chautauqua Institution. The club attracted influential Zimbabweans to discussions where they met people from other sectors of the society and different political backgrounds. This provided embassy access to interesting contacts and also helped Zimbabweans get to know new people in a neutral space.[33] The IIP bureau at State also produces "eJournals" in a number of languages that help posts with their book efforts.

## Exhibitions

Exhibitions mounted by or supported by the embassy can have significant public diplomacy impact. Even a primarily commercial exhibition, in which US commercial companies display their latest material goods, can be helpful to the post's public diplomacy program.

The classic example is the American exhibition in Moscow in 1959, during the Cold War, which was visited by 2.7 million Soviet citizens. It displayed American consumer goods, many of which were unknown to them. Simply the portrayal of a typical American supermarket with its abundance and variety of goods, which contrasted with the usual Soviet market, carried a message about American economic success. American media focused on and made famous the so-called Kitchen Debate on capitalism versus socialism between Vice President Nixon and Premier Khrushchev. From a public diplomacy standpoint, the 75 young American Russian-speaking guides, who engaged with the visitors, were especially helpful because they added an element of personal engagement with Americans.[34]

Exhibitions are expensive and not many are undertaken nowadays. However in 2010, the United States participated in the Shanghai Expo that was a very large undertaking, but it was made possible because it was essentially privately funded. The former US Consul General in Shanghai said, "[W]e created a successful public-private partnership that presented public diplomacy on a massive scale and proved a bright spot in an otherwise testy year for U.S.-China relations." The Expo lasted for six months and it attracted 7.3 million visitors, and it also reached hundreds of millions more through traditional media and social networking. Senior American officials including four cabinet members and ten members of congress visited it, plus ten governors and twelve American mayors who came to promote tourism and investment in their states. But as the Consul General explained, Shanghai Expo also served broader public diplomacy goals. "For many millions of Chinese citizens, this was their first time to meet an American in person or to watch a video of President Obama welcoming them to visit the United

States." She added: "Our 160 Mandarin-speaking U.S. student ambassadors represented 38 states. Pavilion staff organized more than 1,000 cultural and entertainment programs featuring 150 different American groups, including Herbie Hancock, Dee Dee Bridgewater, Harry Connick, Jr. and Quincy Jones visited the pavilion.... The pavilion improved perceptions of the United States and promoted study in the U.S."[35]

Embassies continue the exhibits tradition in a more modest way by bringing photographers and artists face-to-face with counterparts and the broader publics abroad. For example, the PAO in Vladivostok, Bridget Gersten, organized an exhibit that featured the life and times of Eleanor Pray, an American who lived in Vladivostok at the turn of the nineteenth century. The exhibit was curated in partnership a leading local museum and with a US academic who worked with Ms. Pray's family, bringing the story alive to Russian audiences, replete with multimedia installations and the translation of a book of Eleanor Pray's letters in Russian. In Riyadh, PAO Gersten also set up an exhibit with a leading American landscape photographer, Tom Till, who traveled to Saudi Arabia to host talks and tours of his "Fifty American States" and "Desert Landscapes" collections. This connecting of cultures is an important way to promote mutual understanding through shared interests.[36]

## Conclusion

Public diplomacy officers at US embassies abroad sponsor programs that demonstrate, with specific examples, the quality and character of American culture, appropriate to local circumstances. They may arrange musical performances, plays, and exhibitions, or they sponsor lectures and workshops by visiting American artists and experts. They support English teaching, giving foreigners access to American publications and help preparing for study in America. They offer American books—translated into local languages—and periodicals to the public. Most of these programs are non-political, emphasizing aspects of America other than its foreign policy, so they provide balance to the picture of the United States, which is especially useful in countries where the bilateral relationship is adversarial.

All of the programs described above require space in the host country to put them on. In some countries, the public affairs section has its own dedicated space for programming, but in many countries partnerships must be arranged for the embassy's programs. As with everything else in public diplomacy, the arrangements depend on local circumstances. The following chapter discusses the different ways in which public diplomacy sections at embassies have solved the challenge of finding and using program space.

CHAPTER NINE

# Centers, Libraries, and Other "American Spaces"

Effective public diplomacy programming in almost any country depends on using local venues or platforms that are available and suitable for reaching the target audience. Over the years, PAOs have made use of several different types of venue, and today there are many different solutions to this problem. The PAO must decide whether or not to program an event in a US government facility. The choice depends on availability of suitable space owned or leased by the embassy, or in a local institution, and also on what kind of audience the post wants to reach.[1] Selection of a venue is not a trivial issue because it can seriously affect the success of a program.

## American Centers

For most of the second half of the twentieth century when USIA existed, one of the most important public diplomacy tools for embassies around the world was an American Center that was free-standing and usually separate from the embassy compound. These centers typically contained a library of American books and periodicals, and space for programming such as lectures, film shows and other public diplomacy services. Reference librarians provided materials that met the interests and needs of the target audience and the country plan. Librarians promoted their materials by sending out announcements of recently received materials, bibliographies and other notices. Many centers offered free counseling for students wishing to study in the United States, and English language lessons. It was not unusual for these centers to house the best library and the best English lessons in the city, as well as the best advising services for study in America.

The first such center was the Benjamin Franklin library that opened in Mexico City in 1942. Then centers were established in Germany, immediately after the end of World War II, when American occupying forces opened what they called "America Houses" (Amerikahaeuser) in a number of cities, starting in 1951. Soon US public diplomacy personnel in other countries imitated this innovation and the idea spread—first to occupied Austria and Japan and then gradually worldwide—because it had multiple advantages. The American center or library combined several services in symbiotic fashion: students who came for English lessons discovered a useful library and interesting film showings, and they had access to free student counseling. But arguably the most important public diplomacy asset of these centers was the presence of trained PD staff, both Americans and local hires. Professionals from the host country who knew the United States well managed the library and other services. In many cases, American FSOs from the public diplomacy section of the embassy often had full time or part time offices in the center that allowed them easy access to important target audiences on a daily basis. Cultural centers attracted large numbers of high school and university students, faculty members, journalists and other professionals who were reluctant or unwilling to visit the embassy so this might be their only contact with Americans and American information. It was always easier to meet people on "neutral" ground than inside an embassy.

## Jointly Operated Centers

PAOs in Latin America developed a different version of the institution, calling it a "bi-national center" (BNC), based on arrangements with local organizations that shared the management and funding of the institutions. Some started before World War II, and English language teaching has usually been the main source of revenue. In 2013 there were 112 BNCs still functioning in nineteen countries.[2] The advantage of a BNC is that costs are shared and sometimes a broader audience can be reached. The disadvantage is that the embassy does not have full control of it.

In Germany, when USIA was disbanded, the embassy turned the original America Houses over to local German control, although the embassy retained a relationship with them providing books and other

American materials on an ongoing basis. However, after unification in 1990, no such facilities were established in the former East Germany.[3] The majority of the funding for America Houses now comes from local, regional and national German authorities, as well as from private donations. Most of their staff members are now German nationals, but they do provide program space for US public diplomacy officers. In Munich, for example, the America House receives 60 percent of its funding from the State of Bavaria, and of the rest from the US embassy and the US consulate in Munich, including in-kind support in the form of speakers and information materials.[4]

## Changes in the 1990s

Starting in the 1990s, however, several new conditions forced the closure of many of the off-site centers. As one the Senate report put it, "American Centers offered a neutral space for foreigners to access information without interference or oversight from repressive host governments as well as a welcoming environment more conducive to engagement with American officials. Yet, despite the significant Public Diplomacy value of these Centers to project America's ideas and images, several events occurred that led to the rapid demise of all but a handful."[5] First, the end of the Cold War and the demise of USIA caused Washington to reduce public diplomacy budgets as part of the so-called peace dividend, and some centers were sacrificed to these cuts. These stand-alone centers were considered too expensive to maintain because of rent and upkeep. Then the advent of the Internet encouraged people in Congress to think (incorrectly) that centers, libraries and direct personal contact were no longer needed. On top of all that, the increase of security concerns in many countries, especially after terrorists attacked US embassies in Kenya and Tanzania in 1998, made stand-alone American centers seem too vulnerable to maintain safely. They were regarded as likely targets for terrorist attacks, so the embassy either fortified them with new barriers, guards, and walk-through metal detectors, or simply shut them down.

Congress reacted to that security risk and in 1999 passed the Secure Embassy Construction and Counterterrorism Act (SECCA). This act imposed considerable restrictions on US public diplomacy efforts abroad. Embassies and cultural centers were forced to move out of convenient and accessible downtown locations in cities, to locations outside town where there was enough space to accommodate the 100-foot setback from the street, but such locations were often difficult for the public to visit, and the structure of the building added obstacles to easy access. As one Senate report put it: "Sites with sufficient acreage to meet these new set-back requirements can only be found miles away from the previously convenient downtown locations of our original Embassies. Such sites by definition tend to be in remote areas poorly served by public transportation. These relocations have resulted in decreases in both the ease and frequency of locals visiting American officials and vice versa—creating a veritable diplomatic lethargy in many locations."[6]

Even the physical appearance of the newly secured American facilities was part of the problem. One study of US presence in Berlin concluded that the American embassy building there, that was opened in 2008, was bad for public diplomacy since it conveyed an unfortunate image because its design was dictated by security needs and German newspaper commentators called it "bunker style" and "a maximum security prison." They noted its narrow-slit windows and its defense tower and said it looked as if it was "planned for another, more unsettled part of the world," conveying the idea that America had become a nation which is so protected by armor that it can no longer see the world.[7]

The SECCA law also imposed requirements on embassies that severely restricted the ability of public diplomacy professionals to use off-site space for their programming. The act applied to "all official diplomatic facilities and all U.S. Government personnel abroad that are under the authority of the Chief of Mission" including "U.S. citizens and Locally Employed Staff" whether direct hire or under contract. It said any new site must co-locate all USG personnel at that site and must be set back at least 100 feet from the perimeter. The only exceptions were for personnel under command of an area commander, Peace Corps Volunteers and VOA correspondents. The law allowed a waiver permitting US government personnel to be posted off site if the Secretary of State "determines that security considerations permit and it is in the national interest of the United States, and notifies Congress of the waiver.[8]

By 2011 there were only 37 traditional, stand-alone, open access American cultural centers, down from hundreds earlier. In those 37 countries, the PAOs continued to enjoy their programming assets, and some of them still work very well.

For example, the Ben Franklin Library in Mexico City has been maintained as a traditional, stand-alone center staffed by US government personnel since it opened in 1942. According to one Senate report, "The Ben Franklin Library has been in operation in downtown Mexico City since 1942 and is a mainstay of our Public Diplomacy efforts. In addition to providing an impressive collection of 23,000 books on America, U.S. law and economics (primarily in English but also Spanish), it boasts 130 periodicals and over 600 videos on American history and culture. It is one of the better-known landmarks in the city and projects an impressive image of the United States.... The State Department estimates that some 1,200 users visit the library every month."[9]

The James Baldwin Library in Rangoon, Burma is another positive example of a classic American center that is still very successful, and this is despite the restrictive nature of the Burmese regime. It has 13,000 books and 23,000 members. It is, according to one report, "open to any Burmese citizen willing to brave the police spies who haunt the area. On one a day in 2008 a reporter saw "young Burmese were sitting on every available piece of furniture" and it has attracted large numbers of dissidents as well as loyalists. The library has a book club, a dozen internet stations, and over 10,000 visitors a month that makes it "easily our most visited public diplomacy facility in the world."[10]

However, most posts do not have such open-access facilities, and most public diplomacy professionals have suffered from the loss of the stand-alone American Centers that were ideal program platforms. They therefore have tried to find new ways to create new institutions that would meet at least some of the original needs. The options selected by the PAO vary from country to country and depend on local conditions.

## Information Resource Centers

One remedy that PAOs have tried in order to deal with the new conditions was to open what they usually called an "Information Resource Center" (IRC) inside the secure embassy building or compound. The facility had American books and periodicals, and because the Internet was now available, it usually had computer terminals with free Internet access.

For example, In Japan, IRCs or "U.S. Embassy Reference Services," are located in the US embassy in Tokyo and consulates in four Japanese cities (Sapporo, Nagoya, Osaka, and Fukuoka). They play a substantial role in US public diplomacy in Japan. The US Embassy website states the goal of IRCs as "to provide specialized, accurate, and authoritative information about the United States."[11]

The major problem for IRCs is their limit on access. Of the 177 IRCs functioning in 2009, 122 (69 percent) were located on a secure embassy compound, and about two thirds of them made access very difficult: about half of them (87) allowed public access only by appointment, and another 11 percent (19) allowed no public access at all. One Senate report noted, "According to data provided by the State Department, those IRCs located off the compound receive significantly *more* visitors than those located on the compound. In the Middle East—perhaps our area most in need of outreach—with 12 IRCs on Embassy compounds and 4 located off, those off the compound received almost six times as many visitors per month (843) as those on the compound (139). IRCs in Latin America, East Asia, South Central Asia have even greater disparities." The report concluded: "Equally impacted has been the foot-traffic in IRCs that are located on Embassy compounds. At the same time, new security architecture has created structures that project a Fortress America environment that seems to say anything but 'Welcome' which has led to a similar inertia in our Public Diplomacy efforts in many of these locations."[12]

Even for the accessible IRC, visitors were usually required to go through embassy security, and that often entailed leaving their personal identification and cell phones at the front gate with the Marine Security Guard. These new barriers cut down on use by the local population. Where access was not permitted at all, anyone wanting information about the United States could only obtain it by phone call to the IRC staff inside the embassy.

In Egypt, for example, the public affairs section for many years maintained an American Center located in a beautiful old villa on loan from the Egyptian government since 1965 that was two blocks from the embassy. It was heavily used by Egyptian students and professionals for decades, but when the government reclaimed it the PAO had to open an IRC inside a new and strongly fortified embassy compound. The American Center in Alexandria (a city of 4 million) has remained open and accessible to the public, and it receives 1,600 visitors/month, while the IRC at the embassy in the much larger city of Cairo receives fewer than 1,000 per month.[13] In Jordan, the American Language Center in Amman opened in 1989 and teaches 2,400 students per year, but on orders of the embassy's Regional Security Officer (RSO) it flies no American flag, and by order of the RSO it allows entry only to registered members not the general public.[14]

Some IRCs suffer from competition from BNCs. One report on the Dominican Republic said:

> The embassy runs a small IRC called the "Ben Franklin Center," which offers limited resources (some 2,400 titles) and is housed in a single room in a small, off the beaten path, bungalow that serves as the Embassy's Public Affairs section. To address their small size, the staff has aggressively compiled an impressive list of on-line databases that members of the IRC...use with great frequency....However, from a Public Diplomacy perspective, this trend is troubling. If true Public Diplomacy work most effectively involves interactions between Americans and foreign nationals, then relegating "contact" to a mere Internet portal to US government documents, however useful, eliminates the "public" in Public Diplomacy. At the same time, the IRC must compete with Santo Domingo's well-established Bi-National Center which offers both a private K–12 school as well as separate English classes for ages 5 to adult. The BNC's library offers a collection of 13,000 titles in English and Spanish, and boasts a gallery and auditorium that seats 300. The BNC is located on a major thoroughfare and a few blocks from a major university.[15]

## American Corners

Some PAOs realized that an IRC located behind embassy walls and security barriers did not provide an adequate response to the need, so they came up with another new concept they called "American corners." The idea was to establish a small American library inside a local institution such as a university, so security would not be a problem. The PAO would identify an institution that was willing to provide space and a local staff to manage the library on a voluntary basis, and the embassy would provide American books and materials for it. American Corners are located in municipal buildings, such as a university. This approach was first tried in the former Soviet Union where it seemed to be fairly successful because the end of the Cold War had left local populations eager to have direct access to American libraries or other public buildings in regions that often have no other US diplomatic presence. Then it spread to other countries to help fill a need. An American Corner typically has 800 books, and half dozen computers connected to the Internet. In 2009 there were 414: 83 in Africa, 59 in East Asia, 166 in

Europe, 22 in Latin America, 39 in the Middle East, and 45 in South Central Asia. Public diplomacy staffs in Russia work in the embassy in Moscow and consulates in three other cities, but they also support 29 Corners throughout the country. Books related to the United States and computers are supplied to each location.[16]

However the biggest problem with American Corners is that because of SECCA, there could be no US government personnel assigned to them, so there were no opportunities for Americans or even FSNs to have sustained direct contact with the target audience. Moreover, the partner institution often failed to provide the level of personal attention to customer service that the traditional American centers had offered. In Cairo, for example, the PAO discovered after the American Corner was opened with fanfare at Cairo University, that it was left closed and locked for most of the day and was not used by students as it had been intended, so the project was dropped.

One 2006 analysis of American corners by a PD professional with experience in Russia, where they started, said that they are "cheap substitutes for the American Centers shut down after the cold war." It added that "they often disappointed people by their limited, modest scale and available resources, including ones pertaining to high art. Not always directly expressed, but often made clear by tactful insinuation, the reaction of many Russians to the corners was: Is that all America has to offer?"[17]

### IRCs versus Corners

Given the access problem with IRCs, some PAOs have found American corners better than nothing. In Hungary, where the first one opened in 2004 and there were four corners spread around the country, they were working fairly well, as one study showed.[18]

The US Embassy in Thailand has five American corners located in major libraries nationwide. One official report says that these American Corners "aim to foster mutual understanding between Thailand and the United States through a variety of means including satellite broadcasts, digital video conferences, hi-speed Internet access, and book and multimedia collections. The Corners are used to stimulate dialogue with individual citizens, organizations, institutions and the media by providing information and cultural activities." In two of them, the post specifically engages in direct dialogues with the Thai Muslims during PD officers' visits to the Southern parts of Thailand,

and develops contacts for the IVLP and other exchange programs, as well as to monitor small grants programs. The post also uses these American Corners annually to conduct a special Muslim outreach program with an imam from the United States who talks about Islam in the United States.[19]

An analysis of public diplomacy in Serbia said: "when the Cold War ended, the libraries were closed and American corners were established in their place. American corners do not have American staff and offer significantly fewer resources.... There is a healthy attendance at events held at American corners, but they do not attract nearly as many people as the libraries did on a daily basis. Thus, in their current form American corners are not as powerful a tool of public diplomacy as the American libraries were during the Cold War Era.[20]

The public diplomacy staff in Sierra Leone maintains a library in the embassy that according to one study its location "makes it difficult to visit, and it is not very welcoming. The location of the embassy also makes access difficult. The embassy, 'up on a hill' is not only off-putting, but the large compound that it sits on doesn't encourage the people of Sierra Leone to want to use it or its facilities." The post therefore also makes use of American corners, located in Sierra Leonean institutions, that provide information on the United States by means of computers, books and magazines, and venues to talk to Americans about America.[21]

In Russia, the United States maintains an IRC in the embassy in Moscow but it is not accessible to the public. In addition, however, it maintains five American centers and a network of 26American corners, so that every significant city in Russia has one or the other.[22] In Hungary, there is an IRC in the US embassy in Budapest that is accessible to the public, and in addition there are five American corners in different parts of the country, the first one established in Budapest in 2004.[23] In Japan, there are American centers in Tokyo and four provincial cities that are all accessible to the public.[24]

In Chile, there is an IRC located inside the embassy that is physically not accessible to the public. It is staffed by professional documentation and reference specialists who provide information by phone or email in response to questions. In addition, the embassy has established four American Corners in four different Chilean universities, three of them in provincial cities. Their facilities are uneven, with some having outdated or nonfunctional websites. At the same time, there is a BNC in Santiago, the Instituto Chileano Nortamericano that was established in 1938, and today it has 15 branches throughout the country. This ICHN is a private corporation that is administratively and financially independent but it works closely with the US embassy.[25]

## The Lugar Report

In 2008, two prominent think tanks published a joint report that said, "We believe the time is right to revive the ACC [American Cultural Center] concept in those countries where the local security situation permits and program environment warrants."[26]

This think tank report reflected a growing concern in Washington about the ineffectiveness of our public diplomacy. In December 2008 Senator Richard Lugar sent a senior staff member, Paul Foldi, to visit a number of public diplomacy field offices in the Middle East and Latin America to see what could be done to improve performance. Foldi came back with concerns that focused on several issues but in particular on the demise of American centers problem that security precautions were causing our public diplomacy programs. In February 2009, Lugar published Foldi's report as an official US Senate document.

The Lugar report expressed skepticism about the effectiveness of American corners, saying:

> the operation, maintenance and programming offered by each Corner is in the hands of a foreign national who is neither paid nor overseen by U.S. Embassy officials and thus amount to nothing less than an outsourcing of U.S. Public Diplomacy. The results in terms of U.S. Public Diplomacy are therefore mixed; some Corners are vital hubs of information, others dusty relics that offered little more than a photo-op for an ambassador at their opening. None offers Americans to be employed there, although American Fulbright English teachers sometimes give lectures there. While appropriate for remote regions where the U.S. has no diplomatic presence, Corners are too small to take the place of American Centers in a capital city.

It adds:

> If viewed not as a *substitute* for a formal American Center facility but rather as a *supplement,* the Corners do in fact provide Public Diplomacy platforms for U.S. programming to have a home— particularly in the more remote areas of larger countries where the

U.S. lacks any formal diplomatic facility. For example in Russia, outside of our Embassy in Moscow, the U.S. has consulates in only St. Petersburg, Yekaterinburg, and Vladivostok, but there are 33 Corners throughout the country. Belarus has 12 Corners; Indonesia has 11 Corners, the Philippines—14, Afghanistan—7. However, because the Corners are not staffed with nor overseen by U.S. officials, they lack the same Public Diplomacy impact of a dedicated, stand-alone brick and mortar facility in a country's capital. Some are excellent projections of American Public Diplomacy with dedicated and motivated staffs, others, can wither on the vine depending on the level of local interest and resources in providing staff willing to push the programming boundaries that may be at odds with officials in more remote locations.[27]

The report concluded: "The Department of State should take a careful look at any requests for additional American Corners to ensure the need is truly justified." The report also criticized what had happened with the BNCs, saying: "As budgetary constraints took hold and later, as USIA was absorbed into the State Department, the U.S. government began to disengage from day-to-day operations to the point that, now, BNCs are completely independent of U.S. operational and budgetary support, oversight, and programmatic direction." It added: "Rather than create competing institutions that offer English language and cultural programming, the State Department should examine cost and policy implications of formally re-establishing U.S. government links with the network of Bi-National Centers (BNCs) in the region. BNCs were originally created by the United States but are now wholly run by independent local boards."[28]

The Lugar report made several other recommendations. It said: "The State Department—working with Congress and host governments—needs to recreate the American Center system in secure facilities outside our Embassy compounds from which we can provide foreign audiences with greater access to information about the United States through libraries, periodicals and an uncensored Internet." It said: "Congressional support is needed for the Department of State to create more accessible Public Diplomacy platforms by pushing Information Resource Centers (IRCs) out of remote Embassy compounds and allowing them to be rebuilt as stand-alone American Centers in more centrally located areas. In order to accomplish this, the so-called 'co-location requirement' should be re-visited to allow these new Centers to be established as well as to permit those few facilities still off-compound to remain as such, as long as appropriate security measures are in place." The report added: "Reinvigorating the American Centers will go far to providing this by offering a more neutral location for our diplomats and visiting scholars to begin to repair the breach that has been created.... Such a program would entail re-locating a small number of Embassy officials outside our diplomatic compounds in those locations where the security climate permits and where we are able to provide them with appropriately secure facilities."[29]

### State Department Changes

Several months after the Lugar Report was issued, the Undersecretary for Public Diplomacy and Public Affairs Judith McHale decided to take an initiative to revive the original American center concept somehow, calling them "American spaces." Her staff did a survey and found that of the 37 traditional American centers still functioning abroad, 21 of them were in cities where the embassy was scheduled to be relocated and the new compound would include an IRC that would replace the off-site facility. The undersecretary decided to work with PAOs to help protect the 21 autonomous centers that were threatened, and also to find ways to establish new centers outside compound that would comply with the SECCA rules. She established a small office at State to promote the idea.[30]

In 2013, her successor, Undersecretary Tara Sonenshine, continued to promote and support American spaces, saying, "American spaces offer each embassy gathering places to connect with young people, foster new ideas, help foreign students pursue studies in the U.S., and promote English language learning"[31] She called them "extension cords for public diplomacy, extending our reach directly to people." In 2013 there were 853 American spaces of all kinds, including Corners and BNCs, in 169 countries. A few of them are mobile, such as the ones in the Philippines and Madagascar.[32]

The State Department Inspector General praised the IIP Bureau for its enhancement of American spaces, saying, "Regularizing support for American Spaces overseas has strengthened these platforms for engagement with foreign publics, a cornerstone of the Department's 21st century PD effort." It added, "The Under Secretary for Public Diplomacy and Public Affairs has underscored the importance of American Spaces by greatly increasing funding for them," and "The 2011 reorganization created the Regional Coordination and American Spaces group, overseen by a deputy coordinator, to create a single point of contact for embassies and Department bureaus and to support the expanded mandate of 850 American Spaces worldwide."[33]

Some PAOs worked to find ways to create new program space outside the compound, or preserve what they already had. One idea that emerged from the discussions was that in order to get permission of the ambassador and regional security officer (RSO) for space that would be open and accessible to the general public, it might have to be located not in a remote location but in a place close to local commercial offices, perhaps on an upper floor of an office building, that terrorists would be more reluctant to attack.

### The Jakarta Experiment

The PAO in Indonesia, veteran public diplomacy officer Dr. Michael Anderson, proposed to solve the problem when he proposed establishing an American center in a downtown commercial shopping mall, something that had never been done before. His purpose was to try to replicate as closely as possible, within the rules, the traditional American center. Anderson worked to persuade the ambassador and RSO plus other members of the country team. PAO Anderson said that @america has revived Edward R. Murrow's idea of the importance of the "last three feet" of people-to-people interaction to facilitate effective information and cultural efforts abroad.[34]

The PAO persuaded Washington to provide funding for the experiment. It was expensive—two million dollars for the building, plus one million annual operating costs (one-third of his budget). Senior officials at State were opposed to the project, but with the help of Ambassador Cameron Hume, Undersecretary for Public Affairs Judith McHale was persuaded to approve it. She attended the opening in December 2010, and it was called "@america."[35]

The PAO was careful to satisfy the security requirements of SECCA and State Department officials in two ways. First, he showed the embassy security officer that such a public location, on an upper floor in an Indonesian mall, was relatively safe from terrorist attack. Second, to comply with the SECCA law prohibiting US government employees from working there, he contracted with an Indonesian private firm to have it staffed by young bilingual and bicultural Indonesians. He arranged for one of his American staff, an assistant cultural affairs officer, to supervise the project by spending much of his time there but to keep his official office at the embassy.[36]

The center offers a wide range of services including cultural programs, English lessons, personalized student counseling and other attractions typical of a traditional American center. It has a multimedia space, and offers information on the US delivered by videos and photographs, videoconferencing, interactive games, professional education counseling, guest lectures, cultural performances, discussions, debates and other programs. According to the PAO, "During its first six months, it attracted almost 44,000 visitors who attended one of more than 270 programs or received information from onsite educational advisers or learned about U.S. society through various technology platforms. By July 2011, daily total visitors reached 368 people, who physically came into the facility each day. Seventy percent were aged 15 to 30, and @america had over 14,000 website members, almost 12,000 Twitter followers and about 3,200 Facebook friends." The PAO realized that it was important to use social media to publicize the facility because its location did not make it easily visible.[37] One study of public diplomacy reported that "the post experimented with their new cultural center @america to reach out to young people where they spend their free time, which is in the malls of Jakarta, and given the size and diversity of Indonesia, they were consciously trying to reach out beyond Jakarta to communicate with second-tier cities and islands other than Java."[38]

The state inspectors praised the project, saying that they considered it to be an outreach tool designed to go to the target audience of Indonesians aged 15–30.[39] *The New York Times* also featured @america as the latest US public diplomacy effort to win over young people, especially in a Muslim country.[40]

## Conclusion

Public diplomacy professionals continue to find ways to replicate, in some fashion, the concept of a stand-alone center that provides a platform combining several programs and is easily accessible to the public, overcoming security barriers. A study by the American Academy of Diplomacy in 2008 said: "Cultural Centers provide PD field personnel with excellent opportunities to engage college students and young professionals in discussions of American society and policies. The centers will have a library facility; computer access; English language instruction; student counseling and cultural programming. We believe that the time is right to revive the ACC concept in those countries where the local security situation permits and program environment warrants. For Missions that prefer a smaller program operation, an alternative is the Information Resource Center (IRC) model that features a research library facility." The Academy recommended that State "Establish 40 American Cultural Centers (or a mixture of ACCs and smaller Information Resource Centers) in order to broaden U.S. daily cultural presence worldwide" and "Re-engage the autonomous pro-U.S. Binational Center (BNC) network in Latin America whose membership is desirous of closer cultural and political ties with the U.S."[41]

In many places establishing the classic cultural center/library is not possible for security reasons, so other approaches have been tried. As of mid-2013, IIP is studying whether the Jakarta experiment can be copied elsewhere. The US embassies in Dhaka and Riga are considering opening a similar model, but the cost may be prohibitive. As of late 2013 the Jakarta experiment of @America is still doing very well, although because it is expensive it has not been replicated anywhere else.[42] PD field officers will however undoubtedly keep trying to find a way to reach out to the public and still abide by the rules that security requires.

CHAPTER TEN

# *Educational Exchanges*

This chapter discusses the US public diplomacy programs that support educational exchanges between the United States and foreign countries, involving not only students but also professionals. Most Americans have heard of the Fulbright program but few know much about it or the other programs by which US public diplomacy supports other exchanges. From the perspective of a PAO at a US embassy, the two most important exchange programs, and among the oldest, are the Fulbright and the International Visitor Leadership Program (IVLP). But there are several others.

## A Variety of Types of Exchanges

### *Fulbright and IVLP*

*The Fulbright program* is the one that is known best internationally. The name is widely recognized and it carries considerable prestige abroad. It offers scholarships for students and grants for established professionals. It is unique in that it arranges exchanges both ways, not only bringing foreigners to the United States, but also sending Americans abroad. Since it was established in 1946, it has arranged tens of thousands of exchanges with the United States each way. Participants in the program for foreigners are selected by the embassy or by a bi-national Fulbright Commission (see further on). The American Fulbright students and scholars are selected by boards in the United States, based on requests from posts.[1]

Some posts have had Fulbright programs for decades. In Thailand, for example, between 1949 when it began and 2009, the Fulbright program has brought 1,698 Thais to America and sent 2,419 Americans to Thailand.[2] The first Pakistani Fulbright participants traveled to the United States in 1951 and since then the program has become the largest Fulbright Program, in terms of funding, worldwide. In 2009, 154 Fulbright grants were issued to Pakistanis for MA and PhD study in America. The US Embassy also supports International Visitors Leadership Grants.[3]

The IVLP brings mid-career foreign professionals to the United States on short-term visits to meet with their American counterparts in several American cities. Originally called the International Visitors Program, it is a highly selective program for mid-career professionals who visit their counterparts and others in several American cities. Most visits last only three weeks—some are shorter—because the participants are busy people. Its stated purpose is to bring "current and emerging foreign leaders in a variety of fields" to the United States to "experience this country firsthand and cultivate lasting relationships with their American counterparts."[4] Participants are chosen by the country team at the embassy, which looks for candidates who seem to be headed for leadership roles in their country.

Grantees meet with professional counterparts, visit US public and private sector organizations related to the project theme and participate in cultural and social activities. They have either individually-tailored programs or they travel in small groups from the same region or the same profession. They are accompanied by an escort or "facilitator" who is language qualified if necessary. The success of the program is usually measured years after they return home, anecdotally with examples, and many countries have seen people rise to in leadership positions who had participated in the program. Because it is expensive, the number of participants each year is relatively small. The US embassy in Japan, for example, sends approximately 50 IVLP grantees to the United States annually, which is the highest number of any post.[5] In total, the IVLP brings more than five thousand foreign visitors to the United States each year. More than 200,000 International Visitors have come here since the program started in 1940, and this includes over 300 and 30 current or former Chiefs of State or Heads of Government.

In France, for example, in 2011 the president, prime minister, and foreign minister were all IVLP returnees. President Nicolas Sarkozy and François Fillon, his prime minister, had been IVLP grantees when they were in their thirties. Valéry Giscard d'Estaing, president of France 1974–1981, and Lionel Jospin, former prime minister, were also visitors in the United States in their thirties. Every year about 30 French people are invited to visit the USA. About one third of them are now selected from minorities.[6] The CAO in Paris has said: "Needless to say, the positive experience they had in the United States on the IVLP while in their 20s and 30s is helping us today advance the bilateral relationship as these officials have now gotten to such leadership positions in their country." He pointed out: "Here in France, our embassy does not single out any one particular group for outreach. Our goal is to be inclusive and to make sure that no group is ignored.... Today thirty percent of our participants in the International Visitors Leadership Program come from our diversity outreach efforts. The Fulbright Commission is attracting exceptional talent from non-traditional audiences."[7]

There is a similar opportunity that has been available to public affairs sections for decades, called the "Voluntary Visitor Program," by which the US embassy can arrange for meetings in the United States for foreign professionals who are planning to travel there anyway. These short-term "VolVis" grants are less expensive than IVLGs, but they can achieve some of the same objectives.

### Newer Targeted or Tailored Programs

Global political developments have led to the creation of new exchange programs in response to new opportunities.

After the Soviet Union collapsed in 1989, the US Government decided to try to reach out to Russian youth, and the *Future Leaders Exchange* (FLEX) program was created to bring approximately three hundred Russian high school students to the United States annually for one year of study.[8] The students are spread out over all 50 states so they have individual experiences. As one State Department official said about the participants in FLEX, "they return to Russia "transformed" after "fabulous formative experiences" speaking "fantastic English," not only with an intimate knowledge of American culture, but also networks of friends who last well past their academic year of study.[9] By 2010 more than 17,000 Russian school children had participated in this program.[10]

After the 9/11 terrorist attack on the United States, the Bush administration created several exchange programs to focus on youth in the Near East, where the terrorists had come from, and from other Muslim countries. The George W. Bush administration shifted the focus of the exchange program in two major ways: giving the Middle Eastern and Muslim countries a high priority and a shift to more youth and "youth influencers" (teachers, coaches, mentors) instead of only opinion leaders. Both shifts were largely a reaction to the 9/11 terrorist attack on the United States. It seemed prudent to focus attention on Arab and Muslim audiences, and to target youth because they constituted up to 50 percent of the populations under 25, and they were assumed to be subject to negative influences and were expected to be future leaders.[11]

Shortly after 9/11, State also created the *Partnerships for Learning Undergraduate Studies* (PLUS) program, intended to bring "non-elite gifted young men and women" from Muslim countries for their junior and senior years at American universities. The program ran from 2003 until 2008 but was then discontinued because the State Department determined that it was not reaching enough of an audience to justify its expense.[12] At the same time, the Bush administration started the *Youth Exchange and Study* (YES) Program as a direct response to 9/11, and it targeted several dozen countries including Arab and non-Arab.[13] It paid for foreign students to spend one year in an American high school. Embassies made the selection of candidates, who lived with a host family in the United States while they were to school there. Placement and monitoring of student progress was outsourced to several American NGOs. Then in 2007, State launched the *Undergraduate Exchange Program* (NESA UGRAD) to bring up to 100 students annually from the Near East and South Asia to spend one or two semesters for non-degree study at an accredited university in the United States. It was expected that some of the students who attended this program would apply for Fulbright grants to continue their study in the United States.[14] In the United States it is administered by American Councils for International Education.

In 2008, State launched a special program for Egyptian students, called the *Community College Initiative* that would bring one thousand Egyptian students over three years to the United states for one or two year terms at community colleges. The program's objectives are to foster mutual understanding between young Egyptians and Americans; and to develop professional level skills and aid youth in finding employment in the Egyptian job market, mostly in technical sectors.[15]

*Smaller Programs*

PAOs also have some smaller exchange programs to choose from. Among the older, established programs that PAOs have taken advantage of is the *Hubert H. Humphrey Fellowship* and the *Salzburg Seminar*. The Humphrey brings foreign graduate students to the US for a one-year non-degree program of academic coursework, independent research, professional affiliations, field trips, special seminars, and consultations with experts in the field. In addition, Fellows attend a Washington DC conference with Humphrey Fellows from across the United States in the fall. Each year US embassies select approximately ten Fellows. Since the program began, more than 205 Fellows from more than 80 countries have participated. The *Salzburg Global Seminar* hosts seminars several times each year at Schloss Leopoldskron in Austria. Its seminars focus on critical issues confronting the global community, covering topics as diverse as health care and education, culture and economics, geopolitics and philanthropy. Sessions last up to one week. Since it started in 1947, it has hosted more than 500 sessions for over 20,000 people. US embassies select participants from the host nation.[16]

Some exchange programs are for very specific types of participants. *The International Writing Program* (IWP) brings to Iowa City a group of 25 to 35 authors, both rising stars and established creative writers who have achieved literary distinction in their own countries, who have demonstrated literary talent. They have a ten-week residency to work on their own projects, to give readings and lectures, and to interact with American audiences and literary communities across the United States. It is funded by the US government but in the United States it is administered by the University of Iowa.

The *American Council of Young Political Leaders* (ACYPL) brings mid-level professionals with experience in governance to the United States for 8 to 14 days to meet American professionals in their fields. The embassy selects the participants but it is administered in the US by ACYPL. The *FORTUNE/US State Department Global Women's Mentoring Partnership* brings emerging foreign women leaders, between the ages of 25 and 43, to the US where they meet with members of Fortune's Most Powerful Women Leaders for a month-long one-on-one internship program. It is administered in the United States by the Fortune Company. The *Study of the US Institutes for Student Leaders* program is for undergraduate student leaders from abroad who spend six weeks at US academic institutions, participating in academic courses and taking educational tours. Candidates have specialties in civic engagement, US government, public policy, women's leadership, journalism, American religious pluralism, and social entrepreneurship.

The *Study of the United States Institute for scholars* (SUSI) program is for foreign university faculty, secondary educators and other scholars to the United States who teach about America. It brings them to the United States for six weeks to strengthen curricula and improve the quality of their teaching. The first four weeks are spent at specific US host universities where they participate in lectures, seminars discussions, and site visits related to learn about American educational philosophies and new teaching methods. The remaining two weeks are on a study tour in another geographic region of the country. The Stateside programs are arranged by several US universities. The *International Leaders in Education Program* (ILEP) brings outstanding secondary school teachers of English, math, science, and social studies from the Near East, South Asia, Southeast Asia, Sub-Saharan Africa, and the Western Hemisphere[17] to the United States to further develop expertise in their subject areas, enhance their teaching skills, and increase their knowledge about the United States. They participate in a five-month academic program at US university graduate schools of education. ILEP is administered by International Research and Exchanges Board.[18]

Finally, the *Teaching Excellence and Achievement Program* (TEA) is a program for secondary school teachers with five years of experience teaching English, social studies, math and science to spend six weeks at a university graduate school of education, learning teaching methodologies and strategies, lesson planning, teaching strategies, leadership, and instructional technologies. The program also includes field experience at a secondary school. In the United States this is administered by International Research and Exchanges Board.[19]

### The Rationale

The public diplomacy rationale concept behind all of the exchange programs that bring foreigners to America is that they usually result in a much greater understanding by the foreign participants in all aspects of America, including not only its foreign policy but also its history, society and culture, and that it often leads to interpersonal connections with Americans. The secondary benefit is that these programs help lead to a better understanding by Americans of foreign peoples and their societies and cultures, that can help United States interests. The exchange programs that send Americans abroad also serve a dual purpose of helping foreigners learn about America while helping Americans learn about a foreign society and culture.

The Advisory Committee on Cultural Diplomacy in its 2005 report said that "cultural exchanges counteract the stereotypes that inform the attitudes of people everywhere, revealing the common ground."[20] A senior USIA official found that "exchanges have generated tolerance and appreciation of foreign values, culture and institutions as well as lasting connections between participants and their hosts."[21] And US ambassadors consistently rate the International Visitor Leadership Program as one of the most useful public diplomacy tools available to them.[22]

Senior State Department officials have consistently promoted educational exchange programs, using different rationales. The Undersecretary for Public Diplomacy in the Bush administration, Karen Hughes, who was a strong supporter of them, found in 2007 during the Global War on Terror, that if she presented her exchange budget to Congress with the justification that these programs helped prevent future terrorist attacks on the United States, they were more likely to be funded, so she did that.[23] In 2013, her successor, Tara Sonenshine, was pointing out in her speeches that the 765,000 foreign students at US colleges and universities contributed $22.7 billion to the US economy.[24] Secretary of State John Kerry, whose daughter was a Fulbright student abroad, calls himself a "passionate advocate" of that program which he called "one of the great programs that exists anywhere in the world." He said it helps break down barriers, take away ideological extremes and "eliminate the simplistic sort of reduction to a stereotype that so many people engage in."[25]

These are the programs over which American officials have the least control, but they are considered valuable assets to our public diplomacy. Edward R. Murrow's famous dictum about the importance of "the last three feet" in public diplomacy applies to educational exchanges even though the three-feet conversations take place between foreigners and private American citizens. They are not responsible for advocating policy but they can represent American views and attitudes that are part of the PD mission.

The fact that most of the exchange programs are carried out in the United States by American private, non-governmental organizations (see below), is actually a major reason for their success. Participants can directly experience American society, culture, and people, so they likely have no suspicion that they are being misled, as can be the case when the information they receive is mediated. They realize that their program, their contacts and their conversations are not controlled by the US government, and this convinces them that they are seeing the "real America" and it also makes the point about American freedom. According to one study, exchange participants remarked on this aspect of the programs.[26]

Public diplomacy professionals generally agree that exchange programs are among the most powerful of all public diplomacy instruments. They are far more effective in enhancing understanding of America than reading about the United States or watching a film or TV program. The impact on public diplomacy goals is almost always positive, because the visitor attains a more nuanced and sophisticated appreciation of the United States in all its aspects, so that misunderstandings as well as false myths and simplistic impressions are dispelled. In a very small number of cases, visitors return home with negative prejudices reinforced, but on balance the program is almost always achieves public diplomacy goals. Visitors usually return home with a much more sophisticated knowledge of the United States in many respects, and they are often willing to explain America to their compatriots in a more sympathetic way.

Opinion poll data in fact indicates that foreigners who have visited the United States tend to have a more positive view of America than those who have not, corroborating what public diplomacy professionals have always known about these exchanges.[27] One exception that proves the rule is Sayyid Qutb, an Egyptian writer who came to the United States in 1948 on an Egyptian government scholarship to study the American educational system. He spent two years in the United States (he studied at Colorado State College of Education and Stanford) but found many aspects of American life repugnant, including its materialism, racism, and mixing of the sexes, that he wrote about in his 1951 essay "The America I Have Seen." When he returned home he became a radicalized Muslim extremist who confronted the Egyptian regime and continued to criticize the United States. Although Nasser had him executed in 1966 he has since been highly revered by violent Islamists.[28]

A detailed study of the IVLP program found that, in interviews with participants, almost every one returned home with a more positive and much better informed view of the United States. They said they were impressed with American open-mindedness and friendliness, and they understood much better the practical applications of such ideals as freedom and democracy. They were especially pleased with their experiences visiting and staying at American homes that gave them a close look at our family life.[29]

As the PAO in Moscow Michael Hurley explained: "We're not only doing [people-to-people exchanges] because it's the right thing to do," he said. "We do it because we believe that opening the doors to conversations that can be facilitated by... exposure to one another's culture is in our interest to have.... It is in the United States' national interest."[30] The PAO in Germany, Bruce Armstrong, addressed the problem of East Germans having less knowledge and more negative views of America because of decades of Communist rule, by arranging educational exchange programs, such as the Eastern German teacher exchange program.[31]

### Each Post Is Different

As with all public diplomacy efforts, each country has an exchange program that is unique.

The general rule is that Washington provides the public affairs section of each embassy with an annual allocation of a specific number of scholarships for young people to study in the United States, and grants for foreign professionals to travel to America for short visits. The study grants can range from one semester to four years, but the professional grants are usually for a few weeks or months because they are busy people and their grants are intended to allow the visitors to become familiar with the people and practices in their particular specialization. Beyond that, there are variations among posts depending on local circumstances.

First, the size of the budget and the importance of the country matter. In India, for example, the PAO has a much larger budget than most PAOs; so he or she has been able to maintain about 15 different exchange programs for Indians to explore education and professional development in the United States.[32] Small posts on the other hand may have only a few Fulbright or IVLP grants.

Second, if a bilateral political relationship improves, opportunities for the United States to undertake educational exchange programs also change. One example can be seen by comparing the Soviet Union during the Cold War with the Russia of today. During the Cold War, Moscow prevented extensive exchanges of persons with the United States. The US government was able to start a Fulbright program with the Soviet Union in 1973, during the Cold War, but it was limited. Then exchanges expanded considerably after the fall of the Soviet Union so that by 2010 more than 55,000 Russian citizens of all types were alumni of these programs. However, scholar exchanges with Russia, which reached a high of about 80 annually in the late 1990s because of the demise of the Soviet Union, then declined to about 40 annually, while the focus of exchanges shifted to younger students.[33]

Another example is Afghanistan, where exchange programs were impossible for many years because of recurring civil wars and difficult relations with the United States. The Fulbright program was suspended in the 1980, and it only resumed in 2003, when the United States again had a major presence in the country. American Embassy Kabul then began a program to send Afghan high school students to America, and it reinstated the Fulbright program after a 23-year suspension.[34] It has grown since then because Afghanistan became a Washington priority (see chapter eleven).

Third, changes in exchange programs can also go in a negative direction because of the bilateral relationship. In Serbia, throughout the Cold War, exchanges were an important American instrument because of that country's standoff posture toward the USSR, and by the1970s, Yugoslavia had the largest Fulbright program in Eastern Europe. But since the end of the Cold War, the bilateral relationship has become more contentious, and Serbia has become less important to Washington, so the exchange program shrank. By 2008, the United States sent only three American Fulbright scholars to Serbia and received five Serbian scholars. In the following year, seven scholars participated in Fulbright exchanges.[35]

Another example is Iran. Under the Shah, the US had a robust exchange program with Iran when Iranians were among the largest groups of students to come to America. Since the 1979 revolution, the US-Iranian political confrontation has prevented a fully functioning exchange program, although some academic exchanges continued until the 2009 Iranian election that was criticized in the US as fraudulent and tensions increased. Since 2009, the State Department has provided online student counseling to Iranian students, but US-sponsored exchanges have been on hold, primarily because of fears that participants could be arrested by the Iranian regime.[36]

Fourth, if domestic political conditions in a country make other public diplomacy programs difficult, the United States may try to increase the exchange of persons to compensate and to keep the dialogue going. One example of that is Syria, in the years just before the 2011 uprising. Syrian Government restrictions on local public diplomacy activities had become pervasive in those years, closing the American Center and American Language Center, and prohibiting the PAO from contacts with the media, which were hostile to US interests. In response, the PAO decided to expand educational exchanges substantially. In the years 2008–2010, when American public diplomacy facilities remained closed, the embassy sent more Syrians to America on the International

Visitor (IVLP) program than in the several years before that. In 2009 the embassy sent 30 Syrians to the US on the IVLP, involved 26 American and Syrian students and scholars in the Fulbright program, two others on the Humphrey Scholarship program, and one Syrian foreign language teaching assistant. For 2010, Washington responded positively to the embassy's request for IVLP slots for Syria, doubling the number from 32 to 64. In addition, the embassy brought seven Americans to Syria to study Arabic under the critical language program. The embassy was however careful not to try to generate media coverage for the individuals participating in the exchange program for fear it would put them in jeopardy with the authorities, and the candidates themselves expressed concerns about receiving publicity.[37] However, starting in 2011 when Syria's civil war broke out, all in-country public diplomacy programs ceased including all educational exchanges.

China is an interesting case. Despite the many years of US-China political confrontation, and extensive Chinese government restrictions on US public diplomacy programs in China, exchanges are now flourishing. Exchanges were suspended between 1949 and 1979 and again in 1979–80. Today however there are more than sixty thousand Chinese students on US university campuses, most of them here on Chinese government scholarships. The number of Chinese scholars in the United States has doubled since 2004, and the Chinese Ministry of Education contributes almost one million dollars to the Fulbright program. There are more than 110 Chinese professionals in the United States on IVLP programs funded by the United States, a large number considering the high cost of that program.[38]

## Local Partnerships

In some countries, the US embassy has established a bi-national educational exchange commission, often called a "Fulbright Commission," to facilitate the exchange program. These commissions usually are composed half of Americans—including embassy representatives and private Americans—and half of local citizens.

Bi-national commissions can provide several advantages to the US government. One is that the local members provide intimate knowledge of their society and can help identify good scholarship candidates. Another advantage to the United States is that commissions often lead to co-financing by the host government and/or private citizens. In France, for example, the foreign ministry co-finances the Fulbright program through the "Franco-American Commission," that sponsors between 30 and 50 American and French exchange grantees every year for studies, research, or to work as teaching assistants.[39] In India, the program is managed by the US-India Educational Foundation (USIEF), and the Indian government contributes to the cost, which is approximately nine million dollars annually and allows the exchange of more than 300 scholars each year. It is the largest in the world.[40] In Japan, the Fulbright program began in 1952 but since 1979 and it has been managed by the Japan-US Educational Commission (JUSEC). The program is funded by both governments and it sponsors exchanges of forty to fifty students, researchers, educators and journalists annually.[41]

The risk for the embassy in having a commission, however, is that the host country members might insist on choosing candidates that the embassy considers unsuitable, or they might veto candidates or study programs that the embassy wants.

One example of such a problem arose in India in 2007. A disagreement arose in USIEF in 2007 when embassy representatives proposed bringing American scholars to India to undertake research projects in Islamic studies—an outgrowth of Washington's post-9/11 focus on Muslims—and the Indians on the commission refused because their government regarded ethnic conflict as politically sensitive. The Government of India regards any form of ethnic conflict as issues of particular sensitivity, and research that probed ethnic conflict was regularly scrutinized very carefully by the Ministry of Higher Education and the Ministry of the Interior. India did not want Fulbright scholars to be seen as somehow political so it simply did not act upon such research proposals. Indian officials stated, "As soon as you start researching the topic you have to go door to door. This would unnecessarily raise ethnic tensions." The publicly stated Indian explanation was that the restrictions on American Fulbright researchers were "for their own safety." The stalemate was resolved when then-Ambassador David Mulford made the case in public statements for freedom of research. He announced to the media that the program would be discontinued unless these bureaucratic delays were addressed. The officials backed down and as a result the reviews of research proposals were streamlined and accepted without further delays.[42]

Problems have also arisen with commissions elsewhere. In Egypt, the United States has conducted a Fulbright program since 1949 and more than five thousand Egyptians have participated in it.[43] The Fulbright Commission there worked well for many years but at one point the embassy became concerned that the commission was following the personal wishes of some of the Egyptian commission members so that the candidates were not qualified by objective criteria that the embassy was trying to adhere to, despite the fact that the commission director was an American. The problem was resolved when the commission director was replaced.[44]

One exchange partnership arrangement that has gone well was started in 2010 by the PAO in Mexico. As he explained:

> The name of the program in Spanish is "Jovenes en Accion" or Youth in Action. It was—it's a program that we initiated in 2010. It is somewhat unique because it's an exchange program that is co-sponsored by the Mexican government, the secretary of education and private sector partners, along with the embassy in Mexico City. The program reaches out to public school high school students, ages 14 to about 18 years old, and brings them to the United States for a five-week period during which they get instruction in leadership, English language skills. They also have a two-week stay with a family in the United States, which includes community service projects. And, during the same time, they develop a project which they take back to Mexico to implement in their communities.... The first round of this program... had 50 students from all over the—all over Mexico. The second round, which was just this summer, has 68 students from 14 different states in Mexico.

He added: "A lot of these kids... arrived in the United States with, you know, stereotypes of what Americans are like, of what America is all about. And it seems that a lot of them went back home very changed, especially because they actually spent time in communities with families and came to see that we have a lot more in common than they thought we did, and that everybody is concerned about, you know, what's happening in Mexico, what's happening in the border, how it affects the United States, how it affects their communities."[45]

In short, bi-national commissions are in some cases problematic, but in other cases they can enhance the public diplomacy program considerably, depending on local circumstances.

## US Private Sector Partnerships

A very important aspect of cultural and educational programming by the US government involves partnerships with private American institutions that serve mutual purposes. This is sometimes called "citizen diplomacy." These partnerships are not widely known by the American public but they are vital to the success of the public diplomacy efforts. Some writers call for more reliance on the American private sector,[46] but already a great deal has been done, quietly, over the years by private-government cooperation on exchanges. Partnership with the private sector has long been established practice of public diplomacy professionals.

It has been declared US policy for decades that our public diplomacy efforts should be carried out with the help of the US private sector. After World War II, President Truman's the State Department opened an Office of Private Enterprise and Cooperation that worked with the private sector on overseas information projects. It cooperated for example with the Advertising Council to help shape commercial advertising overseas in a useful direction.[47] The Reagan administration's USIA mission statement on public diplomacy acknowledged the private sector role.

Congress has also stressed this point. When it passed the Smith-Mundt Act in 1948 it added provisions in order to satisfy members who were concerned to protect American private institutions. One provision said: "In carrying out the provisions of this chapter it shall be the duty of the Secretary to utilize, to the maximum extent practicable, the services and facilities of private agencies, including existing American press, publishing, radio, motion picture, and other agencies, through contractual arrangements or otherwise. It is the intent of Congress that the Secretary shall encourage participation in carrying out the purposes of this chapter by the maximum number of different private agencies in each field consistent with the present or potential market for their services in each country." Another provision said: "In authorizing international information activities under this chapter, it is the sense of the Congress (1) that the Secretary shall reduce such Government information activities whenever corresponding private information dissemination is found to be adequate; (2) that nothing in this chapter shall be construed to give the Department a monopoly in the production or sponsorship on the air of short-wave broadcasting programs, or a monopoly in any other medium of information."[48] It has therefore been the clear intent of Congress to protect the private sector from any harm that might be done by public diplomacy. But the actual practice of public diplomacy over the years has developed very strong partnerships with private organizations and individuals that have been mutually very beneficial.

In implementing its exchange programs the State Department partners with several different American nongovernmental organizations, such as the Institute for International Education (IIE), the National Council for International Visitors (NCIV), America-Mideast Education and Training Services (AMIDEAST), and others.[49] After the embassy selects the participants, the American NGO carries out the US-based arrangements. The NCIV, for example, that manages all of the stateside programs of the International Visitor Program, was established in 1961, and is an umbrella organization for seven National Program Agencies that work with hundreds of Committees of International Visitors all across the United States. The CIVs are responsible for the local programs of the foreign visitors, greeting them upon arrival, and making arrangements for their official meetings with counterparts and their home-stays, as well as other contacts. The forty-two thousand people who work at the CIVs are almost all unpaid volunteers. Partnership with the NCIV not only gives a private face to the NCIV program, it also saves the US government money; the volunteer hours were estimated in 2011 to be worth more fifteen million dollars.[50]

## Educational Advising

One important function of the public affairs section of the US embassy traditionally has been the provision of educational counseling services to students wishing to study in America. Helping foreign students understand how to apply for entry into American educational institutions is an important public diplomacy tool as an adjunct to the exchange program. For those students who can afford to pay their way to America, it is still difficult to figure out the American educational system, since it is usually much more complicated than the one they are used to at home. Counseling services also are less expensive than study scholarships, although to be done correctly they must include a professional counselor who knows the US system very well.

American education is highly respected around the world, and study in the United States is a strong magnet that pulls many foreigners to the United States, or to the few US-style universities and colleges located abroad. As the American scholar John Waterbury says, many foreigners see American educational institutions as significantly better than the local educational institutions in their own countries, and they are also attracted to other aspects of American society, so despite political differences with Washington, they want to study in the United States.[51]

In the past, student counseling was done almost entirely by US government employees, mostly local employees, who worked in embassy facilities. In 2013, the State Department provided support to student advising programs in 170 countries,[52] but much of that is actually carried out now by others on behalf of the US government. Over the years, because of budget and staff cuts, it has been increasingly outsourced to non-governmental organizations, some of them American. In the Arab world, for example, the State Department has a contract with AMIDEAST, an American NGO with headquarters in Washington DC that has field offices all over the Middle East and North Africa, to do student counseling on behalf of the US government. Washington has also tried to use the new information technology to support student advising by creating the website Education USA, which provides basic educational counseling information to foreign students.[53] In addition, some posts run their own online Q&A "webinars" where locals tune in to get questions answered live with the Public Affairs and Consular Sections teaming up. In some countries, trained local employees and language-qualified Americans handle questions in the local language.[54]

In Indonesia, student counseling is a high priority for the post. According to the PAO: "[O]ne of the major goals of the comprehensive partnership with Indonesia is to double the number of Indonesian students coming to America and double the number of Americans coming to Indonesia." He explained that "@america helps accomplish part of that goal" because "@america has EducationUSA counselors available...so if you walk in you can talk to a live human being and get advice about studying in the United States."[55] The embassy in Nairobi sponsors a student counseling center that advises approximately 4,500 Kenyans annually on studying in the United States. This service is larger than any in sub-Saharan Africa except Nigeria, and as a consequence there are more Kenyans studying in the United States than from any sub-Saharan country except Nigeria.[56]

### Returnee Followup

Returnees from exchange programs can be valuable assets because they can help explain aspects of America to their compatriots who have never been to the United States. They often become unofficial surrogates who help the public diplomacy professionals achieve their objectives. They may write newspaper articles or speak on television about the United States in ways that are helpful to the public diplomacy program. In any case, what they say in public or in private about the United States is likely to be regarded as more credible than information and comments coming from Americans.

PAOs try to engage with exchange participants when they first return home, and encourage them to write of their impressions or give interviews. Some posts have developed alumni associations to maintain contact with returnees.

In Egypt, for example, the PAO organized what he called "an extremely active alumni association," that turned out to be helpful to the embassy when the uprising broke out in January 2011 that toppled President Mubarak. "Many of these youths were actual participants in the January 25th movement. So when Tahrir Square was going on, when the protests were going on—these massive demonstrations that were organized—we were able to contact them—be in touch with them. We knew these people, many of them quite well. And many of them had been on our programs—on exchange programs that looked at American civil society."[57]

Visitors usually return home with a much more sophisticated knowledge of the United States in many respects, and they are often willing to explain American to their compatriots in a more sympathetic way. One problem however is that returnees who are criticized for appearing to have been brainwashed or to be sudden converts to a pro-American view, may have to defend themselves. As the US PAO in Islamabad recently reported: "Everywhere you went when you met these Pakistanis who had been off in the United States and you saw how it changed them and they would say: 'Yes, I'm out there advocating for the United States all the time. I love Pakistan. This is my country. But people accuse me of being a lackey for the United States. I say: No, we're not. I'm just trying to explain what I saw in the United States.'"[58]

Often the participants from an exchange program stay in touch with the Americans they have met during their stay in the United States, and some even form business or professional relationships with them. In some countries, the returnees form associations with each other. Public affairs sections try to keep in contact with the returnees but this effort does not always work well, partly because they move around and their contact information gets lost.[59] Yet because of the value of returnees to public diplomacy programs, many PAOs try to find ways to stay connected with them after their programs end. The State Department also tries to help returnees stay connected online with a website.[60]

## Conclusion

American diplomats regard the programs they arrange that bring students and professionals to the United States and send Americans abroad as among the most effective of all public diplomacy programs. These programs allow foreigners to gain a first-hand experience in America that helps them understand our society, culture and politics, and even the fundamentals of our foreign policies. Fulbright is the best-known exchange program but there are many others, both short and long term, to choose from. Partnership with private American organizations reduces the cost to the embassy, and sends an implicit message to visitors that we have nothing to hide. Returnees can help tell our story credibly back home, and public diplomacy officers make efforts to follow up with them as part of the process.

# PART V
*Pentagon Communications*

CHAPTER ELEVEN

# Defense Department Communications: Changing Role

For decades, the US Department of Defense has undertaken systematic communications with selected audiences. Prior to the September 11, 2001, terrorist attack on the United States, these DOD communications were very different from the civilian communications carried out by civilian agencies (USIA and State) as public diplomacy. After September 11, when the US government declared a Global War on Terrorism, the Pentagon expanded its communication efforts in a number of ways, some of which seemed to resemble civilian public diplomacy. This chapter will first review DOD's traditional means of communication, and then examine how that agency's communication practices have changed during the past decade.

## DOD Communications Practices before 9/11

### Public Affairs

One form of traditional DOD communications is called "public affairs" (PA).

The Pentagon's public affairs effort includes briefings, interviews, and press conferences by DOD officials, as well as radio and TV broadcasts and the publication of print media. The best-known side of DOD's public affairs effort is the daily briefing that the Pentagon spokesperson conducts in Washington for the press corps. Less well known are the broadcasts that the Pentagon has been conducting since World War II.

Since 1942, the Pentagon has managed radio broadcasts for American military personnel stationed abroad, and in 1953 it added television. By 1992 the Armed Forces Radio and Television Services (AFRTS) operated in 130 countries and was reaching more than one million Americans abroad. These programs are narrowly targeted for US military personnel and their families, and are not intended for foreign audiences. Sometimes however these broadcasts reach unintended audiences in the area, as happened in Saudi Arabia during Desert Shield/Desert Storm in 1990–91. In cases where DOD's broadcasts might reach such a "shadow audience," DOD asks the American embassy to provide a list of "Host Country Sensitivities" for AFRTS to avoid.[1]

All aspects of DOD's public affairs function are very different from public diplomacy, because it is primarily intended for American domestic audiences.[2] Public affairs is also unlike public diplomacy because it tends to be more of a monologue rather than a dialogue;[3] unlike civilian PD officers who regard engagements with journalists and others as opportunities for dialogue and learning about local attitudes as well as for explaining US policy and society.[4]

## PSYOP

A second form of DOD communication that on the face of it seems to resemble public diplomacy because its target is a foreign audience is called psychological operations or "Psyop." The Pentagon classifies PSYOP as a form of "Information Operations (IO)," that are intended to "influence, disrupt, corrupt or disrupt adversarial human and automated decision making while protecting our own." The purpose of PSYOP specifically is "to induce or reinforce foreign attitudes and behavior favorable to the originator's objectives."[5]

The Pentagon used PSYOP during military operations in the Vietnam War (1960–75), in Panama (1989) and in the Persian Gulf War of 1991. The US Army maintains an active duty army unit called the "Fourth Psychological Operations Group (POG)," a subordinate element of the US Special Operations Command (USSOCOM) based at Fort Bragg, North Carolina, that develops and produces PSYOP materials, and develops communication programs of various kinds for foreign audiences. For example, the Air Force maintains a squadron of six specially configured EC-130 aircraft operated by the Pennsylvania Air National Guard, which are used for leaflet drops and as platforms for broadcasting.[6]

Although PSYOP is directed at a foreign audience, it has in the past been very different from public diplomacy. PSYOP is targeted only at a specific region or narrow audience for a short term purpose, and has the limited goal of seeking to influence foreign public opinion to support of a specific military mission.[7] Moreover its planning and operation are classified while PD is unclassified. The Pentagon's PSYOP function is short-term and, unlike public diplomacy, does not support long-term programs such as libraries, cultural centers, or cultural presentations. As one Pentagon officer said, PSYOP is meant to "influence," whereas education and cultural centers are truly the rubric of USAID and the State Department.[8] A PD official notes that it would be counterproductive for the military to sponsor such programs, just as if the People's Liberation Army sponsored such centers.[9]

### Truthfulness and Deception

One distinction that DOD makes between these two types of traditional DOD communication—public affairs and PSYOP—is in the question of whether the source of information that they provide is disclosed. For public affairs, DOD's doctrine says that it must be truthful. It explains that while America's adversaries may use lying, deception, and creating false causes" the United States must "stick to the truth" to preserve legitimacy."[10]

PSYOP, on the other hand, is permitted in some circumstances to use deception. DOD policy on PSYOP says it may use not only white propaganda (in which the source is truthfully identified) but also it can use black or grey propaganda, when "the intent is to confuse or deceive" the target audience. Black propaganda deliberately falsifies the source, while gray propaganda deliberately hides the source of the information. DOD says that these "require exceptional coordination, integration, and oversight. The operations are planned and conducted in such a manner that the responsible agency or government is not evident, and if uncovered, the sponsor can plausibly disclaim any involvement. Gray and black products are employed in covert operations."[11]

As one senior military officer put it while explaining the purpose of PSYOP, "The military has to be able to misinform on its own, not to the media but directly to the enemy. We just try to overload the enemy with information coming from you and coming from us. And he doesn't know what's true."[12] One analyst says that the covert aspect of PSYOP has a long history, going back to the Revolutionary War when Benjamin Franklin wrote letters under fake names to set other nations against the British.[13] Another commentator says that senior officers recognize that deception and false information can only be effective in the short term.[14]

DOD says that because it can be covert and deceptive, PSYOP must be carefully segregated from public affairs "for fear that PSYOP tactics and techniques would undermine the credibility of public affairs efforts." DOD notes that State's public affairs practitioners have expressed such "reservations" about PSYOP."[15]

Not all PSYOP is covert and deceptive, however. DOD points out that in the past, it has been used in nonadversarial situations in support of PD and information operations, such as anti-drug, demining, and AIDS awareness campaigns, justified as "support to military campaigns."[16]

PSYOP is restricted by DOD policy and by executive order from addressing domestic audiences. However, DOD recognizes that there is a danger that PSYOP deceptive messages might reach American audiences so DOD says PSYOP should minimize that by limiting itself to "aggressive behavior modification at the operational and tactical level of war" and focus on support to military endeavors (exercises, deployments and operations)... when adversaries are part of the equation."[17]

Although DOD's Information Operations including PSYOP are basically focused on "creating effects against adversaries for the joint war fighting commander," PSYOP can be used for what DOD calls a "broader set of DOD information activities that serve US Government interests." DOD says PSYOP can support public diplomacy, for example, to support civilian international broadcasting.[18] One example of that occurred in 1990 during the confrontation with Iraq, when the Pentagon flew aircraft that relayed Voice of America broadcasts to Iraq and the region. A more recent example is DOD funding for a transmitter in Afghanistan for VOA. DOD policy documents foresee expansion of that function by establishing a global website, disseminating third party views that support US policy positions and maintain a quick response public affairs team with linguistic capabilities. They also have advocated the use of covert PSYOP programs to disseminate radio, TV, print and Web materials, including foreign language products in adversarial situations to help the local combatant commander.[19]

### *IMET*

Another DOD program that seems to resemble public diplomacy, but is basically different, involves educational exchanges. The Defense Department has longstanding exchange programs that bring foreign military officers to the United States for training and familiarization with America. Many of the programs are actually funded by the US State Department as part of the US security assistance program, and the most important of these is the International Military Education and Training (IMET) program, created by Congress in 1976. IMET goals are to increase military-to-military relations and defense cooperation, provide training to support combined combat operations and interoperability, and to instill democratic values and internationally recognized human rights values. IMET facilitates personal and professional relationships that provide access to a critical sector of society, and "introduces military and civilian participants to elements of US democracy such as legislative oversight, free speech, equality issues and US commitment to human rights." In Fiscal Year 2009, for example, nearly 7,000 foreign military and police personnel from 136 countries participated in the IMET exchange programs, attending courses in some 150 US schools and installations.[20]

The IMET exchange programs in some ways resemble public diplomacy exchanges in that they bring foreign visitors to the United States to provide them some exposure to American life and culture. But they are unlike public diplomacy in three ways. First, they are only for foreign military personnel. Second, they are justified as military training programs, and the exposure to American culture is only a subordinate goal. Third, they are one-way programs, bringing foreigners to the United States, and do not involve sending Americans abroad.

## *CAHA*

A final form of traditional DOD communication is nonverbal, namely, the conduct of "civil and humanitarian affairs" (CAHA) missions as well as "presence" exercises overseas. These are designed to build relations with the host nation and are carried out in coordination with the embassy. For example, they involve port visits by the US Navy, or joint exercises with foreign militaries. The humanitarian missions include various forms of disaster relief, humanitarian assistance, and civic action programs around the world that serve to cultivate general goodwill toward the United States and its armed forces. These activities are made possible by the fact that the US military has a very large presence abroad. In 2003, DOD had 255,000 military personnel at 725 bases in thirty-eight countries, plus personnel stationed in one hundred other countries.[21] CAHA efforts have been conducted from many of those bases over the years. In addition, DOD's combatant commanders have small budgets under the Combatant Commander's Emergency

Response program (CERP) that they have used to help win local public support for the presence of US military personnel.

The CAHA missions and CERP are like public diplomacy in that they are intended to influence foreign public opinion about the United States in a positive direction. But the activities themselves are deeds, not words, that are usually in response to specific local needs, and in that way they are more akin to USAID programs than to public diplomacy.

The traditional Pentagon programs as described above therefore have differed from the public diplomacy programs conducted by USIA and the State Department is several respects. As one DOD document puts it, none of the DOD categories is identical with public diplomacy.[22]

### Within an Embassy

In the past, if any US military personnel assigned to an American embassy abroad were involved with carrying out any of these communication activities, they would normally do so independently from the communication activities of the civilian public diplomacy staff. It is true that the civilian PAO might consult with the military officers on his or her public diplomacy programs if they involved military issues, for example in cases where there was a US military base whose presence attracted negative attention from the local media, that needed to be addressed. But otherwise the PD and military communication functions were quite separate.

There has been only one significant occasion prior to 9/11 where there was very close coordination between the Pentagon and civilian PD officers at the embassy. In 1965, during the US war in Vietnam, USIA and DOD set up a Joint United States Public Affairs Office (JUSPAO), which included USIA civilians and uniformed military personnel, all under the Ambassador's supervision. It was headed by a senior USIA officer and had 153 Americans and about 400 Vietnamese staff, including some 54 USIA officers. This arrangement ended in 1972 when USIA director Frank Shakespeare dismantled JUSPAO in order to remove military personnel from under USIA control.[23]

## DOD Communications after 9/11

After the 9/11/2001 terrorist attack on the United States, the communications role of the Department of Defense expanded considerably.

The Pentagon continued the basic communications functions mentioned above, but some were enhanced and other functions were added that in sum constituted a substantial change in its role abroad. The main impetus for this expansion was President Bush's Global War on Terrorism and his designation of the Pentagon as taking the lead role in Iraq and Afghanistan since 9/11, along with his administration's related counter-insurgency efforts in those countries.

DOD's mission since 9/11 has been not only to communicate with foreign publics in support of a conventional war, but also in support of America's fight against terrorism and extremism. Beyond that, when Pentagon officials have identified the target audience for this new type of DOD communication they have not limited it to terrorists and extremists who might be a direct security threat to the United States, but they also include a much broader public that might be sympathetic to terrorists and extremists and who could be helpful in countering them. After 9/11, DOD developed a detailed counterinsurgency (COIN) doctrine that describes COIN as "a battle of ideas." It says, "Insurgents seek to further their cause by creating misperceptions of COIN efforts. Comprehensive information programs are necessary to amplify the messages of positive deeds and to counter insurgent propaganda."[24]

The Pentagon continued psychological operations (PSYOP) but changed its name in 2010 to "Military Information Support Operations" (MISO) because of the negative connotations the word had taken on, and the idea that the term PSYOP was insufficient to cover all current PSYOP activities.[25] The biggest change however was in DOD's public affairs function. Prior to 9/11 this function was intended essentially for the US domestic audience. PA is now defined as communication of DOD themes and messages clearly and credibly to domestic *or* foreign audiences, and to counter misinformation and false conceptions regarding US policy.[26]

According to Pentagon doctrine issued in 2005, PSYOP can now be used either in peacetime or during hostilities. During hostilities, the geographic combatant commander is in charge but he "works closely with the Department of State (DOS) to ensure unity of effort and commonality of message." In peacetime, the US ambassador is the command authority in the host nation.[27]

The Pentagon's shift to a broader target audience has led to a situation where DOD's communication activities aimed at foreigners have overlapped with the traditional civilian public diplomacy efforts conducted by the State Department. Although the State Department is the

US government's agency officially charged with carrying out public diplomacy, State was not able to catch up with DOD because Defense has far greater financial and personnel resources to draw on. Moreover, the DOD leadership under President Bush sought to employ tools resembling traditional public diplomacy to do its job in Afghanistan and Iraq, and elsewhere. Some at the State Department regard this as unwarranted "mission creep" encroaching on State's turf (see next chapter for details on that view).

*Iraq*

When President Bush launched a war against Iraq in 2003, he gave the Pentagon not only the responsibility for conducting the war, but also the leading responsibility of managing the postwar situation in that country, a decision that had an important and subsequently far-reaching impact on America's civilian public diplomacy effort abroad.

In March 2003, American forces entered and quickly occupied Iraq. They set up an occupation they called the "Coalition Provisional Authority" (CPA) that took over the function of the defeated Iraqi government and that was controlled by the Pentagon. From March 2003 and June 2004, the State Department was essentially excluded from responsibility for any activity, such as communicating with the Iraqi public, despite the fact that State had experts who knew Iraq well, and DOD did not.[28]

Pentagon officials in Iraq immediately became involved in a variety of communication efforts aimed at the Iraqi audience as well as non-Iraqi audiences concerned with events there, such as the international press corps covering the story. DOD set up new Iraqi media systems, and sought to influence their content. Through private US contractors, they quickly established local media in Arabic that they controlled, including FM and TV stations, and a daily newspaper.[29] Through the CPA, they also influenced other Iraqi media by issuing decrees requiring all news media to be licensed and provided that license could be revoked if the organization incited violence or civil disorder, violence against the CPA, advocated the return of the Baath Party, or for false reporting.[30]

DOD personnel established a Strategic Communications Unit (Stratcom) to monitor Iraqi and other Arab media and draft guidance for CPA briefers to correct perceived errors. They found that the US invasion and occupation had evoked criticism of the United States in the Middle East and elsewhere, and they tried to counter it.[31] Some of the bad press was caused by actions by American soldiers. One Arab scholar explained that "the image of an American flag draped over Saddam Hussein's statue was transmitted to tens of millions of Arab viewers and contributed to a sense of the humiliation of their Arab brothers and their fears of American imperialism."[32] Pentagon officials, not State Department officers or Iraqis, gave the daily briefings for Iraqi reporters and foreign journalists in Iraq. Arab commentators however criticized them for alleged bias and a lack of credibility. One said this was a "bad model" for the Americans to adopt because it because resembled state-controlled media that was widespread in the Arab world but mistrusted.[33]

In June 2004, the US officially transferred sovereignty to the Iraqi people, the Coalition Provision Authority was abolished, and an American embassy formally took over the responsibility for conducting US official relations with Iraq. Experienced State Department public diplomacy officers were assigned to Baghdad, and they tried to carry out traditional public diplomacy programs as best they could. They undertook a full range of PD activities, including information dissemination and educational exchange programs such as Fulbright grants. They did so despite the security restrictions they faced due to ongoing violence in the country. But their efforts were significantly overshadowed by tens of thousands of DOD personnel who remained heavily involved in communicating with the Iraqi public and other foreign publics, until they left in 2011.

DOD personnel used printed media such as leaflets, posters, handbills, and billboards and they also used radio broadcasts.[34] By 2008, they had translated over 300 "good news" articles into Arabic and disseminated them, with "market penetration" over 50 percent, and they were working with 11 Iraqi radio stations, 13 TV stations, 27 newspapers, and many websites.[35] DOD officials continued to hold press conferences, they reached out to Iraqi and other regional journalists, and they conducted town hall-style meetings for both Iraqi and international media, and they issued press releases. They distributed books, magazines, and pamphlets, intended not only for Iraqi and foreign journalists but also local educators—books and videos to libraries—and to the general public.[36]

DOD officers also carried out other "nation building" tasks for civilians. As one study noted, "these tasks came to include reconstruction projects, agricultural sector development programs, governance and rule of law training programs, urban and rural energy distribution efforts, and anticorruption campaigns among many other critical post-conflict responsibilities. The Pentagon also authorized projects under the Commanders' Emergency Response Program (CERP) to enable military commanders to initiate small-scale community-based programs."[37]

### Covert Placement

DOD officials in Iraq hired an American private contractor, the Lincoln Group, which secretly paid Iraqi media outlets to carry stories favorable to the United States. This company created and distributed radio and TV ads, articles and website content "to inform the Iraqi people of the coalition's goals and gain their support."[38] The Pentagon reportedly paid the contractors $897,000 in 2005 and more than $697,000 in 2006 for that purpose.[39] Christian Bailey, one of the Lincoln Group's founders, said, "We have cultivated a unique nationwide network—Iraqi artists, businessmen, journalists, scholars, activists and local leaders—to tell the story of Iraq.... The 'pay-for-placement' program provides some measure of compensation for those Iraqis brave enough...to assume the risk of running stories that make Americans and our Coalition partners look good. Concealing the ultimate paymaster was a tactical decision."[40] This activity came to light in November 2005 when the *Los Angeles Times* broke the story and members of Congress criticized the practice. The Pentagon investigated and found the Lincoln group had broken no rules, but nevertheless ended its contracts by July 2006.[41]

When the story of Lincoln group's clandestine placement project was revealed, a senior US military officer in Iraq defended it by saying that getting information out was necessary in a war environment, and it had to be kept secret to protect the Iraqis who were taking American money.[42] Another US military officer explained: "The information environment is very much a contributing factor to how the US forces and multinational forces are accepted in this emerging democracy. It is a direct threat to the troops if we don't participate in this information environment." He said that the Pentagon's "information operations" [IO] was a defensive measure against the successful efforts of insurgents to spread untrue stories about the coalition and encourage violence against US forces and Iraqis. He said, "We are not about to surrender the information environment to the enemy. This program is a counterweight to the intimidation and threats Iraqi journalists face." So the military opted for an information campaign to tell its stories while quietly supporting its media friends.[43]

*Afghanistan*

In Afghanistan, as in Iraq, the Pentagon's information effort was aimed at civilian audiences, and there too it was primarily focused on media. Because of low literacy rates and poverty, the preferred channels were radio first, cell phones second, and television third. Data in 2010 showed that 82 percent of Afghans owned a functioning radio and 59 percent of households claimed to have a cell phone. The vast majority of urban residents (86 percent) enjoyed access to a cell phone, and even 52 percent of rural households did, with access growing rapidly. Print media and the Internet were much less useful tools because the literacy rate was only 28 percent,[44] only 9 percent of households had computers[45] and less than 1 percent of these computers were connected to the Internet.[46]

DOD information officers created "Radio in a Box" for rural Afghans, a 200 pound low power FM transmitter that broadcast to a five kilometer radius, and they persuaded large commercial independent stations in key markets to buy their programs.[47] It retransmitted feeds from headquarters in Dari and Pashto, and sometimes had a local call-in show with the governor or other local person. DOD also installed mobile cell towers on forward operating bases in many rural areas to compete with Taliban communications there. DOD focused on television because it was expanding with several large new TV stations established in Kabul. DOD officers for example created a cartoon called Captain Peace, which promoted the Afghan National Security Force. And they constructed a series of new terrestrial TV towers in rural areas.[48]

DOD also engaged in nation building in Afghanistan. Between 1991 and 2012 DOD carried out 16,000 development projects there and disbursed over eighteen billion dollars in development aid. DOD's counterinsurgency policy drafted by Generals David Petraeus and James Amos in 2006 states in the introduction: "Soldiers and Marines are expected to be nation-builders as well as warriors"[49]

State Department civilian public diplomacy officers were assigned to Afghanistan shortly after the defeat of the Taliban and the reopening of the US embassy in Kabul in January 2002, (it had been closed in 1989). They tried to carry out as many traditional public diplomacy programs as they could, given the circumstances of continuing violence and unrest. Like the DOD officers, they gave priority to radio and television because of the illiteracy problem. They arranged several radio programs, and some on television. They broadcast in Dari,

Pashto, and Special English, via the a surrogate station called Radio Free Afghanistan, managed by the US government's Broadcasting Board of Governors (BBG), and the VOA's Radio Ashna and Radio Deewa. Their combined listenership among Afghans rose to the highest of any international broadcaster. PD officers also managed exchange programs that DOD did not do, taking Afghan reporters to cover US reconstruction efforts, and sending some to the US on familiarization tours of America. They reinstated a Fulbright program in 2003 that had been suspended 23 years earlier, and they started special programs like the "Initiative to Educate Afghan Women" and the Afghanistan Undergraduate Fellowship.[50]

Once the embassy re-opened, Public diplomacy officers in Afghanistan also began managing American cultural centers, English language training programs, educational exchanges, press interviews and even some cultural events sponsored by the US Embassy. While security concerns limited the frequency and location of these events, the State Department did its best to introduce Afghans to American culture through displays and exhibits.[51]

State's PD officers also established "Lincoln Learning Centers" or "LLCs" (named after Abraham Lincoln). Similar to American Corners in other countries, they were intended to facilitate engagement between Americans and Afghans and provide a place for Afghans to learn about American democracy and culture.[52] They have been used as venues for community meetings, English and computer classes, film screenings, a speaker series, and most of them had a library with Internet access. In 2010 they were located in Kabul and in seven provinces: Bamyan, Gardez, Herat, Jalalabad, Khost, Kunduz, and Mazar-e-Sharif.[53] By 2013, the number of LLCs had increased in number to fourteen. In 2008, the centers had 71,000 visitors and in 2009 they had 148,000 visitors despite increased violence across the country. Because they were located in an active war zone their operating costs were high—25,000–30,000 dollars annually—and they had different staffing structures from a typical American Corner. The embassy contracted with non-governmental organizations to supervise their day-to-day operations and they in turn hired local staffs to run them, and a three-person staff at the embassy's Information Resource Center spent approximately 80 percent of their time supervising the Lincoln Learning Center program. State's inspectors considered them a resounding public diplomacy success and encouraged the embassy to expand them to more locations.[54]

Afghan youth quickly saw English proficiency as a means to improve their economic status and engage with the large multinational community, given the size of the International Security Assistance Force (ISAF) mission. The US Embassy in Kabul began instituting a number of English teaching programs and resources in Afghanistan, including direct English teaching under the auspices of the "English Access Microscholarship Program" that State had started in 2004 (see chapter eight). A public diplomacy professional who was involved in it believes that this program gave Afghan youth an appreciation for American culture and democratic values, increased their ability to participate successfully in the socioeconomic development of their countries, and allowed them to compete for and participate in future US exchange and study programs. The Access program in Afghanistan has grown to include over 3,000 students in 16 locations, compared to the over 70,000 student program graduates in more than 85 countries worldwide.[55]

A myriad of public diplomacy programs burgeoned as staff size and budgets increased. This included integrating the use of social media into the Embassy's public diplomacy outreach strategy, through the Embassy's and USAID's websites that carry policy messages, media resources, short reports on US-Afghan collaboration, and cultural information. The US Mission set up a Facebook page, a Twitter account (@USEmbassyKabul), a YouTube channel, and other social media sites to foster a two-way exchange of ideas, using English and the local languages, providing a venue for tweets by the US Ambassador. Thus, digital technology became a medium to carry good news or success stories that demonstrate good deeds directed at improving the lives of Afghan citizens, despite limitations on access.

In 2007, the US Embassy worked with other international organizations and embassies in Kabul to set up a Government Media & Information Center (GMIC). The purpose of this media center, modeled in part on the US PD operations, was to help the Afgan government provide a steady stream of official Afghan policy information to the Afghan public and media—as well as policy pertaining to other national and international stakeholders. Endorsed by an Afghan presidential decree, the purpose of the GMIC was to build trust among the Afghan publics and other stakeholders—through the provision of timely information, and to facilitate coordination and information sharing among Afghan ministries and other Afghan organization, as well as the Afghan independent media. It sought to build the capacity of government spokespersons, including at the provincial and local level. In partnership with the Afghan government, the US Embassy and ISAF staffed the GMIC with a small team of advisors that worked in tandem with the largely young and talented Afghan staff. The GMIC continues to function as a central hub for press conferences where Afghan, United States, and other international officials address the cameras side-by-side. GMIC also uses social media to deliver policy messages to the Afghan and international public.[56]

## Embeds

The Pentagon also revived and gave special importance to the practice of "embedding"—allowing reporters to deploy with military units. DOD had used this practice in Bosnia in the early 1980s,[57] and in the US-led 1991 attack on Iraq (Desert Storm).[58] In Afghanistan and Iraq, the Bush administration allowed embedding to become widespread mainly because it helped lead to stories in the US press that were favorable to DOD.[59]

Although embedding was primarily intended to help American reporters cover the story of the war, it was also offered to some non-American reporters as well, so it had an impact on foreign publics. In the 2003, DOD offered four embed slots to al-Jazeera reporters, for example. Also they participated actively in the press briefings that the US Central Command officers held in Doha (al-Jazeera coverage however became somewhat less favorable when a US air strike on Baghdad hit its Baghdad office and killed reporter Tariq Ayoub, which many in al-Jazeera believed was deliberate.).[60]

## Civilian-Military Coordination after 9/11

After 9/11, in Afghanistan and Iraq, with DOD and State personnel working side by side, they learned to cooperate more, and they developed some coordinated projects. In Iraq after July 2004, PD civilians at the embassy began working closely with DOD personnel on communications matters so they would not work at cross-purposes, since the dividing line was unclear.[61] In Afghanistan, the US ambassador created a single unit for that purpose. He established the position of Director of Communication and Public Diplomacy—informally called an "UberPAO"—to supervise all civilian and military information programs, and he recruited for it the experienced and respected American CNN journalist, David Ensor, who later became Director of VOA. State's inspector in 2010 criticized the decision, saying that the PD structure "has been modified to accommodate the addition of particular individuals chosen for their specific expertise. This has created lots of overlap and specific work requirements need to be defined."[62] Under him was a career State PD officer who supervised three deputies (including an army officer) and they in turn supervised almost 30 FSOs and the same number of FSNs. The civilian FSOs engaged in the traditional form of public diplomacy, while the DOD staff's task was to assist the military in accomplishing its mission.[63] However, they did work together on a few projects, for example to develop some original programming for Afghan radio and television.

Two devices, new since 9/11, that facilitated DOD-State coordination were the Provincial reconstruction Team (PRT) and the Military Information Support Team (MIST).

PRTs were first fielded in 2003 in Afghanistan as a US-sponsored effort to extend the reach and enhance the legitimacy of the central government into the provinces at a time when most assistance was limited to the nation's capital. They were intended "to strengthen the capabilities of provincial governments, assist in coordinating US government reconstruction and development assistance efforts, provide enhanced reporting on political and economic developments." The PRT was approved by the ambassador and usually included 50 to 300 troops plus officers from DOD, State and USAID, DOD and USAID collaborated to develop and coordinate the policies, strategies, and activities of each agency towards a common goal.[64] DOD provided logistical support and security for PRTs.

In Iraq there were 31 PRTs in 2008 at the height of the surge of US forces there, but all were disbanded when the military left in 2011.[65] In Afghanistan the United States established PRTs at five regional commands outside Kabul. Each one had State PD officers plus DOD Information Operations representatives, who had had only taken a mandatory half-day course in public diplomacy.[66] The Helmand PRT ran training programs for journalists by contracting with an NGO called Media Solutions Partnership Afghanistan (MSPA) to manage a month long course in Lashkar Gah covering the basics of professional journalism. The PRT found that it helped improve professionalism of reporting.[67]

The Military Information Support Team (MIST) is another vehicle for DOD-State coordination. It is a small unit of US military personnel assigned to the embassy by the unit's headquarters in Ft. Bragg, North Carolina. It is funded by the Pentagon but it operates under the authority of the ambassador and it is usually collocated with, and coordinated with, the embassy Public Affairs Section.[68] In Afghanistan the MIST team at the embassy in Kabul focused on radio and TV and comic books since so few Afghans can read.[69]

## DOD Expansion beyond Afghanistan and Iraq

Since 9/11, DOD has expanded its information operations for civilians beyond Afghanistan and Iraq. The rationale used is that DOD has a role not only in combat situations but also in post-conflict and pre-conflict situations because US national interests could be threatened by terrorists or other hostile elements. As one military officer put it, DOD's outreach to foreign audiences outside war zones serve as a "non-kinetic force multiplier" that could help mitigate or even resolve emerging challenges.[70]

In May 2004, the Deputy Secretary of Defense explicitly outlined an expansion plan for the Pentagon's information efforts, saying: The US "military expeditions to Afghanistan and Iraq are unlikely to be the last excursions in the global war on terrorism." He spelled out an extension scenario going considerably beyond conventional war fighting: "We may need to support an ally under attack by terrorists determined to replace the legitimate government; we may need to effect change in the governance of a country that is blatantly sustaining support for terrorism; or we may need to assist an ally who is unable to govern areas of their own country." He said the US would need to "shape" the situation "in the years before the outbreak of hostilities as well as exploiting the capabilities not traditional to our armed forces in the period following hostilities."[71]

DOD doctrine issued in 2006 confirmed that the military's information effort can now target non-adversarial audiences as well as adversaries. It says: "In peacetime, IO [DOD's Information Operations] supports national objectives primarily by influencing adversary perceptions and decision-making. In crises short of hostilities, IO can be used as a flexible deterrent option to demonstrate resolve and communicate national interest to affect adversary decision-making. During post conflict or stability operations, IO continues to support national objectives and influence foreign perceptions." It gives examples of non-adversarial cases like demining, anti-drug and AIDS awareness in friendly countries where it was "justifiable as support to military operations."[72]

DOD by 2009 had deployed MIST teams to eighteen different countries and by 2013 had them in more than 30. One senior US public diplomacy practitioner regards them as the most significant contribution that DOD has made to the goals of public diplomacy. Each MIST team brings an estimated one million dollars to the embassy along with the manpower of the two to six person DOD team. As of 2013 here were several teams in Afghanistan but by then most of the MIST teams were in Africa and other areas.[73]

DOD must secure embassy agreement for MIST activities, and the rationale has usually been to support counter-terrorism or counter-insurgency. In one case, the embassy in Mali rejected a DOD request to install FM transmitters throughout the country to broadcast US messages because it did not want to involve the military and feared losing control of the transmitters.[74] But the embassy there did approve a MIST team project that created a series of radio dramas in 270 episodes that were produced in four local languages aimed at four Malian ethnic groups. The purpose was to promote peaceful conflict resolution, ethnic tolerance, and health and education, and the programs were intended primarily to counter Tuareg rebel groups suspected of ties with al Qaida and other radical Islamic groups. The series was produced by three Americans working with 350 Malian social scientists, artists, and others, with a secondary goal of training the Malians to do subsequent projects. Scripts were first written in French and English for review by the embassy's subject matter experts.[75]

The normal rotation for one MIST team is 179 days (DOD considers them on "Temporary Duty" or TDY which by their regulations must be less than 180 days or else it is "Permanent Change of Station," or PCS.) The first team can however be followed by others. Because of the fast turnaround, and the fact that the members of the MIST team usually have no knowledge of the local language or culture, they take guidance from the embassy's PAO on development of their programs. The PAO usually welcomes that arrangement because MIST projects often end up being ones that closely resemble something the PAO would do if funding were available, and the DOD budgets are generous. To the PAO, this is a useful opportunity to expand the PD program.[76]

For example in Yemen, a MIST team worked in close coordination with the PAO, carrying out educational programs for civilians such as how to develop democratic activities in Yemeni society, or such as funding a women's political rights forum, or governance and volunteer organizations. The Pentagon's rationale in supporting such programs was to combat terrorism based in Yemen, which had become a serious US problem there. The DOD personnel had no Arabic language skills or public diplomacy training, so they tended to take the strategic and tactical advice of State's public diplomacy officers.[77]

In the Philippines, DOD in 2005 deployed a MIST team to a remote southern province, where Islamist insurgents made it dangerous for embassy civilians. With the ambassador's permission, a MIST team coordinated with the Philippine government and set up projects there. One was to make a comic book for boys aged 8–14, which was written in the local language and drawn by a local artist. It featured a local story about a boy whose family members were killed by terrorists, and it was effective.[78]

Another DOD communication expansion since 9/11 was the creation of six new regional websites for foreign audiences. The first was in 2002, for Southeastern Europe called www.setimes.com, and today it has content in ten languages. As of 2009 there were six DOD regional websites. For Latin American and the Caribbean it is www.infosurhoy.com. For the Afghan-Pakistan region and former parts of the USSR known as "the stans" it is www.centralasiaonline.com, and it is in English, Russian, Farsi, and Urdu. For the Persian Gulf it is www.al-shorfa.com in English and Arabic. For Iraq it is www.mowtani.com. For North Africa it is www.magharebia.com. All indicate they are sponsored by DOD but they are not always strictly objective sources of news, often carrying anti-terrorist or human rights messages. They have been criticized, even by US officials. One unidentified VOA official called them "insidious" because DOD was claiming to be a legitimate provider of objective news and information which was dangerous because that was misleading.[79] In 2005, the DOD spokesman Larry DiRita said, "We have a lot of skilled people, a lot of energy and a lot of money. But I question whether the DOD is the best place to be doing these things."[80] In 2006, the Centcom Commander, General Abizaid, turned down a proposal to create a website for the Middle East and Persian Gulf because he thought it would be ineffective and because of the negative media commentary at the time surrounding the Lincoln Group's efforts in Iraq. But later, one was established anyway.[81]

DOD's Special Operations Command also now produces a quarterly magazine for foreign readers under the "Trans Regional Magazine Initiative" that appears in twelve different languages and is distributed in 171 countries. The magazine varies in content from one combatant command to another. It has from 60 to 80 pages per issue, and a three-year budget of $29 million. It promotes "themes and objectives relating to any overseas contingency operations or any Special Operations activities in support of U.S. government objectives." One commentator said, "This appears to be a Pentagon version of what the old U.S. Information Agency once did."[82]

Finally, DOD developed a monitoring service to track foreign communications around the globe on a 24/7 basis, and produce detailed reports for the Secretary of Defense on media materials that might in some way give clues to people who had hostile intent toward the United States. These "Global issues reports" were initially unclassified documents of about 20 pages each day that were initially posted on the Pentagon's website, but they were later classified.

## Conclusion

The Department of Defense has a long history, going back well before 9/11, of communicating in two ways with two very different audiences. First, with domestic American audiences and second, using communications against the enemy in wartime, including psychological operations where deception is allowed. After 9/11 however, DOD expanded into communicating with civilian audiences during President Bush's Global War on Terrorism and the wars in Iraq and Afghanistan. DOD's counterinsurgency operations included measures to reach civilian populations, which work in parallel with the public diplomacy activities being carried out by State Department public diplomacy professionals. There was and is some coordination between the two agencies but DOD had far more ability to fund and staff these communication efforts. Yet the goals and methods of DOD and State to communication with foreign audiences remain quite different. The following chapter will analyze the DOD rationale for its mission's expansion and will compare the approaches of the two agencies.

CHAPTER TWELVE

# Defense Department Communications Abroad Compared with Public Diplomacy

This chapter will analyze the changes in Defense Department communications abroad since 9/11 and discuss why, in some respects, DOD activities have come to resemble public diplomacy carried out by the State Department so that the two agencies now overlap to a degree. Pentagon officials have justified the expansion of their involvement in communications to foreign non-combatants. As this expansion has taken place, they have modified their policies in dealing with foreign audiences in various ways, based on lessons learned. Yet the Pentagon and the State Department continue to have very different approaches to foreign audiences in a number of ways.

## Rationale for the DOD Mission Creep

The Department of Defense has had several justifications for expanding its communication efforts abroad.

### GWOT and COIN Are DOD Functions

President George W. Bush assigned primary responsibility for his Global War on Terrorism to the Pentagon because he saw it as a military function. When in Iraq and Afghanistan the Bush administration added counterinsurgency (COIN), to support those governments, that too was considered a DOD responsibility. As Pentagon officials learned the importance of success in dealing in "non-kinetic" ways with civilian populations, they expanded their efforts beyond simply killing combatants, so that communicating with civilians became part of the overall American GWOT and COIN strategy. As one DOD participant explained, "Influencing Iraqis is central to managing a favorable outcome in this war."[1] The special US envoy to Afghanistan and Pakistan, Ambassador Richard Holbrooke, also put the Afghanistan conflict in military terms, saying the problem was that the US was "losing the information war" in that country, and General Stanley McChrystal, commander of US forces there, said the conflict in Afghanistan was a "war of ideas and perceptions."[2] General David Petraeus' 2007 counterinsurgency manual said: "by properly shaping the information environment, IO [Information Operations] makes significant contributions to setting conditions for success of all other lines of operations." It said that DOD's information goals were to gain local support for counterinsurgency operations, publicize insurgent violence and discredit insurgent propaganda and provide a compelling alternative to the insurgent ideology and narrative.[3]

One analyst added in 2010:

> In the last ten years or so, as irregular warfare became better understood, military commanders realized the need for something they began to call "information preparation of the battle space. That is, to employ all available tools—political (including diplomatic), informational... psychological, educational an economic means—to prepare for military action to win and defeat the insurgency. Indeed, some commanders even advocate that if you do the 'information preparation of the battle space' well enough, you might never need to use deadly force, or at least much less of it.... the military commander... is justified in using information and other non-kinetic means of achieving his goals. And he is especially likely to do so if it reduces the danger to his own troops.[4]

DOD policy documents from 2006 say PSYOP has been used to support PD with non-adversarial audiences for issues like demining, anti-drug and AIDS awareness in friendly countries where it was "justifiable as support to military operations." However they say PSYOP is "the most aggressive" form of communication that can use "psychological manipulation and personal threats." They warn that PSYOP must not be confused with PA and public diplomacy, to avoid undermining the latter's credibility, and says the State Department has historically expressed concern about that problem.[5]

In Iraq, for example, the Pentagon focused heavily on Iraqi insurgents who opposed the United States and on terrorists supported by al Qaida. They did so, as one PD official in Baghdad said, because the insurgents reportedly had "camera ready" short video clips for the satellite TV news channels that can be turned around and put on the air with a minimum of editing; longer-form videos including a feature on the legendary sniper of Baghdad who reportedly has killed more U.S. troops than anyone; poetry and songs for all ages, written texts and backgrounders for the printed press; all provided by "groups and individuals sympathetic to the insurgency."[6] That threat was regarded as requiring a vigorous US response.

### *It's Too Dangerous for Civilians*

The related argument for DOD involvement was that only the Pentagon has a special capability of operating in conflict zones because such areas are too dangerous for others. Military officers argue that in conflict zones that are unsafe for routine civilian activities, DOD can provide security and logistics for communications efforts that is appropriate to the risk.[7] The Army Field Manual written by General Petraeus in 2006 says: "The degree of violence in the [area of operations]...affects the ability of civilian agencies to operate. The more violent the environment, the more difficult it is for civilians to operate effectively."[8] Even when Iraq had a functioning US embassy with civilian public diplomacy officers, DOD argued that it was uniquely qualified to deal with civilian populations because violence was continuing there.[9] Most PD officers would agree. According to the State Department inspector's report on Iraq, "depending on the definition of support staff, it takes a minimum of 15 and possibly up to 60 security and life support staff to support one substantive direct-hire position."[10] That imposes a significant practical burden on public diplomacy. As one PD veteran described his engagement with Iraqis in Baghdad, contacts often rejected or delayed his meetings because his visit would require a "full military complement including humvees, helicopters, and the like. It would make it look like a military operation and that was something that Iraqis did not want to be seen cooperating with."[11]

### *New Technology Compels Us to Get Involved*

The Petraeus counterinsurgency manual argued that the United States should use new communications technology because our adversaries are doing so. He said, "With the free flow of information present in all theaters, such as television, phone, and Internet, conflicting messages can quickly emerge to defeat the intended effects."[12] DOD's Quadrennial Defense Review Report (QDRR) issued during the Obama administration in 2010 put it this way: "As technological innovation and global information flows accelerate, non-state actors will continue to gain influence and capabilities that, during the previous century, remained largely the purview of states." Therefore, it said: "We will need to improve our ability to understand the concerns, perceptions, and attitudes of foreign governments and populations, as well as the ways in which our words and actions may affect allies and partners. Thoughtful engagement, communication, and collaboration with allies and partners who share our interest in fostering peace and security remain essential."[13]

## Somebody Has to Do It

Pentagon leaders were concerned that if State Department and other civilian agencies could not engage in a sufficiently aggressive manner in the War on Terrorism, they should do so. As the Army Field Manual put it: "To confine soldiers to purely military functions while urgent and vital tasks have to be done, and nobody else is available to undertake them, would be senseless. The soldier must then be prepared to become...a social worker, a civil engineer, a schoolteacher, a nurse, a boy scout. But only for as long as he cannot be replaced, for it is better to entrust civilian tasks to civilians."[14]

DOD doctrine in 2005 said: "Durable policy success [in counterinsurgency] requires balancing the measured use of force with an emphasis on nonmilitary programs. Political, social, and economic programs are most commonly and appropriately associated with civilian organizations and expertise; however, effective implementation of these programs is more important than who performs the tasks. If adequate civilian capacity is not available, military forces fill the gap."[15] DOD doctrine concedes that an extensive COIN operation normally requires "civilian oversight," but adds: "However, given the limited resources of the Department of State and the other US government agencies, military forces often represent the country team in decentralized and diffuse operational environments. Operating with a clear understanding of the guiding political aims, members of the military at all levels must be prepared to exercise judgment and act without the benefit of immediate civilian oversight and control."[16]

Public diplomacy practitioners and others outside DOD do not necessarily disagree with this rationale for the Pentagon's wide-ranging efforts in Afghanistan and Iraq. Ambassador Richard Holbrooke famously asked, "How can a man in a cave outcommunicate the world's leading communications society?"[17] This was an obvious criticism of State's failure to undertake a more vigorous public diplomacy information effort to deal with al Qaida. And one experienced senior public diplomacy officer argues that State was not pushing back effectively against the terrorist threat.[18]

## DOD Has the Resources

Another reason the Pentagon undertook significant information programs for civilians was simply because it had the manpower and the budget to do it. Pentagon doctrine conceded that engagement with civilian populations is primarily a State Department function and therefore coordination with State is in order. One DOD policy document says that State "maintains the lead for public diplomacy"[19] Another says, "The Department of State maintains the lead for public diplomacy with the Department of Defense in a supporting role."[20] Yet as a practical matter, there is a striking imbalance in the resources the two agencies can bring to bear on communications issues.

Until 2009, DOD's total budget had no identifiable amount for communications. These costs were hidden, included in larger functions or in specific mission categories and this helped prevent comparison with State's budget. In 2007, the global DOD budget (excluding operations in Iraq and Afghanistan) was nearly half a trillion dollars, in contrast to State's foreign affairs budget of $36 billion.[21] By 2011 DOD's budget was $708 billion while State and USAID budget was $52.8 billion,[22] and the public diplomacy budget was only $1.3 billion. In 2009 DOD submitted its FY 2010 budget in which the request for strategic communications and information operations was specified for the first time. It asked for $988 million, more than four times what it had estimated for those programs in 2007. But when questioned by Congress they reduced the number to $626.2 million and then they cut it by $100 million more. The request included $243.8 million for Afghanistan.[23]

Congress is always very generous to DOD because supporting the military is popular, while State and public diplomacy have no domestic constituency.

In Iraq even after July 2004, when the embassy opened there, DOD simply overwhelmed State in budgets and in sheer numbers of personnel.

In 2003 there were 150,000 American troops on the ground, and that surged to 172,000 in 2008.[24] Also, many DOD personnel were easily assigned to information duties. US Embassy Baghdad in 2009 did have a budget for PD that was very large by normal standards ($7.65 million including $2.5 million for Fulbright grants)[25] but these numbers were dwarfed by DOD resources. The Pentagon had a multibillion dollar Iraq budget, and logistical capabilities that the State Department could not begin to match, including security, transportation (ground and air) and intelligence assets, which according to one PD officer who served there at the time meant that "the military had better means for direct engagement with the Iraqis."[26] State Department inspectors in Iraq found that the differences in "resources, structures, and approaches [between the military and the State Department] could hardly be more different."[27]

In Afghanistan, the State Department's budget for Public Diplomacy grew to be the largest in the history of civilian public diplomacy. What began as a $1.2 million program in 2001 grew rapidly over the past nine years; finally hitting a high in 2010 of $113 million with an additional $95 million budgeted for FY 2011. The embassy increased its public diplomacy grant spending by tenfold in 2009, allocating $380,000 for 680 projects. Each PRT was also given a $50,000 grant for their own PD programs.[28] This was very impressive in terms of State's budget. But in fact the DOD budget for communication identified for communication in Afghanistan has been just as large. In 2011 it showed $100 million for information operations, including $30 million for PSYOP, $30 million for reporting on local issues, $10 million for public affairs and $10 million for other programs.[29]

## DOD Personnel Learned New Approaches

The Bush administration expected that the US military interventions in Iraq and Afghanistan would be brief, but the US presence in both countries dragged on for years. During this extended period of military involvement, DOD personnel learned some lessons that were familiar to civilian public diplomacy practitioners.

### Cultural Awareness

The army's counterinsurgency doctrine of 2006 written by General Petraeus recognizes the need for local cultural awareness, saying: "Successful communication requires... understanding the social setting, appropriate behaviors towards people of different statuses, and nonverbal cues, among other things. An understanding of the social environment can facilitate effective communication, even if counterinsurgents do not speak the local language and must work through translators or interpreters." It adds, "In-depth knowledge and understanding of the national, regional, and local cultures, norms, moralities, and taboos are needed to understand the operational environment and reactions of the insurgents and populace."[30]

DOD adopted the term "social network analysis (SNA)" which it says is "a tool for understanding the organizational dynamics of an insurgency and how best to attack or exploit it. It allows analysts to identify and portray the details of a network structure. Its shows how an insurgency's networked organization behaves and how that connectivity affects its behavior. SNA allows analysts to assess the network's design, how its member may or may not act autonomously, where the leadership resides or how it is distributed among members, and how hierarchical dynamics may mix or not mix with network dynamics." It adds: "For an insurgency, a social network is not just a description of who is in the insurgent organization; it is a picture of the population, how it is put together and how members interact with one another."[31]

DOD doctrine in 2006 stressed the importance of "social network analysis," as a "powerful threat evaluation tool" that it says is "for understanding the organizational dynamics of an insurgency and how best to attack or exploit it. It allows analysts to identify and portray the details of a network structure."[32]

Before that, the idea was put forward in a 2004 Defense Science Board study that was already arguing that the US should adopt an information policy based on "in-depth knowledge of other cultures and factors that motivate human behavior," it should "search out credible messengers," and "engage in a respectful dialogue of ideas that begins with listening and assumes decades of sustained effort." It said that foreign "opinions must be taken into account when policy options are considered and implemented."[33] The DSB's 2008 follow-up report reinforced the idea. It expressed "heightened appreciation that success in strategic communication depends on deep comprehension of the identities attitudes, cultures, interests and motives of others" and recommended taking "existing government collaboration with civil society to a new level...[and] strengthening traditional partnerships with nonprofit organizations in exchanges, broadcasting, and other government functions."[34]

Secretary of Defense Robert Gates emphasized this change in 2009, when he told Congress: "Effective strategic communication requires active listening and sustained engagement with relevant stakeholders; given this, some in DOD are using the term 'strategic engagement and communication' instead of the term 'strategic communication' as the latter term is often misinterpreted to a narrower concern with media, messaging and traditional 'communications' activities." He added that cultural factors and "perception effects" of non-kinetic actions, and "trying to understand selected audiences thoroughly" were now important.[35]

In Afghanistan and Iraq, the Pentagon established what it called a "Human Terrain System," that embedded social scientists with brigades to improve the US military's knowledge of local culture and populations, because the ethnographic information was thought to improve the army's war fighting capabilities. The program began in 2006, primarily in Iraq, and by 2009, 25 teams had been deployed there. Some American scholars actively participated in the project while others opposed it, objecting on the grounds that that the army was using independent academics to "collect intelligence."[36]

In Afghanistan DOD personnel called the effort TRADCOM" for Traditional Communication, collecting data on "Key Leader Engagements" (KLEs) that they used to create a database of Afghan leaders that were labeled friendly or unfriendly. This was intended to help build trust with Afghan communities through face-to-face interactions, although this was what FSOs have always considered normal contact work. They also undertook a mosque mapping project that combed through hundreds of PSYOP sermon reports and utilized GIS software that mapped 300 mosques in Kandahar City, with information about each mullah, but this turned out to have questionable operational value.[37]

*Surrogates*

DOD officers in Iraq and Afghanistan gradually discovered the importance of using surrogates. One DOD officer in Iraq explained: "Influencing Iraqis is central to managing a favorable outcome in this war. Putting an Iraqi face on news to help counter anti-GOI [Government of Iraq] or anti-coalition propaganda will ultimately be necessary to attain the best outcomes. Having Iraqis produce and report news stories is the best vehicle for eliminating culture and language barriers in communication. News important to improving a public spirit thereby gains a measure of instant credibility that coalition information operations and reporting cannot impart. Using native news reporters will increase chances of acceptance by the Iraqi population by relaying credible stories of progress that can resonate favorably through communities. Media communication Iraqis to Iraqis thus has the potential to sway even the most stubborn of anti-GOI and anti-coalition critics, strengthening resolve and commitment to resist terrorism."[38]

Another participant in the effort put it this way: "Social networks will be needed to engage effectively with appropriate audiences.... The message must be relayed through a messenger that is seen as credible and likeable by the recipients."[39]

### *Decentralization*

Experience in Iraq has also led to some decentralization of DOD's procedures. As the Field Manual indicates: "Local commanders have the best grasp of their situations. Under mission command, they are given access to or control of the assets needed to...manage information operations and civil military operations."[40] DOD communicators now advise: "Make strategic communication approaches more agile, decentralized, and local. Clearly...the top-down approaches will not always work in the present and future information environment."[41] They also found that a dialogue is more effective than a monologue. As one observer put it, "A key element of long term strategic communication is 'strategic listening.' It is not enough just to deliver the message."[42] Another commentator made a similar point: "We must begin by listening to that audience, because if we do not understand what resonates with them we have only a serendipitous chance of succeeding. Much of the current U.S. effort concentrates on delivering 'the message' and omits the essential first step of listening to our targeted audiences."[43]

These techniques—cultural awareness, the use of surrogates, and decentralization—had all been used by civilian public diplomacy professionals for many decades before 9/11. Since 9/11, public diplomacy officers working with DOD counterparts in the field came to appreciate their willingness to learn and to adapt their approaches in these ways, as well as their can-do spirit. Nevertheless, fundamental differences remained between the two approaches.

## Fundamental DOD/State Differences Remain

Despite the fact that DOD personnel in conflict zones have learned lessons similar to those familiar to public diplomacy professionals, and that working side by side with PD officers the two agencies have cooperated in some respects, their fundamental approaches still remain quite different. Following are the main characteristics of the DOD outlook that distinguishes it from public diplomacy practice.

### Narrow DOD Focus

The focus of the DOD information effort continues to be much narrower than that of State's. DOD tends to concentrate only on areas of conflict or serious threat (although under GWOT the latter has expanded geographically). In contrast, State's civilian public diplomacy officials deal with virtually every country in the world and their task relates to any issue affecting US national interests, including political, economic, and cultural.[44] They use educational exchanges, English teaching, libraries and cultural presentations that DOD does not. One senior PD professional says: "Public diplomacy efforts ultimately are intended to promote greater understanding of the U.S. and the American people on the part of those in the foreign country where the efforts are undertaken. The underlying assumption—which has proven correct in my experience over the past 30 years—is that better understanding of our country and its people improves the views and attitudes of foreigners towards the U.S. and Americans. This goal, and the efforts that need to be undertaken to pursue this goal, do not have a military dimension, and thus should be in the hands of civilians."[45]

### Short Time Frames

DOD personnel assume that a communication task is limited in duration, with specific start and finish dates. Their tours are short, sometimes only four to six months, not enough time to know any country well.[46] One PD officer said: "for the military, the goal is to succeed in the current military operation, which will last only for a finite time. Thus, the information activities are developed and implemented with that in mind."[47] An Army Public Affairs Officer who served three tours in Iraq, agreed, saying: "The military's mindset was 'what do we need to do to get out of here?'"[48] PD personnel on the other hand have mostly long-term goals, with no predictable end-points. They regard communication as a process of ongoing engagement that requires listening to local opinion and give-and-take. They focus on coming to mutual understanding rather than simply conveying facts. In addition to short-term tools like press releases or speeches, they use long term ones such as educational exchanges and English teaching, but they assume that their work is part of a long term ongoing task that will be handed off to the next FSO after two or three years in one country.

### Unilateral Information Dissemination

DOD personnel focus almost exclusively on the media, and their tendency is to use unilateral communication. As one study points out, the Pentagon's Information Operations (IO) are intended to be a short-term and a "one-way blast of information,"[49] that differentiates it from public diplomacy, which is both long and short term, and not only one way but communication through dialogue. They make this analogy: "If they confront an enemy tank they fire at it until it is destroyed. Then if they confront a person who attacks the US with words, they fire information at him until he changes his mind."[50] Military personnel also tend to regard communication as information determined and coordinated from higher levels. One says: "When the brigade commander says this is the message, it is conveyed down the chain of command and it is done."[51]

### Counterproductive Techniques

Experienced PD officers concede, as one says, that "in a war situation there is an important role for certain elements of 'public diplomacy' to support the war effort, and these are and should be undertaken by the military."[52] But they tend to believe that these are exceptional cases, and DOD has gone too far, using techniques they regard as counterproductive. The most common example cited is the decision of US military personnel in Iraq (described in the previous chapter) to hire a contractor to pay Iraqi media secretly for placement of favorable stories in the press.[53] One veteran PD officer called that "the most damaging thing DOD did in Iraq."[54] Another noted that he had never paid for foreign media placement because that would jeopardize his credibility with local media contacts.[55] PD officers want editors to accept the information on its merits, not for money. Also, when payments become known, the price goes up; one Iraqi editor reportedly commented that, had he known the stories were being paid for by the US government, he would have charged "much, much more" to publish them.[56] The practice also undermined US efforts to engender good journalistic practices. Another PD veteran said DOD's anti-terrorism placements on Iraqi TV "were frightening and counterproductive; they were strange productions that the Iraqis knew were coming from the outside."[57] State's PD officials insist on truthfulness because they believe it enhances credibility, and they reject deception as counterproductive. DOD information operations however allow for deceptive sourcing practices. In Afghanistan, some DOD information products disseminated by DOD hid the US origin of the material.[58]

### Presenting the Wrong Image

Another criticism is that security measures sometimes undermined PD efforts, as one official report noted when it said that private contractors' "use of deadly force, the killing of allegedly innocent Iraqi civilians by [their]...employees, and the State Department's alleged lack of concern about accountability...have undermined U.S. foreign policy and specifically U.S. standing in Iraq."[59] Aaron Snipe, deputy spokesman for US Embassy in Baghdad 2008–09, argued that "the [military] uniform is a barrier, it communicates a message that is a barrier to genuine dialogue. The military has a rank structure that can be very intimidating. A civilian face is important because it can communicate things that a military face can't." A civilian face conveys a normal and enduring relationship rather than a temporary military relationship between the US and foreign audiences, while "the military face comes with a lot of baggage,"[60]

### Detailed Planning and "Metrics"

The two agencies differ in planning and measurement. DOD has special planners and planning divisions ("J-5") who focus on specific countries for which they try to anticipate all possible contingencies and measure results that they like to call "metrics." DOD doctrine now says Information Operations should "Identify all the audiences (local, regional, and international), the various news cycles, and how to reach them with the HN [host nation] government's message."[61] For Iraq and Afghanistan DOD established categories for audiences, such as Female

Engagement, Religious Engagement, or Key Leaders Engagement.[62] In 2010 DOD created "female engagement teams" of females dedicated to engaging local women.[63] Civilian PD officers, on the other hand, seek to retain operational flexibility. They do participate in the embassy's Mission Strategic Plan but they are more likely to revise operations on the spot due to changing circumstances. They regard performance measurement as very difficult or nearly impossible, and they usually offer anecdotal evidence instead of hard metrics. They know it is difficult to prove effectiveness since usually multiple factors are at work, so they resort to anecdotes.

For example, Matt Lussenhop, who was PAO in Kabul 2010–2011, says that PD officers generally admire the can-do attitude of their military colleagues, but they approach their tasks in different ways. He says they like to do a lot of planning, setting specific dates, times and precise goals, defining expectations, bring their own resources and doing evaluations afterwards, in a formal way. He said when he was PAO and wanted to call on a university president he simply got in a car with a driver and went. If a DOD officer wanted to visit the same person, he would plan carefully in advance and then go in an armed convoy, in uniform with flak jackets, and carrying weapons, causing a big commotion on campus. That often created a negative impression of America, but the officer would nevertheless write up a formal report about his successful "Key Leader Engagement."[64]

### *Differences in Training*

Some DOD officers have pointed out that military personnel are not prepared to do public diplomacy. One said: "[No] template or structure existed for incorporating the routine or special engagements that military leaders conducted with members of the host nation who had the ability to impact their area of responsibility.... [So most of the American military personnel who conducted these operations] "had little or no preparation for conducting strategic engagements and/or brokering dialogue."[65] Even Secretary of Defense Rumsfeld criticized DOD's inadequacies, saying that a DOD public affairs assignment is not career enhancing.[66]

In Afghanistan, at one point State's cultural affairs and press offices at the embassy each had at least six experienced and fully trained FSO's and approximately eighteen FSNs, while the DOD personnel responsible for communication with the public had only temporary direct hire contractors who had received no prior training in public diplomacy and were only in Afghanistan for between three and six months at a time.[67]

In 2008, however, DOD installed two military Public Affairs officers at the Government Media and Information Center (GMIC) in Kabul, in an attempt to coordinate crisis communications messaging with Afghan media counterparts. The impetus behind this move was to streamline and verify security incident reporting from the field and place Afghans, not the US military, at the center of the reporting process. The thought was that communications about joint Afghan-ISAF operations should come from the Afghans themselves directly to the Afghan people, rather than having the international coalition forces messaging to Afghans, to build capacity as well as credibility between the Afghan government and the Afghan people. To this end, the GMIC built up a robust Public Awareness Campaign unit, so that the Afghan government builds up credibility in communicating on security issues, while they transitioned to taking the lead as foreign forces were scaled down.[68]

The Pentagon's use of American anthropologists to help the military understand the local culture expanded greatly in 2007 with the explicit encouragement of General Petraeus.[69] Despite the Pentagon's effort to provide "cultural awareness" to its personnel and send Human Terrain Teams to help them, they have not been able to match the skills of FSOs in this regard, who depend heavily on a nuanced understanding of the local culture they are working in.

According to a senior FSO who served in Iraq 2004–2005, a successful public diplomacy section in the embassy there must have American career officers who are fluent in the local language.[70] DOD has few foreign area specialists, and DOD personnel assigned to information tasks tend to receive little or no prior communications training. The Joint Forces Staff College has a Joint IO Orientation course but it lasts only one week (38 hours).[71] Ft. Bragg has a scenario-based course for Information Officers that has included State officers as well. Also, the number of mid-level officers receiving foreign language training has reportedly increased in recent years, an indication of the Pentagon's recognition that language skills for its own personnel are important.[72]

Secretaries of Defense Gates and Rumsfeld recognized that some DOD personnel were doing tasks civilians should be doing. Gates said: "The Department of Defense has taken on many of these burdens that might have been assumed by civilian agencies in the past,... forced by circumstances, our brave men and women in uniform have stepped up to the task, with field artillerymen and tankers building schools and mentoring city councils—usually in a language they don't speak. They have done an admirable job. But it is no replacement for the real thing—civilian involvement and expertise."[73] And Rumsfeld said, "In some cases, military public affairs officials have had little communications training and little, if any, grounding in the importance of timing and rapid response, and the realities of digital and broadcast media."[74]

Retired FSO Thomas E. McNamara quoted Joint Chiefs of Staff Chairman Admiral Mike Mullen admitting that "U.S. foreign policy is still too dominated by the military." And he quoted former Secretary of Defense Robert Gates as saying that military operations "should be subordinated to measures aimed at promoting better governance, economic programs that spur development, and efforts to address the grievances among the discontented." McNamara added: "That sounds like what diplomats do every day."[75]

## No Long-Term Local Staff

Americans doing public diplomacy tasks at US embassies abroad always have locally-hired professional local staffs who are long term employees that support the Americans very significantly because they are bilingual and have a deep knowledge of the local culture and can provide continuity. In contrast, US military personnel deployed abroad rarely have such local employees to support them and they depend on hiring short-term ad hoc interpreters. They often end up hiring Americans for the task for security reasons.[76]

## Mission Creep

As a consequence of the war on terrorism and the funding imbalance, DOD has expanded its communication effort beyond the war zones in Afghanistan and Iraq. Public diplomacy career veterans question whether expansion to that extent is necessary. As one of them said, "I think that no one questions the validity of the DOD going into war zones and interacting in ways that are necessary to winning wars. [But] In places that people aren't shooting at us, the DOD probably has very little business going... "[77]

One study in 2008 concluded: "The 'militarization of diplomacy' is noticeably expanding as DOD personnel assume public diplomacy and assistance responsibilities that the civilian agencies do not have the trained staff to fill. In the area of security assistance—traditionally the authority of the Secretary of State but implemented largely by the Defense Department—a number of new DOD authorities have been created, reducing the role of the Secretary of State even more in this vital area of US foreign policy.[78]

### Continuing DOD-State Funding Imbalance

One PD professional said: "We are (personal opinion) shooting ourselves in the feet by overfunding DOD and underfunding DOS in this area. It boils down to credibility and also touches on very basic issues of the American identity. Are we, like ancient Rome, a militarized superpower that engages with the world through our military? Or are we a different kind of country than that?... In this day and age where too many people in the world think of helicopters and people in fatigues killing Muslims, are military channels really the most effective and credible ways to influence people?"[79]

One retired ambassador expressed the frustrations that many career diplomats have felt, when he said, "During the Bush administration's eight years in power, the military has come to dominate U.S. foreign policy, while other arms of the U.S. government operating abroad—such as the State Department and the U.S. Agency for International Development (USAID)—have been ignored, underfunded and gravely weakened." He said DOD received 26 percent of the US foreign assistance budget in 2008, "But the Pentagon has no comparative advantage or particular expertise in post conflict stabilization and reconstruction, and its nation-building attempts often fail."[80]

Defense Secretary Robert Gates expressed concern about the global funding and staff imbalance with State.[81] Joint Chiefs Chairman Admiral Mike Mullen in 2010 expressed concern about DOD mission creep: "U.S. foreign policy is still too dominated by the military, too dependent upon the generals and admirals who lead our major overseas commands. It's one thing to be able and willing to serve as emergency responders; quite another to always have to be the fire chief."[82] The Obama administration's Defense Department went further and said that, as a matter of policy, " the 'soft power' options and capabilities are given equal priority and considered in coordination with hard power alternatives"[83] but this did not change the budget and staffing imbalance.

## The Obama Administration

Under the Obama administration, the situation has changed very little. In 2010, the Pentagon conceded that its view of "strategic communications" had evolved, and "emphasis on strictly 'informational' activities has decreased. It told Congress that "DOD is shifting to viewing strategic communication as an adaptive, decentralized process of trying to understand selected audiences thoroughly, [and] hypothesizing physical or informational signals that will have the desired effect on those audiences." It noted that "all DOD activities have a communication and informational impact," so it was important for DOD personnel to understand "the perceptions, attitudes and beliefs of potential audiences," know "complex social communication systems" and be able to "formulate timely and culturally attuned messages."[84]

Obama's DOD also retained the Bush-era concept that the role of the military extended well beyond wars: "DOD's responsibilities and operational missions give DOD a unique role to play, ensuring the Department's strategic communication processes support major military operations, shape the environment to prevent conflict, and if conflict occurs, ensure it occurs on terms favorable to the realization of U.S. national security interests." Nevertheless, DOD asserted that it did "not engage directly in public diplomacy, which is the purview of the State Department, but numerous DOD activities are designed specifically to support the State Department's public diplomacy efforts and activities." As examples, it cited the MIST teams and "key leader engagements" that "closely resemble State Department public diplomacy efforts." But it added the caveat that "during combat operations or in other nonpermissive environments, DOD often takes the lead out of necessity, as civilian actors may be unable to perform their usual activities."[85]

DOD's Quadrennial Review of 2010 also recognized the new situation, saying: "As technological innovation and global information flows accelerate, non-state actors will continue to gain influence and capabilities that, during the previous century, remained largely the purview of states." Therefore: "We will need to improve our ability to understand the concerns, perceptions, and attitudes of foreign governments and populations, as well as the ways in which our words and actions may affect allies and partners. Thoughtful engagement, communication, and collaboration with allies and partners who share our interest in fostering peace and security remain essential."[86]

By 2014, President Obama had ended the major US military involvement in Iraq and he was winding it down in Afghanistan. He has altered the US approach to terrorism and to counter-insurgency that Bush espoused and he has indicated that he is not planning to support nation building by DOD of the kind his predecessor undertook. In June 2011 for example he said "The tide of war is receding" and "it is time to focus on nation building here at home."[87]

These are signs that the greatly increased involvement by the Department of Defense in communication and engaging with foreign civilian audiences will be scaled back. But the momentum that shifted during the Bush decade in favor of such Pentagon involvement with civilians abroad may be difficult to turn around quickly and DOD is likely to continue to devote resources and personnel to this new task for some time. Meanwhile, in the judgment of some experienced senior diplomats, the public diplomacy professionals at State may have lost their edge, due to the fact that DOD has been in the driver's seat in key areas of importance to American national interests for more than a decade.

During the USIA years, a cadre of public diplomacy professionals in the senior and middle ranks of the profession were highly focused on their tasks, and they spent a career consistently and exclusively dealing with PD issues and honing their skills as they went from one assignment to the next; they learned from mentors and then mentored others in PD, developed best practices that they shared with their USIA colleagues. Since the merger into State and the post-9/11 growth of the Pentagon's direct involvement in communication with foreign audiences, this specialized skill has become somewhat diminished.

## Conclusion

DOD justified its expansion into communicating with foreign civilians by arguing war zones are too dangerous for civilians, "somebody has to do it," and DOD has the capability. In the process, DOD personnel learned lessons long known to PD professionals such as the importance of cultural awareness. Yet fundamental differences remained between the DOD and State approaches. DOD tends to have a shorter time frame, a narrower focus and prefers unilateral information dissemination, and it seeks metrics, while State PD officers also undertake long term and short term projects and can be satisfied with anecdotal evidence of effectiveness. DOD is likely to remain engaged in communication with foreign civilian audiences, however, as long as the United States remains concerned about terrorist threats.

# PART VI
*Conclusion*

CHAPTER THIRTEEN

## *Changes and Enduring Principles*

For nearly 80 years, the US government has systematically undertaken programs abroad that serve the national interest by communicating with foreign publics. We call that public diplomacy. During these eight decades public diplomacy has in some ways undergone significant changes. At the same time, certain basic principles have evolved and endured among practitioners who have learned best practices in the field. This chapter briefly reviews the fundamental changes and then lists some of the enduring principles of public diplomacy

### Changes

Some of the changes have come in the way the US government has structured public diplomacy. Others have been external forces that have required adaptation.

One structural development is that the responsible Washington agency for public diplomacy has changed several times. The State Department had the responsibility, and then in quick succession the Office of Strategic Services, the Office of War Information and State again, followed by the US Information Agency (USIA) for most of the second half of the twentieth century. In 1999, USIA was abolished and the main responsibility for public diplomacy returned to the State Department, although broadcasting was separated and given to the Broadcasting Board of Governors. For a while, some advocated the return of the function to an independent agency such as USIA, while others suggested privatization of public diplomacy.[1] But after 14 years neither has happened.

At this point it seems the function will stay with State for the foreseeable future. Some old career hands still miss USIA because they regarded it as an efficient and flexible agency not constricted by the larger bureaucracy at State. For example, in 2005, four former USIA directors declared that shutting down the agency was a "major mistake" and urged that something like it be recreated.[2] But as time passes and new generations rise in the ranks of PD professionals to take on leadership roles, the sentiment for the old agency has died out. An effort during the George Bush administration by some retired USIA officers to modify the role of public diplomacy at the State Department, by consolidating it into a more cohesive bureau, failed to gain support because non-PD personnel at State saw no reason to alter the situation.[3] More importantly, there is no interest at all in Congress or the White House to reopen the issue of organization and inertia is carrying the status quo with no change in sight.

The Voice of America (VOA) and other civilian broadcasting channels such as Radio and TV Marti were for most of the twentieth century under USIA which was therefore able to coordinate broadcasting with the other types of public diplomacy. When USIA was abolished in 1999 this link was severed and broadcasting was put under an independent Broadcasting Board of Governors. The Secretary of State has a seat on the broadcasting board of governors (BBG) but in practice State has exercised almost no influence over broadcasting. Criticism of the BBG's management has continued from several quarters, but there is no sign that broadcasting will be reconnected with the rest of public diplomacy any time soon. Thus for PD field officers at embassies, broadcasting is not anything they are remotely responsible for, and that is likely to remain the case for the foreseeable future. However, the VOA Special English division and the Office of English Language Programs at State continue to reinforce the mission of using English as a means to build mutual understanding and open opportunities to different facets of society through quality English language sites such as VOA's "Learn America English"[4]

Another major structural change is that since 9/11, as outlined in this book, the Department of Defense has significantly expanded its involvement in communicating with foreign civilian publics. In several ways this involvement resembles civilian public diplomacy, but it is not certain to what extent that will continue. Much of this DOD expansion was the result of the way the George W. Bush administration prosecuted the Global War on Terrorism and wars in Afghanistan and Iraq. President Obama ended the US military involvement in Iraq, wound it down in Afghanistan, and narrowed the scope of the American fight against terrorism. He has indicated that he does not intend to give high priority to nation building abroad. In his 2014 State of the Union address he said, "America cannot remain on a permanent war footing," and he promised to focus instead on diplomacy. By 2013, most of the American public had also become wary of military intervention abroad. For example, polls showed that a significant majority of Americans (68:24) opposed any US military intervention in Syria, despite civilian suffering there, and a large majority preferred diplomacy over military action in Iran, although they had an 87:13 unfavorable view of that country.[5]

The priority that the Pentagon has given to communicating with foreign civilian populations is therefore likely to be much less in the future than it has been in recent years. It will however probably remain for some time as a DOD function, particularly since terrorism is unlikely to disappear completely, and DOD has accepted a key role in combating it. In any case, DOD will continue to have more resources to devote to the task, and the two agencies will continue to coordinate some of their outreach.

Meanwhile two major external issues have arisen since about the turn of the century that have affected the conduct of American public diplomacy at our embassies abroad.

One is the increase in security concerns for our embassies and American diplomatic personnel. Throughout most of the second half of the twentieth century, American embassies and cultural centers around the globe were for the most part fully open to the public and this was of considerable advantage to our PD programs because it facilitated easy contact between embassy personnel and local audiences. The security concerns that began in the 1990s at some embassies and increased on 9/11 and afterward, led to the erection in many countries of barriers between embassies and the local public that severely hampered local contact. PD personnel in many places were compelled to find ways to work around these new obstacles, but it was not easy.

Another external issue that affects PD conduct is the dramatic growth in electronic communication technology including social networking media. During the twentieth century, PD personnel at American embassies abroad had access to information about various aspects of the United States, including American policy, society, and culture, that was otherwise unavailable abroad, and they could use this information to good advantage in communicating with local audiences. Today, however, because of the new technology, in so many countries the people have access to a great deal more information about America than they had in the past, and therefore what can be provided by the embassy is less unique than it once was. In addition, the public debate has expanded exponentially as more actors take the stage to make their viewpoints about US foreign policy a part of the larger public debate. The problem for PD professionals however is that they must still deal with a considerable amount of misinformation about America, whether deliberate or from ignorance. In fact, the many news reports and commentaries about America that flood the airways nowadays on a 24/7 basis have increased the number of distortions that PD officials must deal with. This has made public diplomacy more important, not less.

## Enduring Principles

Public diplomacy officers working at US missions abroad often share best practices with each other and with Washington, but they have not been codified into a formal theory of PD field operations. Nevertheless, from the empirical studies of field posts operations that are now available, and from comments made by veteran PD practitioners, it is possible to identify a set of approaches that seem to have worked well over time. These have been discussed in the previous chapters, but they are enumerated here as thirteen enduring PD principles.

### 1. Understand Local Concerns

Communication with the public in a foreign country must start with an understanding of their attitudes and perceptions on issues of importance to the United States. American PD professionals in that country must know their audience in order to advocate US policies, explain American society and culture, and engage in productive discussions about issues of mutual concern.

The basic principle is akin to Congressman Tip O'Neill's famous saying, "All politics is local." PD officers taking up an assignment at a US embassy abroad quickly seek to gain an understanding of local attitudes toward issues of concern to the United States, by consulting with local staff and other embassy colleagues as well as local contacts, and following the local press. FSOs assigned to the Middle East, for example, hear about local attitudes toward Palestine and Israel and American-Muslim relations, while FSOs assigned to Turkey hear about Kurds,

Armenians, and Cyprus. The FSOs assigned elsewhere hear about still different specialized local concerns.

Public diplomacy professionals try to determine what kinds of public diplomacy programming and activities would be most appropriate to the local culture and society, and most effective in communicating American ideas. If they are posted to Riyadh, for example, they learn that bringing an American ballet would be inappropriate, but a college choir might work. If they are in London they might learn that bringing a symphony orchestra might be redundant while a Supreme Court judge would attract an audience. They assess the level of English, or the sophistication of the local information technology might affect programming. And they carefully evaluate any restrictions the host government may impose on programs or activities by the US embassy and its personnel, in order to avoid violating the local rules. In highly restrictive environments they try to work out ways to engage with the public despite the barriers.

The effort by the PAO and the public diplomacy staff to create a sophisticated understanding of the local culture is akin to the approach that Pentagon personnel have developed that they call situational or cultural awareness, but they generally see it as a short-term problem. State Department public diplomacy professionals however consider this a long-term effort, building on the work of their predecessors and others in the embassy to comprehend local perceptions that are important for effectively functioning in a foreign environment.

### 2. *The Last Three Feet Rule*

The most effective way for the United States to communicate, persuade, and reach mutual understanding across cultures, is by direct personal conversation between an American and a foreign individual or group.

Edward R. Murrow remarked that "the real art" in information dissemination was not to move it five or 10,000 miles but "to move it the last three feet in face-to-face communication." He made that comment in 1963, but it has been quoted often by public diplomacy professionals ever since then, because they know from experience how true it is.

Experienced PD professionals also know that they can learn a great deal about local attitudes by talking face to face with local people who represent different shades of opinion. The public diplomacy section monitors the local press, especially the vernacular media, and the local staff helps keep abreast of local attitudes that are not in the media. They also know that it is essential for them to engage in sustained conversations with key local opinion leaders and to probe them for what they really think in order to develop an accurate picture. In some countries there may be opinion polls that help provide an understanding of local views, but in many countries such polls are inaccurate or misleading and in any case they tend to be few and far between so they serve only as supplemental data. Personal engagements with key interlocutors remain the essential means to understand local views accurately.

If these engagements are sustained and developed over time they usually become more productive and the conversations become more candid. Moreover, if a situation arises in which the American diplomat wants to lodge a complaint, for example to an editor who has published damaging misinformation, the complaint tends to be more effective if the two have already established an ongoing personal relationship and the American can simply engage the reporter on a one-to-one personal basis to try to solve the problem.

### 3. Use Dialogue

Public diplomacy field officers have long known that mutual understanding and persuasion can best be achieved through dialogue, rather than monologue. That means listening carefully and responding to the other's views. Honest and open exchanges can foster an intellectual effort to build bridges between differing perceptions.

Experienced PD officers know that in a foreign country when they are in discussion with a local citizen they can best respond to criticisms and misunderstandings of America by dealing with them directly, responding to the local views rather than simply parroting official US statements. It is important for the American officer to listen very carefully to what their local interlocutor has to say, what arguments he or she brings to bear, and try to understand what fundamental misperceptions may lie behind those arguments. It is much more effective to deal directly with those arguments and assertions of fact, in order to help correct the ones that need correcting, rather than simply stating what the policy is that has been enunciated in Washington, or what the standard American view is. Moreover, listening first conveys respect for the other's opinions, and sets the discussion in a positive direction. It is also important to choose the proper moment to make a point.

Perhaps instinctively, experienced PD officers know that the nineteenth-century philosopher John Stewart Mill was right when he said that he "who knows only his own side of the case, knows little of that," because it is in open-minded engagements with local citizens rather than monologues, that the public diplomacy officer best develops his or her skill at making a convincing case for understanding aspects of America.

### 4. Be Truthful

Always be truthful. Edward R. Murrow explained why: "To be persuasive we must be believable; to be believable we must be credible; to be credible we must be truthful."

Public diplomacy officers know that deception undermines the trust and credibility that are essential in sustained communication and persuasion. Discussions in this book (chapters eleven and twelve) about the Pentagon's covert payments to editors in Iraq, and DOD's view of PSYOP (psychological operations) that allows for some deception in communication, have highlighted the fact that civilian PD practitioners regard these practices as unacceptable. They believe that they must always stick to the truth.

For them, this rule can theoretically create a conflict with another obligation that they have, which is to be loyal to their employer, the US government. This may arise when they speak publicly about American foreign policy, if they happen to have disagreements with some aspects of that policy. In cases where they are unable to resolve the conflict, they may feel compelled to resign, as John Brady Kiesling and John Brown did in 2003 (see chapter five). But usually the American diplomat can find creative ways to deal with this dilemma if it presents itself. He or she is not compelled to tell the "whole truth," only not to lie or mislead, and in a discussion it is possible to do that and not express direct criticism of current policy. It is acceptable to decline public comment on a sensitive issue. And there are established means of internal communication that allow for dissent from policy, but transmitted in classified channels to US policy makers.

In cases where the American diplomat wishes to help a reporter with a story by providing some information that is not strictly classified but would nevertheless be unhelpful if it appeared in print as coming from an official US government source, the diplomat can use the standard devices of making the statements on background, deep background or off the record. In this way the official would still be maintaining loyalty while adhering to the truth. But the diplomat must be confident that the reporter will respect those rules.

### 5. Reach Out

Public diplomacy officers should make efforts to expand their contacts as much as possible among opinion leaders.

It is important to engage with people who represent a broad spectrum of opinion, not just those who are well disposed to the United States, but also to those who criticize America. PD officers in particular should reach out, beyond the official channels that exist between the United States and the host government, to interact with a wide variety of people. In this way, they can build a more comprehensive picture of local public opinion, and they can open opportunities to help more people understand America better.

American diplomats are in an excellent position to be able to gain access to all, or nearly all, segments of the local society. Unlike private Americans, US diplomats are sought after as an authoritative source of US policy. Moreover, for any local person who has complaints about that policy, US diplomats are a conduit back to Washington for those complaints. Even the harshest critics of the United States are usually accessible for these reasons, if the Americans make an effort to be in touch with them. Only in very few instances, might a dedicated critic of the United States avoid contact with US officials for fear of losing his or her local reputation, but this is rare. Moreover, because American diplomats must represent all of America, they are unlike private American citizens, who usually have a narrow commercial or other purpose.

Restrictions on local contacts by the American side are usually a mistake, unless the contact risks expulsion by the host government. Karen Hughes cancelled the boycott on talking with al-Jazeera Television because it hampered the ability of American officials to present their side of the story to a wide-reaching media outlet. She also urged PD officers and other officials at our embassies abroad to "think advocacy" and engage with local media to the extent possible. These were sensible instructions.

### 6. Promote First-Hand Knowledge

Educational exchange programs are among the most valuable of all public diplomacy tools.

American embassies sponsor students and professionals to travel to the United States because the visitors learn directly about many aspects of America that they otherwise cannot learn from books, magazines, films, or videos. These exchanges almost always enhance their understanding of America because first-hand knowledge is powerful. Unfettered access to a variety of private Americans sends a message about American openness. US embassies also support student advising for privately-sponsored students for the same reason.

A similar purpose is served by State Department programs that send American experts abroad as Fulbrighters, or on speaking tours, or to teach English, because they help bring the Americans into contact with foreign audiences in ways that facilitate better mutual understanding through personal engagement. The private American experts Washington sends abroad are chosen for their expertise and fairness, not their politics, and even if they may have some criticisms of the United States, this can add to their credibility and send a valuable message about American society.

### 7. Collaborate with Others

The US government collaborates with private institutions in the United States to manage and implement exchange programs. The work of the staffs of National Council on International Visitors and other private American nongovernmental organizations, many of them volunteers, has been invaluable to the US government's exchange programs. They save the State Department money, and they enable foreign visitors to have experiences in America, including home-stays, that almost always make a positive impression on them.

Another example of effective collaboration occurs when American PD officers serving abroad partner with local institutions to undertake cultural presentations or other programs. The embassy may not have appropriate program space that it owns or controls, and if a local governmental or private institution is willing to offer space and other support to the embassy for a program, that can be a mutually beneficial arrangement. This kind of partnership can even work well if bilateral relations are strained, if the host government is willing to cooperate because the program is non-political.

### 8. Find Surrogates

Individual local citizens can be helpful to a public diplomacy program.

The public diplomacy staff may be able to identify individual members of the local society who are reasonably balanced and fair-minded about the United States, and willing to express their views to their compatriots. If these individuals can be encouraged to participate in radio or television programs, or write in local newspapers, their credibility as local nationals can substantially enhance their message. Logical candidates for this role are returnees from visits to the United States, whether they have been sponsored by the US government or privately. If they are willing to talk about their personal experiences in America, this is valuable because they are likely to be trusted, and they have firsthand knowledge that they can recount from a local perspective, and in the local language. This is one of the reasons that PD officers try to stay in touch with returnees from visits to the United States.

### 9. Employ Social Media Thoughtfully

Social networking media can be a great asset in public diplomacy, especially for reaching younger audience members, but local conditions should help determine which ones to use.

American diplomats are now using a variety of social networking media for public diplomacy purposes. The State department in Washington supports their use in several ways. The International Information Programs bureau distributes large amounts of material that in some cases goes directly to audiences and in other cases are adapted by PD officers locally. Washington also makes daily use of the rapid response bulletins to get policy guidance out quickly, Digital Outreach Teams to engage key audiences where they are talking, and several regional media hubs positioned abroad to allow fast responses to breaking stories.

At embassies abroad, PD personnel evaluate the local availability and level of use of these media to determine which ones reach their target audiences best. In the most wired countries like Japan they may use the most sophisticated types, while in many African countries the embassy may focus on SMS or other means because of the low degree of Internet connectivity. Where the host government blocks many social media channels, as in China, they work around that barrier as best they can. However, PD professionals have realized that, valuable as they are, there are some practical limitations to the continued expansion of the use of these new media. They take time and attention from the PD staff that would otherwise be doing other things, and they sometimes raise expectations when they engage in discussions that they are unable to keep up with, causing disappointments. But if properly managed, and costs and benefits are weighed, social networking media can be a great asset to the PD program.

## 10. Use Teamwork

Collaboration within an embassy with other American diplomats is always essential.

Public diplomacy is a special skill, but interagency collaboration maximizes the effectiveness of a PD program. Ambassadors of course have unique access and attract more audiences when they speak, so it is important for the public affairs section to be involved, as appropriate, in ambassadorial public performances and social media efforts. Other embassy officers can extend the reach of the PD effort through speaking and interviews on subjects related to their expertise, such as the economy or trade. The PD staff can help publicize the economic assistance program if there is one, and can help the consular officer get the word out, for example on special visa matters. Representatives of the Defense Department may have resources that can enhance PD programs if properly coordinated, and the PD staff can help if there are public relations aspects of the military relationship. But the public diplomacy professionals should be involved in all decisions on public affairs activities of others in the embassy.

## 11. Use Local Staff

The public affairs section at every embassy depends heavily on local staff.

They are indispensable sources of information about local attitudes and behavior, and they play essential roles in outreach, contacts, and translation. They are language interpreters and cultural interpreters. They are often effective at helping to explain American society and its policies. They also provide an institutional memory and program continuity, a great asset to transitioning officers newly arriving at the embassy.

## 12. Remember Cultural Programs

American cultural presentations can be a very valuable asset to a public diplomacy program.

Although the US government does not send nearly as many cultural presentations abroad as it did in the past, they should not be forgotten because they can be very useful depending on local circumstances. In countries where bilateral political relations are tense and the host government prevents programming that has any political content, or restricts contacts, arranging a musical or theatrical event or an art or photography exhibit, or a sports envoy, can circumvent these barriers and enable the embassy to reach a significant segment of the public. English teaching is in great demand in many countries and can serve this purpose also, and it carries cultural freight. Such "Americana" programs can provide balance to the political relationship, and soften the American image. The cultural programs must however be carefully selected to fit local cultural and social norms, and reinforce positive aspects of America.

### 13. Balance Long- and Short-Term Goals

Public diplomacy programs should carefully balance long- and short-term goals.

The USIA-State merger, the anti-terrorism campaign and the post-9/11 expansion of Pentagon involvement in communication abroad, have tilted the emphasis of public diplomacy activities to favor short-term information and media efforts, at the expense of educational and cultural programs. American public diplomacy must retain a short-term quick response capability to be able to knock down false accusations that are gaining traction, so media hubs and rapid-response bulletins are useful. But the Public Affairs Officer at the embassy remains responsible for the overall orchestration of all types of program according to local circumstances, and he or she should keep the long term tools in mind.

## Conclusion

Public diplomacy is likely to remain an important feature of American diplomatic practice for as far as we can see into the future. Its funding and staffing may continue to be increased or decreased as in the past, depending on how the Congress and the administration see threats to the United States from abroad. But professional diplomats know that the perceptions of foreign publics on issues of importance to America's national interests are always important because they affect the attitudes and behavior of foreign governments toward the United States. Therefore US officials should take those perceptions into account in our foreign policy, and to do what we can to achieve understanding of our policies, society and culture.

The American public tends to have very limited knowledge of what its country's PD professionals actually do when they work at embassies abroad. Some of the thirteen principles listed above, such as truthfulness and dialogue, may not conform to their concept of what public diplomacy is, and they may not appreciate the fact that American diplomats usually have excellent access. The skills of a successful practitioner of public diplomacy are to a large extent learned on the job, at a US mission abroad, under the tutelage of experienced mentors.

The young officers who enter the Foreign Service today will face many challenges in their careers. There is no question that they are a special group, having been selected in a highly competitive examination process, and they undoubtedly will be conversant with the new social media communications methods. But the FSOs who are assigned to public diplomacy duties will also need a variety of other communication skills and techniques as well, many of which have been developed over the years as enduring principles. It will be important for them to learn effective communication principles from the mentors they work for, although they will also develop their own PD methods to cope with local circumstances.

# NOTES

## Introduction

1. William A. Rugh, *American Encounters with Arabs: The Soft Power of American Public Diplomacy*, New York: Praeger, 2006; and William A. Rugh, Ed., *Engaging the Arab and Islamic Worlds through Public Diplomacy*, Washington DC: Public Diplomacy Council, 2004.
2. William P. Kiehl, Ed., *The Last Three Feet: Case Studies in Public Diplomacy*, Washington, DC: Public Diplomacy Council, 2012, Washington DC: Public Diplomacy Council; and William A. Rugh, Ed, *The Practice of Public Diplomacy*, New York: Palgrave Macmillan, 2011.
3. Hans Tuch: *Communicating with the World: U.S. Public Diplomacy Overseas*, Washington DC: Institute for the Study of Diplomacy, 1990; Wilson Dizard, *Inventing Public Diplomacy: The Story of the U.S. Information Agency*, Boulder, CO: Lynne Rienner, 2004.
4. Nicholas J. Cull, *The Cold War and the U. S. Information Agency: American Propaganda and Public Diplomacy 1945–1949*, New York: Cambridge University Press, 2009; and Nicholas J. Cull, *The Decline and Fall of the U.S. Information Agency: American Public Diplomacy 1989–2001*, New York: Palgrave Macmillan, 2012.

## 1  Legacy: Public Diplomacy's Philosophy and Legal Basis

1. Bruce Gregory, "Public Diplomacy: Sunrise of an Academic Field," in *The Annals of the American Academy of Political and Social Science*, March 2008, pp.279.
2. Nicholas Cull, *The Cold War and the United States Information Agency*, Cambridge: Cambridge Press, 2008, pp.6–9.
3. Cull, pp.12–13.
4. Walter R. Roberts, "The Voice of America: Origins and Recollections," *American Diplomacy Online,* October 2009.
5. Cull, pp.13–19.
6. Cull, p.32.

7. Cull, p.35.
8. Barton Paulu, "The Smith-Mundt Act: A Legislative History," *Journalism Quarterly*, p.313, See the text of the law, title 22, Chapter 18, as amended up through 2008 in http://www4.law.cornell.edu/uscode/22/usc_sec_22_00001461/.
9. Some of these points have been made by Matt Armstrong in various essays, http:mountainrunner.US/smith-mundt.html; and Matt Armstrong, "Rethinking Smith-Mundt," Small Wars Journal, 2008; also www.smallwarsjournal.comhttp://publicdiplomacy.wikia.com/wiki/smith_mundt_act/.
10. "Modernization Act FAQ" Mountainrunner blog, June 5, 2012, www.mountainrunner.us. The Smith-Mundt Modernization Act, HR 5736, passed in 2012, http://thomas.loc.gov/cgi-bin/query/z?c112:H.R.5736; and Emily T. Metzgar, "Smith-Mundt Reform: In with a Whimper?" *Columbia Journalism Review online*, January 21, 2013.
11. Cull, pp.81–82.
12. Wilson P. Dizard, Jr., *Inventing Public Diplomacy: The Story of the U.S. Information Agency*, Boulder CO: Lynne Rienner, 2004, p.55.
13. Cull, p.196; it was passed as US Code title 22, Chapter 33, in 1961.
14. Public Law 87–256, September 21, 1961, 75 Stat. 527.
15. Edward Gullion, quoted in Delaney, Robert F., and John S. Gibson, eds. *American Public Diplomacy: The Perspective of Fifty Years*, Tufts University: Lincoln Filene Center for Citizenship and Public Affairs, 1967, p.31.
16. Joseph S. Nye, Jr., "Public Diplomacy and Soft Power," *The Annals of the American Academy of Political and Social Science* (March 2008) 94–95. See also Joseph S. Nye, Jr., *Soft Power: The Means to Success in World Politics*, New York: Public Affairs Press, 2004, and Wlliam A. Rugh, "The Case for Soft Power," in Philip Seib, *Toward a New Public Diplomacy: Redirecting U.S. Foreign Policy*, New York: Palgrave Macmillan, 2009, Chapter 1.
17. Howard Cincotta, "Wireless File to Web," in William A. Rugh, Ed., *Engaging the Arab and Islamic Worlds through Public Diplomacy*, Washington DC: Public Diplomacy Council, p.140–41; and Hans N. Tuch, Communicating with the World, Washington DC: Institute for the Study of Diplomacy, 1990, p.58.
18. Cincotta, p.144.
19. Tuch, pp.60–6; Dizard, p.165; and Cull, pp.65, 73, 77.
20. Lucija Bajzer, "Ameliorating Strained Relations: U.S. Public Diplomacy in Serbia," in William A. Rugh, Ed., *The Practice of Public Diplomacy*, New York: Palgrave Macmillan, 2011, pp.10–11.
21. Dizard, p.165.
22. Cincotta, pp.146–47.
23. Elise Crane, "Finding the Right Media Formula—from the Soviet Union to Russia," Chapter 12 in William A. Rugh, Ed., *The Practice of Public Diplomacy*, New York: Palgrave Macmillan, 2011.
24. Cull, p.187.
25. For examples of CIA propaganda see Hugh Wolford, *America's Great Game*, New York: Basic Books, 2013.

26. Kenton Keith, "Troubled Takeover," *Foreign Service Journal*, vol.76, no.9, September 1999, pp.19–20.
27. For example, the American public diplomacy staff in Egypt in 1965 was 12, but by 1988 it was down to 8. Later, in 2008, it was back up to 11, but that was because of the Mideast crises and staffing levels at most other posts remained much lower than in the 1960s.
28. Keith, pp.19–20.
29. Crane, Chapter 12.
30. Cincotta, pp.146–47; see also Dizard, pp.166–67.
31. Keith, p.20; William P. Kiehl, "Seduced and Abandoned: Strategic Information and the National Security Process," Chapter 8 in Gabriel Marcella, *Affairs of State: the Interagency and National Security*, December 2008, pp.354–55; and Peter Galbraith, "The Decline and Fall of USIA," *Foreign Service Journal*, vol.76, no.9, September 1999, pp.30–34.
32. The Foreign Affairs Reform and Restructuring Act of 1998, section G of the FY2008 Omnibus Appropriations legislation, PL-105–277, pp.761ff, http://frwebgate.access.gpo.gov/cgi-bin/getdoc.cgi?dbname=105_cong_public_laws&docid=f:pub1277.105.pdf.
33. Keith, p.22
34. Joe Duffey, former USIA director, interview by the author, 2007
35. Keith, p.22.
36. Kiehl, pp.354–55.
37. Kathy R. Fitzpatrick, *The Collapse of American Public Diplomacy: What Diplomatic Experts Say About Rebuilding America's Image in the World—A View from the Trenches*, Hamden CT: Quinnipiac University 2008, pp.10–11.
38. Foreword, Reorganization Plan and Report, Foreign Affairs Reform and Restructuring Act of 1998, PL 105–277, Division G.
39. Leonard Marks, Bruce Gelb, Charles Wisk, and Henry Catto, "America Needs a Voice Abroad," *The Washington Post*, February 26, 2005.
40. Secretary of Defense Robert Gates, address delivered at Kansas State University, Manhattan, Kansas, November 26, 2007, www.defenselink.mil/speeches/speech/aspx?speechid=1199/.
41. Senator Richard Lugar, "U.S. Public Diplomacy—Time to Get Back in the Game," Report to members of the Committee on Foreign relations, United States Senate, February 13, 2009, USGPO, pp.vi and 15.

## 2 Public Diplomacy Professionals

1. http://www.state.gov/documents/organization/208938.pdf. http://www.state.gov/s/d/rm/rls/statecbj/2014/pdf.htm. The numbers of these types of positions at State have remained almost exactly constant from 2012 to 2014.
2. Nicholas J. Cull, *The Cold War and the United States Information Agency*, Cambridge: Cambridge University Press, 2008, p.187.

3. http://www.state.gov/documents/organization/207305.pdf/.
 4. Secretary of Defense Robert Gates, address delivered at Kansas State University, Manhattan, Kansas, November 26, 2007, www.defenselink.mil/speeches/speech/aspx?speechid=1199/.
 5. J. Anthony Holmes, "Where are the Civilians? How to Rebuild the U.S. Foreign Service," *Foreign Affairs*, vol.88, no.1, Jan/Feb 2009, pp.10–57.
 6. See http://careers.state.gov/officer/selection-process for details.
 7. Harry W. Kopp and Charles A. Gillespie, *Career Diplomacy: Life and Work in the U.S. Foreign Service*, Washington, DC: Georgetown University Press, 2008.
 8. US Department of State and the Broadcasting Board of Governors, Report of the Inspector General, OIG Report No. ISP-I-09-44, Review of Locally Employed Staff Compensation Issues, April 2009, p.2.
 9. *Chronicle of Higher Education*, Volume 53, Issue 34, April 27, 2007, p.A24.
10. James A. Baker III and Lee H. Hamilton, *The Iraq Study Group Report*, New York: Random House, 2006, p. 92.
11. "Why the Pool of Arabic Speakers is Still a Puddle; Six Years After the U.S. Awoke to the Need for its Citizens to Learn Arabic, Obstacles Remain," *Christian Science Monitor*, May 17, 2007—http://www.csmonitor.com/2007/0517/p13s01-legn.html/.
12. Michael Canning, "The Overseas Post: The Forgotten Element of our Public Diplomacy," unpublished paper, Washington DC, September 15, 2008.
13. Ibid.
14. Ibid.
15. David D. Pearce, *Wary Partners: Diplomats and the Media*, Washington, DC: Congressional Quarterly, 1995, p.133.
16. Kathy R. Fitzpatrick, *The Collapse of American Public Diplomacy: What Diplomatic Experts Say About Rebuilding America's Image in the World—A View from the Trenches*, Hamden CT: Quinnipiac University 2008, p.13.
17. Canning.
18. Peter Galbraith, "The Decline and Fall of USIA," *Foreign Service Journal*, vol.76, no.9, September 1999, pp.30–34.
19. James L. Bullock, "The Role of the Embassy Public Affairs Officer After 9/11," Chapter 4 in William A. Rugh, Ed., *Engaging the Arab and Islamic Worlds through Public Diplomacy*, Washington, DC: Public Diplomacy Council, 2004, pp.35–48.
20. Pearce, p.134 quoting an unnamed PAO.
21. U.S. Advisory omission on Public Diplomacy, "Getting the People Part Right: A Report on the Human Resources Dimension of Public Diplomacy," Washington DC, 2008, sections VI and I.
22. There were 1,332 American public diplomacy positions at State, including 263 in IIP, 362 in ECA, 49 in R, and 658 assigned to the regional bureaus, with 96 percent of the latter serving abroad. American Academy of Diplomacy and the Stimson Center, "A Foreign Affairs Budget for the Future: Fixing the Crisis in Diplomatic Readiness," October 2008, pp.14–15.
23. Canning, p.9, http://www.publicdiplomacycouncil.org/uploads/canningoverseasposts.pdf/.

NOTES                    239

24. American Academy of Diplomacy and the Stimson Center, ibid., p.15.
25. U.S. Advisory Commission on Public Diplomacy, "Getting the People Part Right," ibid., pp.4, 8–10, 12–13.
26. Unclassified State Department telegram number 00049422 sent to all diplomatic and consular posts on March 28, 2006 entitled "Public Diplomacy and the EER Process."
27. Pearce, p.ix, quoting Lawrence Eagleberger, former Secretary of State.
28. Ibid., p.83.
29. See a more detailed discussion of this topic in William A. Rugh "PD Practitioners: Still Second-Class Citizens," *Foreign Service Journal*, October 2009.
30. Edward R. Murrow talking about USIA, quoted in Wilson P. Dizard, Jr., *Inventing Public Diplomacy: The Story of the U.S. Information Agency*, Boulder, CO: Lynne Rienner, 2004, p.86, was citing Thomas C. Sorenson, *The Word War: The Story of American Propaganda*, New York: Harper and Row, 1967, p.134.
31. U.S. Advisory Commission on Public Diplomacy, "Getting the People Part Right," http://www.publicdiplomacycouncil.org/uploads/canningoverseasposts.pdf, pp.4, 14, and 16.

## 3  The Public Affairs Officer

1. US Department of State, Office of the Inspector General, "Inspection of Embassy Jakarta, Indonesia and Constituent Posts," March 2011, pp.31–32.
2. Brianna Dieter, "Public Diplomacy in India," term paper, December 5, 2011, Fletcher School, Tufts University, public diplomacy course, unpublished, pp. 12–13, quoted by permission.
3. US Department of State, Office of Inspector General, "Report of Inspection, Embassy Beijing and Constituent Posts," September, 2010.
4. Dana Schübe, "Neuer Schulvergleich unter den Bundesländern—Der Süden schneidet am besten ab," in: http://www.rp-online.de/panorama/deutschland/Der-Sueden-schneidet-am-besten-ab_aid_872831.html, last visit: November 30, 2010, cited in Matthias Kaufmann, "U.S. Public Diplomacy in Germany: Challenges and Opportunities," term paper, December 6, 2011, Fletcher School, Tufts University, public diplomacy course, unpublished, pp. 3–5, 16–17, quoted by permission.
5. Blair Rapalyea, "The Future of United States Public Diplomacy in Brazil, *American Diplomacy*, March 2013, http://www.unc.edu/depts/diplomat/item/2013/0105/ca/rapalyea_uspd.html.
6. Dan Sreebny, "Public Diplomacy: The Field Perspective," in William P. Kiehl, Ed., *America's Dialogue with the World*, Washington, DC: Public Diplomacy Council, 2006, pp.98–101.
7. Comment to the author by a senior public diplomacy official.
8. John Rahaghi, "New Media or Old in Egypt and South Korea?" in William A. Rugh, Ed., *The Practice of Public Diplomacy*, New York: Palgrave Macmillan, 2011,

pp.176–77; and Huh Huh, Yoon-Jeong, "The Staying Power of Personal Contact in South Korean Public diplomacy," in William A. Rugh, Ed., *The Practice of Public Diplomacy*, Palgrave Macmillan, 2011, pp.110–12.
9. Nicole Farina, "Revitalizing Relations with Turkey," in Rugh, p.23.
10. Rahaghi, p.181.
11. Matt Lussenhop, PAO in Afghanistan, 2010–2011, interview Washington DC, October 13, 2011, Public Diplomacy Council website, accessed January 27, 2012, http://publicdiplomacycouncil.org/public-diplomacy-videos-us-missions-around-world/.
12. William Horsley: "Polls find Europeans oppose Iraq war" (BBC News World Edition, February 11, 2003, http://news.bbc.co.uk/2/hi/europe/2747175.stm), last visit: November 3, 2010.
13. Thomas Darnstädt: "Torturing for America" (Spiegel Online International, January 5, 2009, http://www.spiegel.de/international/world/0,1518,622382-2,00.html), last visit: November 13, 2010.
14. Gregor Peter Schmitz: "Europeans Back Obama but Not Necessarily His Policies—'Transatlantic Trends' survey 2008," in: Spiegel Online International, http://www.spiegel.de/international/world/0,1518,577449,00.html, last visit: October 25, 2010.
15. Pew Report June 17, 2010, "Obama More Popular Abroad than at Home, Global Image of U.S. Continues to Benefit," http://www.pewtrusts.org/our_work_report_detail.aspx?id=59555, last visit: November 13, 2010.
16. Telephone interview with Pamnela DeVolder, former Cultural Affairs and Press Officer in the US Embassy in Berlin, October 26, 2010, cited in Kaufmann, pp.11–12, 19.
17. "Iran Gains as Arabs' Obama Hopes Sink," Zogby International, Accessed November 30, 2010. http://www.zogby.com/Soundbites/ReadClips.cfm?ID=19331. cited in Jeffrey Fine, "U.S. Public Diplomacy in Lebanon: Challenges and Opportunities," December 2010, Public Diplomacy Council website, http://publicdiplomacycouncil.org/tufts-papers, pp.13–14.
18. For details, see: Pew Global Attitudes Project reports, http://pewglobal.org/reports/display.php?ReportID=263.; http://pewglobal.org/reports/display.php?ReportID=5;andhttp://pewglobal.org/reports/display.php?ReportID=206/. Cited in Sarah Riley, "Iran and the United Kingdom: A Study in Contrasts," Chapter 3 in Rugh, p.50.
19. *Horizon Chinese Opinion Poll: Eyes On The World, Future In Hand*, December 14, 2006, cited in Liang Pan, "U.S. Public Diplomacy in China," term paper, public diplomacy seminar, Fletcher School, December 6, 2011, unpublished, p.10, cited by permission.
20. Sarah Riley, "Iran and the United Kingdom: A Study in Contrasts," in Rugh, p.38.
21. August 2009 Pew Global survey. The Pew Global Attitudes Project, "Pakistani Public Opinion." Washington, DC: Pew Research Center, 2009.
22. http://www.pewglobal.org/2012/06/27/pakistani-public-opinion-ever-more-critical-of-u-s/.

23. Rachel E. Smith, "Afghanistan and Pakistan: Public Diplomacy During Instability," in Rugh, pp. 55–60.
24. Walter Lippmann, *Public Opinion*, New York: Free Press/Simon and Schuster, 1997, p.18.
25. Email to the author from a PD field officer, October 2013.
26. Marc Lynch, "Public Opinion Survey Research and Public Diplomacy," in Joshua S. Fouts, "Public Diplomacy, Policy Makers and Public Opinion," Report of the Public Diplomacy and World Opinion Forum, pp.33–35.
27. Walter Douglas, PAO Islamabad, transcript of a talk given at the November 3, 2011 conference sponsored by the Public Diplomacy Council and George Washington University, http://publicdiplomacycouncil.org/keynoter-panelist-information-and-transcripts/.
28. Atu Yudhistru Indarto, "U.S. Public Diplomacy in Indonesia Post 9/11: A Case of Concerted Muslims Outreach," term paper, December 5, 2011, Fletcher School, Tufts University, public diplomacy course, unpublished, cited by permission, p.41, quoting email and phone interview with former US Foreign Service Officer, October 18, 2011 on November 24, 2011.
29. Quote attributed to USIA Director Carl Rowan.
30. Dawn McCall, talk at the USC Center Forum, Washington DC, February 4, 2013 also Susan McHale's remarks at the opening of @America in Jakarta, December 1, 2010, for example.
31. See http://www.state.gov/j/gyi/.
32. Emilie Falguieres, "Public Diplomacy towards France: Engaging Diversity," term paper, December 5, 2011, Fletcher School, Tufts University, public diplomacy course, unpublished, pp.15–16, quoted by permission.
33. Fine, p.24.
34. Mabel Ntiru: "Kenya's 'Native Son' and Enduring Local Issues," in William A. Rugh, Ed., *The Practice of Public Diplomacy*, New York: Palgrave Macmillan, 2011, p.86.
35. United States Department of State, Office of the Inspector General, "Report of Inspection: Inspection of Embassy Bangkok and Consulate General Chiang Mai, Thailand," November 2010. http://oig.state.gov/documents/organization/152595.pdf.
36. Dieter, citing phone interview 10/24/2011 with Adnan Siddiqi. Counselor for Cultural Affairs, India, New Delhi 2004–8.
37. Christine Schoellhorn, "U.S. Public Diplomacy and the Egyptian Revolution," term paper, December 8, 2011, Fletcher School, Tufts University public diplomacy seminar, unpublished, quoted by permission, p.25.
38. Tulani N. Elisa, "Sierra Leone: Public Diplomacy Unwired," in William A. Rugh, Ed., *The Practice of Public Diplomacy*, New York: Palgrave Macmillan, 2011, p.95.
39. See http://state.gov/s/srmc/c45088/htm.
40. Ibid.
41. David G. Kirkpatrick and Steven Lee Myers, "U.S. Hones Warnings to Egypt as Military Stalls Transition." StarAdvertiser.com, November 17, 2011.

## 242  Notes

42. Garett Martin, "In Smart-Power Shift, U.S. Now Actively Cultivating Muslim Minorities in the EU," The European Institute, http://www.europeaninstitute.org/EA-April-2011/in-smart-power-shift-us-now-actively-cultivating-muslim-minorities-in-the-eu.html (April 3, 2011).
43. Katrin Bennhold, "U.S. Courts the Support of French Muslims," *The New York Times,* May 26, 2008, http://www.nytimes.com/2008/05/26/world/americas/26iht-paris.4.13227713.html; and Paul Patin, Information Officer in U.S. Embassy in Paris, quoted in Christophe Ayad, "L'Amérique Prend Ses Quartiers," *Libération,* October 26, 2010. http://www.liberation.fr/monde/01012298482-l-amerique-prend-ses-quartiers; both cited in Falguieres.
44. Elisa, p.95.
45. Ontira Amatavivat, "U.S. Public Diplomacy in Thailand," term paper, December 5, 2011, Fletcher School, Tufts University, public diplomacy course, unpublished, quoted by permission.
46. Ntiru, pp.82–83.
47. Lussenhop.
48. Fine, pp. 9 and 23–24 quoting CAO Jennifer Williams.
49. Stanley McChrystal, "COMISAF Initial Assessment (Unclassified)—Searchable Document," *The Washington Post,* August 30, 2009, http://www.washingtonpost.com/wp-dyn/.content/article/2009/09/21/AR2009092100110.html (ed., sec. 2009: November 1, 2009). cited in Rachel E. Smith, "Afghanistan and Pakistan: Public Diplomacy During Instability," in Rugh, pp.57–58).
50. Lussenhop. For details on security restrictions on our American centers and libraries, see chapter eight.
51. Raul Chavez, "Public Diplomacy and Nationalistic Leaders: The Dangers of Applying Strategies in Cuba to Venezuela," April 23, 2008, Public Diplomacy Council website, http://publicdiplomacycouncil.org/tufts-papers, pp.28 and 38.
52. This list omits CIA which, if represented, is under cover of another functional title.
53. Edwin Eichler, "U.S. Public Diplomacy in Hungary, Past and Present," April 25, 2008, Public Diplomacy Council website, http://publicdiplomacycouncil.org/tufts-papers, p.49.
54. Yohei Ogawa, "Economic Issues and Anti-Americanism in Japan," in. Rugh, p.132.
55. Atu Yudhistru Indarto, pp.23–25.
56. Ibid., pp. 20–21, citing Former US Foreign Service Officer, Interview by email on October 18, 2011 and by telephone on November 24, 2011.

## 4   Contacts and Personal Networking Techniques

1. Edward R. Murrow, on ABC TV's "Issues and Answers," August 4, 1963, quoted by John Brown in "Enjoy This Killer App for the Holidays!" Public diplomacy press and blog review, December 31, 2011, http://publicdiplomacypressandblogreview.blogspot.com.html.

# Notes

2. The Public Diplomacy Council in 2011 organized a conference with that title and in 2012 published a book with that title: William P. Kiehl, *The Last Three Feet: Case Studies in Public Diplomacy*, Washington, DC: Public Diplomacy Council, 2012.
3. John Brown, "Enjoy This Killer App for the Holidays!" John Brown Blog, posted December 31, 2011, 11:18 am ET.
4. John Stuart Mill, "On Liberty," 1859.
5. USIA mission statement approved by the NSC on October 24, 1953, quoted in Nicholas Cull, in *The Cold War and the United States Information Agency*, Cambridge: Cambridge University Press, 2008, pp.101–2.
6. US State Department unclassified telegram no.006202, for COMs, DCMs and PAOs from Karen Hughes, subject: "Speaking on the Record," January 12, 2006.
7. US State Department unclassified telegram from Karen Hughes, subject "Speaking on the Record," October 2006, reproduced in the Washington Post, November 8, 2006, p.A25.
8. Shaun Riorden, "Dialogue-Based Public Diplomacy: A New Foreign Policy Paradigm?" Chapter 10 in Jan Melissen, Ed., *The New Public Diplomacy: Soft Power in International Relations*, New York: Palgrave Macmillan, 2005.
9. Business for Diplomatic Action, "America's Role in the World: A Business Perspective on Public Diplomacy," October 2007, pp.10–11; see also Reinhard, Keith, "American Business and its Role in Public Diplomacy," Chapter 16 in Nancy Snow and Philip Taylor, Eds., *The Routledge Handbook of Public Diplomacy*, New York: Routledge, 2009.
10. Kristin M. Lord, "Voices of America: U.S. Public Diplomacy for the 21st Century," Washington, DC: Brookings, November 2008, pp. 19–21.
11. Geoffrey Cowen, and Amelia Arsenault, "Moving from Monologue to Dialogue to Collaboration: The Three Layers of Public Diplomacy," in Geoffrey Cowan and Nicholas Cull, Eds., *Public Diplomacy in a Changing World*, in The Annals of the American Academy of Political and Social Science, March 2008, 616, p.11.
12. Paul Lazarsfeld and Elihu Katz, *Personal Influence*, New York: Free Press, 1955.
13. David D. Pearce, *Wary Partners: Diplomats and the Media*, Washington, DC: Congressional Quarterly, 1995, p.100.
14. http://vostokmedia.com/n46746.html?print; http://vladivostok.usconsulate.gov/mariachi.html.
15. Helen Thomas, *Watchdogs of Democracy?* New York: Scribner, 2006, p. 57.
16. Pearce, p.13.
17. Pearce, pp. 82, 95–97, 103.
18. Edward R. Murrow, statement as USIA director, in testimony before Congressional committee, May 1963.

## 5 Traditional Information Channels

1. David D. Pearce, *Wary Partners: Diplomats and the Media*, Washington, DC: Congressional Quarterly, 1995, p.104.

2. As explained in chapter eleven on the Pentagon, American military personnel violated this rule when they made clandestine payments for placement to Iraqi editors.
3. Wah Kwan-Lin, "Obstacles to U.S. Communication Efforts," unpublished paper, Fletcher School, Tufts University, December 11, 2012, cited by permission.
4. US Agency for International Assistance, "From the American People: Why the Story That U.S. Foreign Assistance Is Working Must Be Told," Washington DC, November 2008.
5. http://www.unesco.org/new/en/communication-and-information/events/prizes-and-celebrations/celebrations/world-radio-day/statistics-on-radio/; http://www.aljazeera.com/news/americas/2012/09/2012923232111323871.html.
6. William A. Rugh, "How Washington Confronts Arab Media," *Global Media Journal*, vol.3, issue 5, Fall 2004, http://lass.calumet.purdue.edu/cca/gmj/SubmittedDocuments/Fall2004/invited/rugh.htm.
7. Ibid.
8. Karen P. Hughes, Interview with Undersecretary Hughes by the Council on Foreign Relations, August 28, 2007, http://www.cfr.org/publication/14089/.
9. Karen P. Hughes, "Presentation to U.S. House of Representatives Committee on Appropriations Subcommittee on State, Foreign Operations and Related Programs, Department of State, April 2007.
10. Marc Lynch in his blog, AbuAaarvark, posted October 22, 2006, www.abuaardvark.typepad.com.
11. US State Department unclassified telegram no.006202, for COMs, DCMs, and PAOs from Karen Hughes, subject: "Speaking on the Record," January 12, 2006; and US State Department unclassified telegram from Karen Hughes, subject: "Speaking on the Record," reproduced in the *Washington Post*, November 8, 2006, p.A25.
12. Marc Lynch, "The Fernandez Problem," Lynch Abuaarvaak blog, October 22, 2006, http://abuaardvark.typepad.com/abuaardvark/2006/10/the_fernandez_p.html; and Craig Hayden, "The Fernandez 'Stupid Storm', Misunderstanding a Diplomat's Candor" CPD Blog, Center on Public Diplomacy, University of Southern California, October 23, 2006.
13. Josh Rogin, "Inside the Public Relations Disaster at the Cairo Embassy," *The Cable/Foreign Policy*, September 12, 2012, http://thecable.foreignpolicy.com/posts/2012/09/12/inside_the_public_relations_disaster_at_the_cairo_embassy; and Max Fisher, "The U.S. Embassy in Cairo's Oddly Informal Twitter Feed," *The Atlantic*, September 13, 2012.http://www.theatlantic.com/international/archive/2012/09/the-us-embassy-to-egypts-oddly-informal-twitter-feed/262331/.
14. John Brady Kiesling, "U.S. Diplomat's Letter of Resignation," *The New York Times*, February 27, 2003; and "Letter of Resignation by John H. Brown, Foreign Service Officer,"http://www.commondreams.org/views03/0312-11.htm/.
15. US State Department, "IIP Print and Electronic Publications," Foreign Affairs Handbook vol.10, 10 FAM 341 and 343, http://www.state.gov/documents/organization/88255.pdf.

NOTES                                                                245

16. Howard Cincotta, "Wireless File to Web," in *Engaging the Arab and Islamic Worlds Through Public Diplomacy*, William A. Rugh, Ed., Washington, DC: Public Diplomacy Council, p.143.
17. http://iipdigital.usembassy.gov/#axzz2dlRPvW6M.
18. Mabel Ntiru, "Kenya's 'Native Son' and Enduring Local Issues," in William A. Rugh, Ed., *The Practice of Public Diplomacy*, New York: Palgrave Macmillan 2011, p.85.
19. Peter Galbraith, "The Decline and Fall of USIA," *Foreign Service Journal*, vol.76, no.9, September 1999, pp.30–34.
20. Rapidresponse@statelists.state.gov.
21. Nicholas Kralev, *America's Other Army: The U.S. Foreign Service and 21st Century Diplomacy*, Lexington, KY: Create Space (Amazon), 2013, p.107.
22. See, for example, the European, East Asian and African media hubs at http://useu.usmission.gov/hub.html, http://www.state.gov/r/pa/ime/eapmediahub/index.htm, and http://southafrica.usembassy.gov/mediahub.html.

## 6  Social Networking Media: Use by Field Posts

1. Facebook, Twitter, and YouTube, were created in 2004, 2005, and 2006 respectively. Flickr, that allows electronic transmission of photographs, began in 2004, as did Vimeo, the video-sharing tool. Tumblr, that allows users to post multimedia content as short blogs, began in 2007, while the photo-sharing devices Pinterest and Instagram started in 2009 and 2010 respectively. Google Plus started in 2011 with Secretary Kerry engaging in outreach using Google Hangouts.
2. American Academy of Diplomacy and Stimson Center, "A Foreign Affairs Budget for the Future: Fixing the Crisis in Diplomatic Readiness," Washington DC, October 2008, p.3.
3. Malcolm Gladwell, "Does Egypt Need Twitter?" *New Yorker* Online, February 2, 2011; among the writers who disagreed was Clay Shirky, see his book *Here Comes Everybody: The Power of Organizing without Organizations*, New York: Penguin Press, 2008.
4. Nicholas J. Cull, "The Long Road to Public Diplomacy 2.0," *International Studies Review* (2013) 123–39.
5. Rachel N. Okunubi, "New Media or 'the Last Three Feet' in Africa?" in William A. Rugh, Ed., *The Practice of Public Diplomacy*, New York: Palgrave Macmillan, 2011, pp.159–60.
6. Retired senior public diplomacy officer, comment to the author by email, February 13, 2013.
7. Donna Winton, Senior State Department officer at IIP, interview July 6, 2012.
8. Okunubi, p.167.
9. Takahiro Yamamoto, "U.S. Public Diplomacy 2.0 in Asia: Beyond Catch-up," in William A. Rugh, Ed., *The Practice of Public Diplomacy*, New York: Palgrave Macmillan, 2011, pp.153–54.

10. www.intelink.gov/communities/state/smp.
11. John Matel and William May, "Digital Diplomacy: IIP Engages New Audiences with Social Media," *State Magazine*, November 2009, pp12–13.
12. Dawn McCall, IIP Coordinator, interview with the author, Washington DC, May 10, 2012, and speech by Dawn McCall before the Public Diplomacy Council, Washington DC, February 5, 13; and Michelle Rabayda, senior State Department official in the IIP bureau, interview with the author, May 30, 2012.
13. Winton, email to the author, July 6, 2012.
14. Alicia M. Cohn, "State Department Shifts Digital Resources to Social Media," *The Hill*, April 24, 2011, http://thehill.com/blogs/hillicon-valley/technology/157501-state-dept-shifts-digital-resources-to-social-media.
15. Ibid.
16. Winton email to the author, July 6, 2012.
17. Winton email to the author, July 6, 2012.
18. See http://alumni.state.gov/; and http://www.state.gov/r/pa/prs/ps/2012/12/201785.htm.
19. http://moscow.usembassy.gov/us/us.php?record_id=irc.
20. "Otkroy Ameriku. October 2007," http://moscow.usembassy.gov/files/discover4.pdf.
21. Aleksey Dolinskiy, "British and U.S. Public Diplomacy in Russia," Spring 2008, Public Diplomacy Council website, http://publicdiplomacycouncil.org/tuftspapers, pp.29–30, citing "Otkroy Ameriku. October 2007," http://moscow.usembassy.gov/files/discover4.pdf, and "Domashnyaya Stranitsa—Vse O USA," http://www.infousa.ru/.
22. U.S. Department of State and Broadcasting Board of Governors, Office of Inspector General, Inspection Report Number ISP-I-10-39, February 2010 on The Bureau of Public Affairs, pp.25–26
23. http://dashboard.php1.getusinfo/smdash/platform, accessed February 7, 2013.
24. John Rahaghi, "New Media or Old in Egypt and South Korea?" in William A. Rugh, Ed., *The Practice of Public Diplomacy*, New York: Palgrave Macmillan, 2011, pp.178–80.
25. Ontira Amatavivat, "U.S. Public Diplomacy in Thailand," term paper, December 5, 2011, Fletcher School, Tufts University, public diplomacy course, unpublished p.24, used by permission.
26. Judith Baroody, Public Affairs Officer in Paris (2009–2011) interview by email, November 3, 2011 by Emilie Falguieres, quoted in her term paper "Public Diplomacy towards France: Engaging Diversity," December 5, 2011, Fletcher School, Tufts University, public diplomacy course, unpublished, cited by permission.
27. PAO Michael Pelletier, phone interview November 2, 2011, cited in Brianna Dieter, "Public Diplomacy in India," term paper, December 5, 2011, Fletcher School, Tufts University, public diplomacy course, unpublished, quoted by permission.
28. "Santiagopress's Channel," YouTube (accessed November 10, 2010); available from http://www.youtube.com/santiagopress; and "Embajada EEUU Chile,"

Twitter (accessed November 29, 2010); available from http://twitter.com/EmbajadaEEUUcl; and Sarah Schaffer, "U.S. Public Diplomacy in Chile: A Study of Instruments, Programs and Effectiveness," term paper, Fletcher School of Law and Diplomacy, December 6, 2010, public diplomacy seminar, fall 2010, unpublished pp.15–16, cited by permission.
29. Winton email to author, July 6, 2012.
30. http://www.videochallenge.america.gov/. See also: http://globalvoicesonline.org/2009/07/22/democracy-video-challenge-winner-showcase/.
31. Winton, email to author, July 2012, cited.
32. Dieter.
33. Rahaghi, pp. 182–86.
34. Yamamoto, pp.154–55.
35. Okunubi, pp.167 and 170.
36. Matel and May, pp12–13.
37. US State Department, Bureau of International Information Programs, Digital Outreach Team, "What's Playing in Cyberspace," March 11, 2009, Vol. 2, Issue 10.
38. Matel and May, pp12–13.
39. Winton July 6, 2012 email to author.
40. http://www.state.gov/documents/organization/116709.pdf.
41. http://dashboard.php1.getusinfo/smdash/platform, accessed February 7, 2013.
42. Brent Blashke in 2008 on NBC Nightly News, quoted in Cameron Bean, "State's Digital Outreach Team May Do More Harm than Good," COMOPS Journal, posted online November 11, 2010.
43. http://iipdigital.usembassy.gov/#axzz2fdxhYNru/.
44. http://dashboard.php1.getusinfo/smdash/platform, accessed 2-7-13; and http://www.facebook.com/eJournalUSA, and Twitter @innovgen; and http://IIP_WE@state.vov.
45. Hadi Barkat, Lisa Jaeggli, and Pierre Dorsaz, "Citizen 2.0," November 2011, p.13, http://citizen20.redcut.ch/Citizen%202.0%20%28EN%29.pdf (accessed March 28, 2012). See also, Office of Inspector General, *Inspection of Embassy Jakarta, Indonesia and Constituent Posts, March 2011,* 31.
46. Alix Browne, "Embassy Suite," *The New York Times Style Magazine,* April 28, 2011; and Paul Patin, Information Officer in Paris, Interview by phone, November 10, 2011.by Emilie Falguires, quoted in her term paper, "Public Diplomacy towards France: Engaging Diversity," December 5, 2011, Fletcher School, Tufts University, public diplomacy course, unpublished, cited by permission.
47. http://france.usembassy.gov/benfranklinparisblog2.html.
48. Dieter, pp. 21–22.
49. Peter Velasco, Bureau of East Asian and Pacific Affairs in 2010, phone interview by Ontira Amatavivat, work cited.
50. http://bangkok.usembassy.gov/news/index.htm.
51. "Santiagopress's Channel," YouTube (accessed November 10, 2010); available from http://www.youtube.com/santiagopress; and "Embajada EEUU Chile," Twitter (accessed November 29, 2010); available from http://twitter.com/EmbajadaEEUUcl; and Schaffer, pp.15–16.

248    Notes

52. Ambassador John Beyrle, interview, undated (ca. October 2011), Public Diplomacy Council website, accessed 1/27/2012, http://publicdiplomacycouncil.org/public-diplomacy-videos-us-missions-around-world/.
53. Wikileaks story reported in AsianCorrespondent.com September 5, 2011.
54. Kristie Kenney, "Viewpoint," April 7, 2011, Online video clip YouTube, http://www.youtube.com/watch?v=e0DdnQPyJ8o&feature=related.
55. Amatavivat, pp.10–12.
56. Kristin L. Kneedler, 'Thailand LIKES Ambassador Kenney," Dipnote, February 8, 2011 http://blogs.state.gov/index.php/site/entry/thailand_kenney_social_media/.
57. Huh, Yoon-Jeong, "The Staying Power of Personal Contact in South Korean Public Diplomacy," Chapter 7 in William A. Rugh, Ed., *The Practice of Public Diplomacy*, Palgrave Macmillan, 2011, p.118.
58. http://usambassadortolaos.tumblr.com/AboutMe; see also http://laos.usembassy.gov/ambio.html
59. African Press International, May 22, 2009.
60. Mabel Ntiru: "Kenya's 'Native Son' and Enduring Local Issues," in William A. Rugh, Ed., *The Practice of Public Diplomacy*, New York: Palgrave Macmillan, 2011, pp.79–80.
61. Lucija Bajzer, "Ameliorating Strained Relations: U.S. Public diplomacy in Serbia," in William A. Rugh, Ed., *The Practice of Public Diplomacy*, Palgrave Macmillan, 2011, p.11, citing *YouTube: Broadcast Yourself,* Cameron Munter Part 1, February 2009; available at http://www.youtube.com/watch?v=dOStIJlKLYg.
62. Takahiro Yamamoto, "U.S. Public Diplomacy 2.0 in Asia: Beyond Catch-up," in William A. Rugh, Ed., *The Practice of Public Diplomacy*, New York: Palgrave Macmillan, 2011, p. 149.
63. Winton 7/6/12 email to author; the US press however focused attention on the fact that he was the first openly gay U.S. ambassador.
64. http://blogs.newzealand.usembassy.gov/ambassador.
65. Pamnela DeVolder, former Cultural Affairs and Press Officer in the US Embassy in Berlin, telephone interview October 26, 2010, cited in Matthias Kaufmann, "U.S. Public Diplomacy in Germany: Challenges and Opportunities," term paper, December 6, 2011, Fletcher School, Tufts University, public diplomacy course, unpublished, cited by permission.
66. ABC News, January 19, 2014.

## 7 Social Networking Media: Factors to Consider in Their Use

1. Takahiro Yamamoto, "U.S. Public Diplomacy 2.0 in Asia: Beyond Catch-up," in William A. Rugh, Ed., *The Practice of Public Diplomacy*, New York: Palgrave Macmillan, 2011, p. 148.
2. http://qz.com/132590/china-has-more-internet-monitors-than-active-army-personnel/.

3. Richard Burkholder, "Internet Use: Behind 'The Great Firewall of China,'" Gallup Poll and Report. February 1, 2005. Accessed online: http://www.gallup.com/poll/14776/Internet-Use-Behind-The-Great-Firewall-China.aspx.
4. Wah-Kwan Lin, "Obstacles to US Communication," unpublished paper, Fletcher School of Tufts University, December 11, 2012, cited by permission.
5. Liang Pan, "U.S. Public Diplomacy in China," term paper, public diplomacy seminar, Fletcher School, December 6, 2011, unpublished, pp.19–21, cited by permission, quoting interviews November 2011 with the PAO at the US embassy in Beijing Thomas F. Skipper and with former US Consul General in Beijing Beatrice Camp; US State Department, Office of Inspector General (OIG), *Report of Inspection, Embassy Beijing and Constituent Posts*, September, 2010.
6. Bea Camp, Consul General in Shanghai at the time, transcript of transcript of a talk given at the November 3, 2011 conference sponsored by the Public Diplomacy Council and George Washington University, posted on Council website, http://public diplomacycouncil.org/.
7. Raul Chavez, "Public Diplomacy and Nationalistic Leaders: The Dangers of Applying Strategies in Cuba to Venezuela," April 23, 2008, Public Diplomacy Council website, http://publicdiplomacycouncil.org/tufts-papers, pp.12, 18–20.
8. Gloria Berbena, Public Affairs Counselor, US Interests Section, Havana, interview, Washington DC September 19, 2011, http://publicdiplomacycouncil.org/public-diplomacy-videos-us-missions-around-world, accessed January 27, 2012.
9. Sarah Riley, "Iran and the United Kingdom: A Study in Contrasts," in William A. Rugh, Ed., *The Practice of Public Diplomacy*, New York: Palgrave Macmillan, 2011, p.43.
10. http://iran.usembassy.gov/.
11. Rachel N. Okunubi, "New Media or 'the Last Three Feet' in Africa?" in William A. Rugh, Ed., *The Practice of Public Diplomacy*, New York: Palgrave Macmillan, 2011, pp.169 and 172.
12. Winton email to author, July 6, 2012.
13. Tulani N. Elisa, "Sierra Leone: Public Diplomacy Unwired," in William A. Rugh, Ed., *The Practice of Public Diplomacy*, New York: Palgrave Macmillan, 2011, pp.96–98
14. Ontira Amatavivat, "U.S. Public Diplomacy in Thailand," term paper, December 5, 2011, Fletcher School, Tufts University, public diplomacy course, unpublished, pp.21–22, quoted by permission.
15. Experienced senior public diplomacy professional, now retired, comments to the author by email, February 13, 2013.
16. Joseph S. Nye, *Soft Power: The Means to Success in World Politics*, New York: Public Affairs, 2004
17. Yamamoto, pp.151 and 155.
18. Yamamoto, p.151.
19. Mabel Ntiru: "Kenya's 'Native Son' and Enduring Local Issues," in William A. Rugh, Ed., *The Practice of Public Diplomacy*, New York: Palgrave Macmillan, 2011, p.80.
20. Ntiru, pp.79–80.

21. Rachel Graaf Leslie, PAO Manama, transcript of a talk given at the November 3, 2011 conference sponsored by the Public Diplomacy Council and George Washington University, http://publicdiplomacycouncil.org/keynoter-panelist-information-and-transcripts.
22. John Rahaghi, "New Media or Old in Egypt and South Korea?" in William A. Rugh, Ed., *The Practice of Public Diplomacy*, New York: Palgrave Macmillan, 2011, p.187.
23. In 2008 South Korea had 14,735,375 Internet subscribers, after the United States (at 70,345,756), Germany (at 28,781,000), Japan (at 32,720,197), and the United Kingdom (at 18,277,047). In terms of broadband share among total Internet subscribers, almost 100 percent are broadband and not dial-up. Also, 80.9 percent of households have access to a computer at home.; and Yoon-Jeong Huh "The Staying Power of Personal Contact in South Korean Public diplomacy," in William A. Rugh, Ed., *The Practice of Public Diplomacy*, Palgrave Macmillan, 2011, p.117 citing http://www.oecd.org/document/23/0,3343,en_2649_34449_33987 543_1_1_1_1,00.html; OECD, "Internet Subscribers in the Total for OECD" (last updated on September 21, 2009); and "Households With Access to a Home Computer" (last updated on July 22, 2009).
24. Huh, pp.115–18; ; and http://cafe.daum.net/usembassy.
25. Rahaghi, pp.186–87.
26. Winton email to author, July 6, 2012.
27. Pat Kabra, Cairo PAO, comment to the author, March 2012.
28. *New York Times*, September 11, 2012 and *Daily Beast*, September 11, 201212.
29. Winton email, July 6, 2012.
30. Yamamoto, pp.154–55.
31. Winton email, July 6, 2012.
32. Rahaghi, pp. 179–80.
33. https://twitter.com/USEmbassyRiyadh and https://www.facebook.com/USEmbassyRiyadh/.
34. Yamamoto, pp. 149–50.
35. Yohei Ogawa, "Economic Issues and Anti-Americanism in Japan," chapter 8 in William A. Rugh, Ed., *The Practice of Public Diplomacy*, New York: Palgrave Macmillan, 2011, pp.129–30.
36. Brianna Dieter, "Public Diplomacy in India," term paper, December 5, 2011, Fletcher School, Tufts University, public diplomacy course, unpublished, quoted by permission, pp. 21–22.
37. US Department of State and Broadcasting Board of Governors, Office of Inspector General, "Inspection of the Bureau of International Information Programs," report ISP-I-13-28, May 2013, p.1.
38. Leslie, transcript of a talk November 3, 2011 cited.
39. Hillary Rodham Clinton, "Internet Rights and Wrongs: Choices and Challenges in a Networked World," at George Washington University, Washington DC, February 15, 2011. See also her similar remarks at the Newseum, Washington DC, on January 21, 2010.

40. Ambassador John Beyrle, interview, undated (ca. October 2011), Public Diplomacy Council website, accessed January 27, 2012, http://publicdiplomacycouncil.org/public-diplomacy-videos-us-missions-around-world.
41. Winton email, July 6, 2012.

## 8  American Cultural Programs

1. The term "cultural diplomacy" has been used in various ways, sometimes to refer to these cultural programs, sometimes to refer to exchanges, and sometimes both.
2. Raul Chavez, "Public Diplomacy and Nationalistic Leaders: The Dangers of Applying Strategies in Cuba to Venezuela," April 23, 2008, Public Diplomacy Council website, http://publicdiplomacycouncil.org/tufts-papers, pp.23–25.
3. Barry Ballow, "Academic Exchanges in the Arab World: an Underdeveloped Tool," in William A. Rugh, Ed., *Engaging the Arab and Islamic Worlds through Public Diplomacy*, Washington, DC: Public Diplomacy Council, 2004, p.112.
4. Information from a knowledgeable field officer, October 2013.
5. Yohei Ogawa, "Economic Issues and Anti-Americanism in Japan," in William A. Rugh, Ed., *The Practice of Public Diplomacy*, New York: Palgrave Macmillan, 2011, pp.129 and 132.
6. Emilie Falguieres, "Public Diplomacy towards France: Engaging Diversity," term paper, December 5, 2011, Fletcher School, Tufts University, public diplomacy course, unpublished, pp.27–35, quoted by permission, citing an American diplomat in Paris, interview by phone, November 4, 2011. See also http://france.usembassy.gov/.
7. Rafik Mansour, Cultural Affairs Officer, US Embassy Paris, interview September 30, 2011, in Paris, Public Diplomacy Council website, accessed January 27, 2012, http://publicdiplomacycouncil.org/public-diplomacy-videos-us-missions-around-world/.
8. Falguieres, source cited.
9. US Embassy Damascus, "Events: US Embassy Damascus Summary of Events February to April 2010," Unclassified report; and "Highlights: US Embassy Damascus Public Affairs Section Highlights," March 2010.
10. For further details see http://exchanges.state.gov/us/search/solr/sports/.
11. Michelle Kwan, interview in Washington DC, September 21, 2011, Public Diplomacy Council website, accessed January 27, 2012, http://publicdiplomacycouncil.org/public-diplomacy-videos-us-missions-around-world/.
12. Ambassador John Beyrle, interview, undated (ca. October 2011), Public Diplomacy Council website, accessed January 27, 2012, http://publicdiplomacycouncil.org/public-diplomacy-videos-us-missions-around-world/.
13. Lucija Bajzer, "Ameliorating Strained Relations: U.S. Public Diplomacy in Serbia," in William A. Rugh, Ed., *The Practice of Public Diplomacy*, New York: Palgrave Macmillan, 2011, pp.8–9.

14. Walter Douglas, PAO Islamabad, transcript of a talk given at the November 3, 2011 conference sponsored by the Public Diplomacy Council and George Washington University, http://publicdiplomacycouncil.org/keynoter-panelist-information-and-transcripts.
15. "Events: US Embassy Damascus Summary of Events February to April 2010," Embassy of the United States Damascus, Syria. Unclassified report; and "Highlights: US Embassy Damascus Public Affairs Section Highlights," Embassy of the United States Damascus Syria. March 2010. Unclassified report.
16. Geoffrey Cowan and Amelia Arsenault, "Moving from Monologue to Dialogue to Collaboration: Three Layers of Public Diplomacy," in *The Annals*, March 2008, p.15.
17. John Kerry, Secretary of State, "Remarks at Fulbright Teaching Assistant Event," Kuala Lumpur, Malaysia, October 11, 2013, http://www.state.gov/secretary/remarks/2013/10/215323.htm/.
18. Erin Hart, "The New Exchanges: Challenges and Opportunity for U.S. Public Diplomacy in the Middle East," April 23, 2008, Public Diplomacy Council website, http://publicdiplomacycouncil.org/tufts-papers, pp. 53–54.
19. Senator Richard Lugar, "U.S. Public Diplomacy—Time to Get Back in the Game," Report to members of the Committee on Foreign relations, United States Senate, February 13, 2009, USGPO, p.2.
20. Falguieres, p.31.
21. http://beijing.usembassy-hina.org.cn/taachers_resources.html, cited in Ivan Willis Rasmussen, "Re-Envisioning US Public Diplomacy: An Analysis of the Challenges to US Public Diplomacy Efforts in China (PRC)," term paper, Fletcher School of Law and Diplomacy, April 30, 2008, public diplomacy seminar, spring 2008, unpublished, pp.31–32, quoted by permission.
22. There were 24 in East Asia, 20 in South and Central Asia, 19 in Europe, 8 each in the Near East/South Asia area and the Western Hemisphere, and 7 in Africa. http://www.elfellowprogram.org/elf/projects13-14.html.
23. In 2009 there were 17 Teaching Fellows in Africa, 28 in East Asia, 33 in Europe, 21 in the Middle East, 13 in South Central Asia and 24 in Latin America; United States Senate, Committee on Foreign Relations, "U.S. Public Diplomacy —Time to Get Back in the Game," A Report to Members, February 13, 2009, Washington DC, pp.12, 32–34, and 40–43.
24. US Department of State, English Language Programs and Resources, http://bangkok.usembassy.gov/education/english-language-program.html. See also Ontira Amatavivat, "U.S. Public Diplomacy in Thailand," term paper, December 5, 2011, Fletcher School, Tufts University, public diplomacy course, unpublished, quoted by permission, pp.22–23.
25. http://exchanges.state.gov/non-us/program/english-access-microscholarship-program#sthash.3rji01rw.dpuf.
26. Brianna Dieter, "Public Diplomacy in India," term paper, December 5, 2011, Fletcher School public diplomacy course, unpublished, quoted by permission, quoting her phone interview with Adnan Siddiqui. Counselor for Cultural Affairs, DoS, New Delhi 2004–2008, on 24 October 2011, quoted by permission.

## Notes 253

27. US Department of State, Bureau of Educational and Cultural Affairs, *Executive summary: evaluation of the English Access Microscholarship Program* (accessed January 31, 2007 available from http://exchanges.state.gov/education/evaluations/execsummaries/Access.pdf (quoted from Hart, Erin, "The New Exchanges: Challenges and Opportunity for U.S. Public Diplomacy in the Middle East," April 23, 2008, Public Diplomacy Council website, http://publicdiplomacycouncil.org/tufts-papers).
28. http://americanenglish.state.gov; https://www.facebook.com/Access ProgramHQ; https://www.facebook.com/media/set/?set=a.534187213282086.1 27541.178121162222028&type=1.
29. Cincotta, p.145.
30. Hans N. Tuch, *Communicating with the World*, Washington, DC: Institute for the Study of Diplomacy, 1990, p.70.
31. Lugar, pp.31, 38–39; and Howard Cincotta, "Wireless File to Web," in *Engaging the Arab and Islamic Worlds through Public Diplomacy*, William A. Rugh, Ed., Washington, DC: Public Diplomacy Council, p.145.
32. US House of Representatives Appropriations Committee, "Changing Minds, Winning Peace: A New Strategic Direction for the U.S. Public Diplomacy in the Arab World," Report submitted by the Advisory Commission on Public Diplomacy for the Muslim World, Edward P. Djerejian, Chair, Washington DC, October 2003, p.37.
33. Bruce Wharton, Deputy Assistant Secretary of State for Africa, transcript of a talk given at the November 3, 2011 conference sponsored by the Public Diplomacy Council and George Washington University, http://publicdiplomacycouncil.org/keynoter-panelist-information-and-transcripts/.
34. Wilson Dizard, *Inventing Public Diplomacy: The Story of the U.S. Information Agency*, Boulder CO: Lynne Rienner, 2004,73–74; and Crane, Elise, "Finding the Right Media Formula—from the Soviet Union to Russia," in William A. Rugh, Ed., *The Practice of Public Diplomacy*, New York: Palgrave Macmillan, 2011.
35. Bea Camp, Consul General in Shanghai 2008–2011, transcript of transcript of a talk given at the November 3, 2011 conference sponsored by the Public Diplomacy Council and George Washington University, posted on Council website, http: //public diplomacycouncil.org/.
36. http://vladivostok.usconsulate.gov/am_eyes.html; plus information from a field officer, October 2013.

## 9 Centers, Libraries, and Other "American Spaces"

1. Hans N. Tuch, *Communicating with the World*, Washington, DC: Institute for the Study of Diplomacy, 1990, pp.65–67.
2. http://www.latinsuccess.org/LocateBNC?id=88.
3. Such institutions are located in Freiburg, Hamburg, Munich, Stuttgart, Nuremberg, Saarbrueken, Tuebingen and Heidelberg. US embassy in Germany website, http://german,germany.usembassy.gov/germany-ger/dais.html.

4. Matthias Kaufmann, "U.S. Public Diplomacy in Germany: Challenges and Opportunities," term paper, December 6, 2011, Fletcher School, Tufts University, public diplomacy course, unpublished, pp.26–28, cited by permission.
5. Senator Richard Lugar, "U.S. Public Diplomacy—Time to Get Back in the Game," Report to members of the Committee on Foreign relations, US Senate, February 13, 2009, USGPO, p.5
6. Lugar, pp. 7, 15 and 17; and http://burma.usembassy.gov/the_american_center.html).
7. "New US Embassy in Berlin triggers architecture debate," 05/11/2008, http://www.dw-world.de/dw/article/0,,3325836,00.html, and "Verdict on the new US Embassy in Berlin," 05/28/2008, http://entertainment.timesonline.co.uk/tol/arts_and_entertainment/visual_arts/architecture_and_design/article4016465.ece.
8. US Government Foreign Affairs Manuel, 12 FAM 311 and 315.
9. Lugar, pp.14 and 19. See also: http://www.usembassy-mexico.gov/bbf/bibliotecs=a.htm/.
10. Lugar, pp.14 and 19; also George Packer, "Drowning: Can the Burmese People Rescue Themselves?" *The New Yorker,* August 25, 2008, http://newyorker.com/reporting/2008/08/25/080825fa_fact_packer, http://www.newyorker.com/reporting/2008/08/25/080825falfactlpacker/.
11. Yohei Ogawa, "Economic Issues and Anti-Americanism in Japan," in William A. Rugh, Ed., *The Practice of Public Diplomacy,* New York: Palgrave Macmillan, 2011, p.129. Also see: http://tokyo.usembassy.gov/e/irc/irc-kisokoza.html.
12. Lugar, pp.6–8.
13. Lugar, p.24.
14. http://www.alc.edu.jo/web.
15. Lugar, pp.19–20, also see http://domincoamericano.edu.do/english/index.asp,
16. Lugar, pp.12, 23–38.
17. John Brown, "Arts Diplomacy: The Neglected Aspect of Cultural Diplomacy," in William P. Kiehl, Ed., *America's Dialogue with the World,* Washington, DC: Public Diplomacy Council, 2006, p.83. John Brown was previously Cultural Attache in Russia.
18. Edwin Eichler, "U.S. Public Diplomacy in Hungary, Past and Present," April 25, 2008, Public Diplomacy Council website, http://publicdiplomacycouncil.org/tufts-papers, pp.47–48, and http://hungary.usembassy.gov/american_corners2.html/.
19. The Corners are located in the main libraries of Prince of Songkla University (Pattani campus), Khon Kaen University, Chiang Mai University, Nakhon Si Thammarat Rajabhat University, and Yala Rajabhat University, Office of Inspector Report, US Department of State and the Broadcasting Board of Governor, *Report of Inspection: Inspection of Embassy Bangkok and Consulate General Chiang Mai, Thailand.*
20. Lucija Bajzer, "Ameliorating Strained Relations: U.S. Public Diplomacy in Serbia," in William A. Rugh, Ed., *The Practice of Public Diplomacy,* New York: Palgrave Macmillan, 2011, p.13.

21. Tulani N. Elisa, "Sierra Leone: Public Diplomacy Unwired," in Rugh, pp.100 and 102.
22. Aleksey Dolinskiy, "British and U.S. Public Diplomacy in Russia," Spring 2008, Public Diplomacy Council website, http://publicdiplomacycouncil.org/tufts-papers, who cites http:/Moscow.usembassy.gov/us/us.php?record_id=irc), accessibility from SFRC report p.6.
23. Eichler, pp.47–48.
24. Ogawa, pp.129–30, who cites http://tokyo.usembassy.gov/e/irc-kisokoza.html.
25. Sarah Schaffer, "U.S. Public Diplomacy in Chile: A Study of Instruments, Programs and Effectiveness," term paper, Fletcher School of Law and Diplomacy, December 6, 2010, public diplomacy seminar, fall 2010, unpublished, pp.12–13, 16–17 and 32–35.
26. American Academy of Diplomacy and Stimpson Center, "A Foreign Affairs Budget for the Future: Fixing the Crisis in Diplomatic Readiness," Washington DC, October 2008, pp.14 and 16.
27. Lugar, pp. 6, 12, 19 and 23.
28. Lugar, pp.3 and 11.
29. Lugar, pp.vi, 2, 7, and 15.
30. Bud Jacobs, US State Department official, interview by the author, May 11, 2011.
31. Tara Sonenshine, Undersecretary of State, "Bottom Line Diplomacy: Why Public Diplomacy Matters," remarks at the Center for Strategic and International Studies, Washington DC, June 18, 2013, http://www.state.gov/r/remarks/2013/210771.htm.
32. Tara Sonenshine, "From Card Catalogues to 21st Century Community Centers: new Dynamics for the American Space," remarks at the John F. Kennedy School of Government, Harvard University, February 27, 2013, http://www.state.gov/r/remarks/2013/205338.htm.
33. US Department of State and Broadcasting Board of Governors, Office of Inspector General, "Inspection of the Bureau of International Information Programs," report ISP-I-13–28, May 2013, pp.1 and 17.
34. Michael H. Anderson, former PAO in Indonesia, transcript of transcript of a talk given at the November 3, 2011 conference sponsored by the Public Diplomacy Council and George Washington University, http://publicdiplomacycouncil.org/keynoter-panelist-information-and-transcripts.
35. Michael Anderson, former PAO in Indonesia, email to the author, February 13, 2013.
36. Ibid.
37. Ibid. Also, Anderson, transcript November 3, 2011.
38. Atu Yudhistru Indarto, "U.S. Public Diplomacy in Indonesia post 9/11: A Case of Concerted Muslims Outreach," term paper, December 5, 2011, Fletcher School, Tufts University, public diplomacy course, unpublished, quoted by permission, p.41, citing email and phone interview with former US Foreign Service Officer, October 18, 2011 and November 24, 2011.

39.. Office of Inspector General, *Inspection of Embassy Jakarta, Indonesia and Constituent Posts*, March 2011, pp.27–28.
40. Michael H. Anderson, "Engaging Audiences—The Story of @America, The First Really Different U.S. Cultural Center in Ages" (presented at the Conference on "The Last Three Feet: New Media, New Approaches and New Challenges for American Public Diplomacy," George Washington University, Washington DC, November 3, 2011), p.9.
41. American Academy of Diplomacy and Stimson Center, "A Foreign Affairs Budget for the Future: Fixing the Crisis in Diplomatic Readiness," Washington DC, October 2008, pp.14 and 16.
42. Anderson, February 13, 2013, email to the author, cited, and interview, September 26, 2013, by the author with an American familiar with @America.

## 10  Educational Exchanges

1. In addition to Fulbright grants, study abroad for Americans is also made possible by the Kennedy-Lugar Youth Exchange and Study program that sends American high school students abroad for one year to countries with significant Muslim populations, where they attend high school and live with host families.
2. Ontira Amatavivat, "U.S. Public Diplomacy in Thailand," term paper, December 5, 2011, Fletcher School, Tufts University, public diplomacy course, unpublished, quoted by permission, pp.19–20.
3. Rachel E. Smith, "Afghanistan and Pakistan: Public Diplomacy during Instability," in William A. Rugh, Ed., *The Practice of Public Diplomacy*, New York: Palgrave Macmillan, 2011, p.65.
4. Information on the IVLP is at http://exchanges.state.gov/ivlp/ivlp.html.
5. Yohei Ogawa, "Economic Issues and Anti-Americanism in Japan," in William A. Rugh, Ed., *The Practice of Public Diplomacy*, New York: Palgrave Macmillan, 2011, p.131.
6. Elsa Vigoureux, "Quand La Diversité Françaises' Exporte Aux Etats-Unis," *Nouvel Observateur*, September 17, 2011, http://tempsreel.nouvelobs.com/societe/20110915.OBS0455/quand-la-diversite-francaise-s-exporte-aux-etats-unis.html. Emilie Falguieres, "Public Diplomacy towards France: Engaging Diversity," term paper, December 5, 2011, Fletcher School public diplomacy course, unpublished, p.30, cited by permission.
7. Rafik Mansour, Cultural Affairs Officer, US Embassy Paris, interview September 30, 11, in Paris, Public Diplomacy Council website, accessed January 27, 2012, http://publicdiplomacycouncil.org/public-diplomacy-videos-us-missions-around-world/.
8. http://americancouncils.spb.ru/main.phb?p=prog_flex&m_n=2/.
9. Ilya Lozovsky, "U.S. Public Diplomacy in Russia: Success of the Past, Hope for the Future," December 6, 2010, term paper, Fletcher School, Tufts University, public diplomacy seminar, unpublished, p.39, quoted by permission.

# Notes

10. Aleksey Dolinskiy, "British and U.S. Public Diplomacy in Russia," Spring 2008, Public Diplomacy Council website, http://publicdiplomacycouncil.org/tufts-papers.
11. Erin Hart, "The New Exchanges: Challenges and Opportunity for U.S. Public Diplomacy in the Middle East," April 23, 2008, Public Diplomacy Council website, http://publicdiplomacycouncil.org/tufts-papers. See also US Department of State, Bureau of Educational and Cultural Affairs, *Request for Grant Proposals*, http://www.exchanges.state.gov/education/rfgps/febu15rfgp.htm. This lists 15 Arab countries as targets.
12. Hart.
13. US Department of State, Bureau of Educational and Cultural Affairs, *Youth Exchange and Study Program* (accessed February 4, 2008); http://exchanges.state.gov/education/citizens/students/programs/yes.htm.
14. Hart. Also Center for International Education and Development, Georgetown University, *Near East and South Asia Undergraduate Exchange Program* (accessed April 5, 2008, http://www8.georgetown.edu/centers/cied/nesa/.
15. The Bi-national Fulbright Commission in Egypt, *Community College Initiative* (accessed April 2, 2008); available from http://www.fulbright-egypt-cci.org/default_e.asp; and Francis J. Ricciardone, "The Solid Impact of Soft Power: U.S. Educational Engagement with Egypt," speech February 22, 2008, http://egypt.usembassy.gov/ambassador/tr022108.html.
16. www.salzburgglobal.org.
17. In 2003 the program was open to citizens of Bangladesh, Brazil, Egypt, Ghana, India, Indonesia, Kenya, Lebanon, Malaysia, Morocco, Philippines, Senegal, and Uganda.
18. irex@irex.org.
19. http://exchanges.state.gov/non-us/find-programs. irex@irex.org.
20. US Department of State, Advisory Committee on Cultural Diplomacy, "Cultural Diplomacy: The Linchpin of Public Diplomacy," Washington DC, 2005, p.10.
21. Barry Ballow, "Academic and Profesional Exchanges in the Islamic World: An Undervalued Tool," in William A. Rugh, Ed., *Engaging the Arab and Islamic Worlds through Public Diplomacy*, Washington, DC: Public Diplomacy Council, 2004, p.113.
22. Giles Scott-Smith, "Mapping the Undefinable; Some Thoughts on the Relevance of Exchange Programs with International Relations Theory," *The Annals of American Political and Social Science*, 616, 2008, p.174.
23. Karen Hughes, Undersecretary of State, comments to the author, 2007.
24. Tara Sonenshine, Undersecretary of State, "Bottom Line Diplomacy," remarks at the Center for Strategic and International Studies, Washington DC, June 18, 2013, http://www.state.gov/r/remarks/2013/210771.htm/.
25. John Kerry, Secretary of State, "Remarks and the Fulbright Enrichment Seminar," made at the George C. Marshall Center, Washington DC, March 15, 2013, http://www.state.gov/secretary/remarks/2013/03/206335.htm; and John Kerry, "Remarks at Fulbright English teaching Event," Kuala Lampur, Malaysia, October 11, 2013, http://www.state.gov/secretary/remarks/2013/10/215323.htm/.

26. Jennifer Mock, "Impact and Evaluation of the International Visitor Leadership Program," Tufts Papers, Public Diplomacy Council website, www.publicdiplomacycouncil.org/tufts-papers/.
27. William A. Rugh, *American Encounters with Arabs: The Soft Power of U.S. Public Diplomacy in the Middle East,* Westport CT: Praeger, 2006, p.18.
28. David von Drehle, "A Lesson in Hate," *Smithsonian Magazine,* February 2006.
29. Jennifer Mock, "Impact and Evaluation of the International Visitor Leadership Program," Tufts Papers, Public Diplomacy Council website, www.publicdiplomacycouncil.org/tufts-papers/.
30. Lozovsky, p.48.
31. Matthias Kaufmann, "U.S. Public Diplomacy in Germany: Challenges and Opportunities," term paper, December 6, 2011, Fletcher School, Tufts University, public diplomacy course, unpublished, quoted by permission, pp. 16–17.
32. US Embassy in New Delhi website. http://newdelhi.usembassy.gov. Accessed October 20, 2011.
33. Dolinskiy, pp. 34–36 and 41.
34. Smith, p.63.
35. Lucija Bajzer, "Ameliorating Strained Relations: U.S. Public Diplomacy in Serbia," in William A. Rugh, Ed., *The Practice of Public Diplomacy,* New York: Palgrave Macmillan, 2011, pp.13–14.
36. Sarah Riley, "Iran and the United Kingdom: A Study in Contrasts," in William A. Rugh, Ed., *The Practice of Public Diplomacy,* New York: Palgrave Macmillan, 2011, p.43.
37. US Department of State, Office of Inspector General, US Department of State and the Broadcasting Board of Governors. Report of Inspection, Embassy Damascus Syria, Report Number ISP-I-10–34A. March 2010.
38. Ivan Willis Rasmussen, "Re-Envisioning US Public Diplomacy: An Analysis of the Challenges to US Public Diplomacy Efforts in China (PRC)," term paper, Fletcher School of Law and Diplomacy, April 30, 2008, public diplomacy seminar, spring 2008, unpublished, pp.26–27, quoted by permission.
39. Falguieres, pp.31–35.
40. Brianna Dieter, "Public Diplomacy in India," term paper, December 5, 2011, Fletcher School, Tufts University, public diplomacy course, unpublished, quoted by permission, p. 19).
41. Ogawa.
42. US Department of State, Office of the Inspector General, "Inspection of Embassy New Delhi, India and Constituents Posts, Report Number ISP-I-11–39A, June 2011," US Department of State and the Broadcasting Board of Generals, June 2011. Also see Dieter, pp.19–20.
43. Ricciardone.
44. Author's personal information.
45. Gabriel Kaypaghian, PAO, US Embassy Mexico City, interview, Washington DC October 13, 2011, Public Diplomacy Council website, accessed January 27, 2012, http://publicdiplomacycouncil.org/public-diplomacy-videos-us-missions-around-world/.

46. For example, see Business for Diplomatic Action, "America's Role in the World: A Business Perspective on Public Diplomacy," New York, October 2007.
47. Nicholas Cull, *The Cold War and the United States Information Agency*, Cambridge: Cambridge University Press, 2008, p.56.
48. Paragraphs 1437 and 1462 of the Smith-Mundt Act, title 22, chapter 18, as amended, in http://www4.law.cornell.edu/uscode/22/usc_sec_22_00001461/.
49. In January 2014, NCIV changed its name to "Global Ties."
50. Mock.
51. John Waterbury, "Hate Your Politics, Love Your Institutions," *Foreign Affairs*, vol.82, no.1, January/February 2003.
52. Sonenshine, "Bottom Line Diplomacy," cited.
53. http://www.educationusa.state.gov/.
54. Information from a currently serving PD officer. For example, the embassy in Riyadh had a Facebook page that had 4,300 followers as of October 2013 and informed the public about webinars and directed their attention to information on the EDUSA website. See https://www.facebook.com/EducationUSASaudiArabia/.
55. Michael Anderson, PAO Jakarta, interview with the author, December 3, 2011.
56. Mabel Ntiru, "Kenya's 'Native Son' and Enduring Local Issues," in William A. Rugh, Ed., *The Practice of Public Diplomacy*, New York: Palgrave Macmillan, 2011, p.85.
57. Haynes Mahoney, PAO, US Embassy Cairo, interview, Washington DC, July 7, 2011, Public Diplomacy Council website, accessed January 27, 2012, http://publicdiplomacycouncil.org/public-diplomacy-videos-us-missions-around-world/.
58. Walter Douglas, PAO Islamabad, transcript of a talk given at the November 3, 2011 conference sponsored by the Public Diplomacy Council and George Washington University, http://publicdiplomacycouncil.org/keynoter-panelist-information-and-transcripts.
59. Mock.
60. http://alumni.state.gov/.

## 11 Defense Department Communications: Changing Role

1. Trent Christman, *Brass Button Broadcasters*, Padukah, KY: Turner Publishing Company, 1992, pp. 8, 105, 136, 205–7.
2. US Department of Defense, "Information Operations Roadmap," October 30, 2003, unclassified (originally Secret/Noforn), p.26.
3. Rachel Greenspan, "Public Diplomacy in Uniform: The Role of the U.S. Department of Defense in Supporting Modern Day Public Diplomacy," *American Diplomacy*, March 2011, http://www.unc.edu/depts/diplomat/item/2011/0104/comm/greenspan_pduniform.html, quoting her interview November 12, 2010 with Col. Carl Ayers, former chief of PSYOP.
4. Robert J. Callahan, "A View from the Embassy," *American Journalism Review*, April/May 2006, http://ajrarchive.org/Article.asp?id=4071/.

5. US Department of Defense, Joint Chiefs of Staff, "Information Operations," Joint Publication 3–13, February 13, 2006. : www.fas.org/irp/doddir/dod/jp3_13.pdf. I-1, I-1, II-1 and 2.
6. Carnes Lord, *Losing Hearts and Minds? Public Diplomacy and Strategic Influence in the Age of Terror*, Westport CT: Praeger, 2006, p.31, and Carnes Lord, "Propaganda and Psychological Operations (Cold War)," unpublished paper, citing Col. Benjamin F. Findley, Jr., USAFR, "US and Vietcong Psychological Operations in Vietnam"; See Col. Dennis P. Walko, USA, "Psychological Operations in Panama during Operations Just Cause and Promote Liberty," and Col. Frank L. Goldstein, USAF, and Col. Daniel W. Jacobowitz, USAF (ret.), "PSYOP in Desert Shield/Desert Storm," in Goldstein and Findley, pp. 249–77, 341–56.
7. Other categories of Information Operations besides PSYOP are Military Deception, which are actions intended to deceive an enemy and Operations Security, or the protection of classified information. These also are very different from public diplomacy.
8. Greenspan, quoting her interview with Col. Carl Ayers.
9. Greenspan, quoting her interview with PD senior official Mark Davidson, October 22, 2010.
10. US Department of the Army, "Counterinsurgency," FM-3-24, MCWP 3–33.5, December 2006, LTG David F. Petraeus and LTG James F. Amos, pp.1–3, 5–8 and 7.2, http://www.fas.org/irp/doddir/army/fm3-24.pdf.
11. US Department of the Army, "Psychological Operations," FM 3–05.30, MRCP 3–40.6, April 2005, Appendix A.
12. Robert W. McCormick Tribune Foundation, *The Military and the Media: Facing the Future*, Chicago: Robert W. McCormick Tribune Foundation, 1998, p.138.
13. Philip M. Taylor, *Munitions of the Mind,* New York: Manchester University Press, 1995, 142.
14. Comment by retired senior US diplomat, email, June 2013.
15. US Department of Defense, "Information Operations Roadmap," October 30, 2003, unclassified (originally Secret/Noforn), p.25.
16. Ibid., p.25.
17. Ibid., p.26.
18. Ibid., p.26.
19. Ibid., pp.27–28 and 71.
20. US Department of State and US Department of Defense, *Foreign Military Training, FY 2009–2010: Joint Report to Congress*, volume I, pp.II-2, http://state.gov/documents/organization/155982.pdf, accessed 4–5–2011.
21. Nick Turse, *The Complex: How the Military Invades Our Every Day Lives*, New York: Henry Holt, 2008, p.50.
22. US DOD, Joint Chiefs of Staff. "Information Operations." Joint Publication 3–13, 2006.
23. Nicholas J. Cull, *The Cold War and the United States Information Agency, 1945–1989*, Cambridge: Cambridge University Press, 2008, pp.219–20, 245–52, 310–11.
24. US Department of the Army, "Counterinsurgency," December 2006, p.2.

25. Greenspan.
26. US DOD, Joint Chiefs of Staff. "Information Operations." Joint Publication 3–13, 2006, cited, II-8.
27. US Department of the Army, "Psychological Operations," April 2005, pp. 1–6; and US DOD, "Information Operations Roadmap," October 30, 2003, p.26.
28. Private information from State Department officials.
29. For details see William A. Rugh, "How Washington Confronts Arab Media," *Global Media Journal*, vol.3, issue 5, Fall 2004.
30. Ibid.
31. Philip Seib, "Hegemonic No More: Western Media, the Rise of al Jazeera and the Influence of Diverse Voices," *International Studies Review* (2007), vol. 7, p. 607, citing Middle East Media Research Institute 2003, 1 and 2. The term "strategic communications" was used by many in the Pentagon for a few years, but was officially dropped in 2012.
32. Seib, p. 606, citing Hussein Amin, "Watching the War" in the Arab World, *Transnational Broadcasting Studies Journal* (Spring–Summer). Available at www.tbsjournal.com/amin.
33. Rugh, "How Washington Confronts Arab Media."
34. US Department of Defense, Field Manual 3–13 "Information Operations," 3–13, 11–28–03, Chapter 2.
35. Frank B. DeCarvalho, Spring Kivett and Matthew Lindsey, "Reaching Out: Partnering with Iraqi Media," *Military Review*, July–August 2008, pp.87–94.
36. Ambassador Richard Schmierer, Minister-Counselor for Public Affairs at US Embassy Baghdad from 2004–2005, interview quoted in Sean Duggan, "Reclaiming U.S. Public Diplomacy from the U.S. Military in Iraq," *Middle East Journal*, vol. 66, no.1, Winter 2012.
37. Ibid.
38. Justin Fox, "Secret No More: Inside the Pentagon's Iraqi PR Firm," *Fortune*, February 23, 2006, http://www.govexec.com/story_page.cfm?articleid=32892, "What Lincoln Group," *Government Executive*, December 1, 2005 [quoted by Cary p.12 -CK].
39. Turse, p. 197.
40. Michael Schrage, "Use Every Article in the Arsenal: Good Press Is a Legitimate Weapon," *Washington Post*, January 15, 2006, p.B3, quoting Christian Bailey, a Lincoln Group founder.
41. Mark Mazetti and Borzou Daraghahi, "U.S. Military Covertly Pays to Run Stories in Iraqi Press," *Los Angeles Times*, November 30, 2005; Griff Witte, "Lincoln Group Out of Military PR Contract," *Washington Post*, July 19, 2006.
42. Lt. Col. Barry Johnson, commander of the Coalition Press Information Center, quoted in Schrage, p.B3; this article also quoted Christian Bailey, a Lincoln Group official, defending the policy.
43. Johnson.
44. Embassy of the United States of America-Kabul, ISAF, and US Forces Afghanistan, "Integrated Civilian-Military Afghanistan Communication Plan," 7 and 12

45. Mohammad Osman Tariq, Najla Ayoubi, and Fazel Rabi Haqbeen, *Afghanistan in 2010: A Survey of the Afghan People*, The Asia Foundation, 2010, 147.
46. Embassy of the United States of America–Kabul, 7.
47. Ibid.
48. Anonymous reliable source, December 6, 2010.
49. *Foreign Affairs* January/February 2012, p.185.
50. Rachel E. Smith, "Afghanistan and Pakistan: Public Diplomacy during Instability," chapter 4 in William A. Rugh, Ed., *The Practice of Public Diplomacy*, New York: Palgrave Macmillan, 2011, pp.63 and 66.
51. Lussenhop, Matt, PAO in Afghanistan, 2010–2011, interview Washington DC, October 13, 2011, Public Diplomacy Council website, accessed January 27, 2012, http://publicdiplomacycouncil.org/public-diplomacy-videos-us-missions-around-world.
52. http://kabul.usembassy.gov/lincoln_center.html.
53. "Lincoln Learning Centers (LLCs)—U.S. Embassy Kabul, Afghanistan," US Embassy–Kabul, Afghanistan, http://kabul.usembassy.gov/llc_kabul.html.
54. US Department of State and the Broadcasting Board of Governors Office of Inspector General, "Report of Inspection: Embassy Kabul, Afghanistan." February 2010, 52.
55. This paragraph and the next two were based on information from a public diplomacy professional who served in Afghanistan, email June 2013. http://kabul.usembassy.gov/english_language.html; http://afghanistan.usaid.gov/en/index.aspx.
56. For additional details on State's programs in Afghanistan, see: http://kabul.usembassy.gov/;http://kabul.usembassy.gov/english_language.html; http://afghanistan.usaid.gov/en/index.aspx; http://www.youtube.com/user/usembassykabul1; http://www.gmic.gov.af/english/about/gmic; https://twitter.com/GMIC; https://www.facebook.com/gmicafghanistan.
57. McCormick Tribune Foundation, p.61.
58. Helen Thomas, *Watchdogs of Democracy?*, New York: Scribner, 2006, p.82.
59. McCormick Tribune Foundation, p.46.
60. Seib, p. 603.
61. Bill Cavness, telephone interview, November 3, 2010, quoted in Duggan.
62. US Department of State and the Broadcasting Board of Governors Office of Inspector General, "Report of Inspection: Embassy Kabul, Afghanistan." February 2010, 46, 52.
63. White, p.46.
64. US Department of the Army, "Counterinsurgency," December 2006, and State Department Office of the Inspector General, "Report of Inspection Embassy Baghdad, Iraq," July 2009, available at: http://oig.state.gov/documents/organization/126600.pdf. Accessed November 15, 2010.
65. US Embassy Baghdad, "2008 Press Release: Provincial Reconstruction Teams (PRT) Fact Sheet," March 20, 2008, available at: http://iraq.usembassy.gov/pr_01222008b.html.

66. Anonymous reliable source, December 6, 2010.
67. Anonymous reliable source, December 6, 2010.
68. "Report of Inspection: Embassy Kabul, Afghanistan," 46.
69. Lussenhop interview.
70. Colonel Stephen P. Perkins, "Strategic Communications: An Expanded IO Role?" Joint Information Operations Center: IOSphere, Winter 2006, p.5 www.carlisle.army.mil/DIME/.../iosphere_win06_perkins.pdf.
71. US Department of Defense, Office of the Undersecretary of Defense for Acquisition, Technology and Logistics, "Report of the Defense Science Board Task Force on Strategic Communication," September 2004, Appendix A, Paul Wolfowitz letter to the Defense Science Board, May 24, 2004. The DSB is a Federal Advisory Committee established to provide independent advice to the Secretary of Defense.
72. US Department of Defense, "Information Operations Roadmap," August 14, 2006, Secret/Noforn, declassified on May 9, 2008 under the Freedom of Information Act, pp. 25–26 http://www.gwu.edu/~nsarchiv/NSAEBB/NSAEBB177/info_ops_roadmap.pdf.
73. Retired senior public diplomacy officer, email to the author, June 2013.
74. Peter Cary, "The Pentagon, Information Operations and International Media Development," Washington, DC: Center for International media Assistance and National Endowment for Democracy October 19, 2010, p.30.
75. Department of State, USAID, BBG, "Interagency Strategic Communication Network Report," March 26, 2010.
76. Interview with the US official in Yemen, interview with the author, November 22, 2011.
77. Ibid.
78. Lussenhop interview. The Philippines has 94 million people, who speak many languages and Tagalog is only spoken by 22 percent; 10 percent of the population is Muslim.
79. Peter Cary, "The Pentagon, Information Operations and International Media Development," Washington, DC: Center for International media Assistance and National Endowment for Democracy October 19, 2010, pp.31–32.
80. Carey, p.65.
81. Personal communication from a US official, March 7, 2006.
82. Walter Pincus in the *Washington Post*, May 9, 2013, p.A-15.

## 12 Defense Department Communications Abroad Compared with Public Diplomacy

1. Frank B. DeCarvalho, Spring Kivett, and Matthew Lindsey, "Reaching Out: Partnering with Iraqi Media," *Military Review*, July–August 2008.
2. Rachel E. Smith, "Afghanistan and Pakistan: Public Diplomacy during Instability," Chapter 4 in William A. Rugh, Ed., *The Practice of Public Diplomacy*, New York:

Palgrave Macmillan, 2011, pp.56 and 57 citing *New York Times*, August 15, 2009, and *Washington Post*, September 29, 2009.
3. General David Petraeus, Lt. General James Amos, and Lt. Colonel John Nagl, "U.S. Army and Marine Corps Counterinsurgency Field Manual," *U.S. Army Field Manual* No. 3–24 (Chicago and London: University of Chicago Press, 2007), 160, 152.
4. Brian E. Carlson, "Who Tells America's Story Abroad? State's Public Diplomacy or DOD's Strategic Communication?" in Shoon Murray and Gordon Adams, Eds., *Mission Creep*, Washington, DC: Georgetown University Press, 2014.
5. US Department of Defense, "Information Operations Roadmap," August 14, 2006, Secret/Noforn, declassified on May 9, 2008 under the Freedom of Information Act, pp-25–26 http://www.gwu.edu/~nsarchiv/NSAEBB/NSAEBB177/info_ops_roadmap.pdf/.
6. Alvin Snyder, "Iraq War's Arabic Youtube," blog June 26, 2007, quoting from Daniel Kimmage and Kathleen Ridolfo, "Iraq Insurgent Media: the War of Images and Ideas," RFE/RL, June 2007.
7. Rachel Greenspan, "Public Diplomacy in Uniform: The Role of the U.S. Department of Defense in Supporting Modern Day Public Diplomacy," *American Diplomacy*, March 2011, http://www.unc.edu/depts/diplomat/item/2011/0104/comm/greensapn_pduniform.html, quoting her interview November 12, 2010 with Col. Carl Ayers, former chief of PSYOP.
8. General David Petraeus and General James Mattis, "Army Field Manual 3:24: Counterinsurgency Operations," available at: http://www.fas.org/irp/doddir/army/fm3-24fd.pdf, Section 2–8.
9. Ambassador Richard Schmierer, Minister-Counselor for Public Affairs at US Embassy Baghdad from 2004–2005, personal email November 25, 2010 quoted in Sean E. Duggan, "Redefining the Relationship: Reclaimng American Public Diplomacy from the Military in Iraq," *Middle East Journal*, 2012.
10. State Department Special Inspector General, "Report of Inspection: Compliance Follow-up Review of U.S. Embassy Baghdad," October 2010, available at: http://oig.state.gov/documents/organization/150507.pdf.
11. Bill Cavness, telephone interview November 3, 2010, cited in Sean E. Duggan, "Redefining the Relationship: Reclaiming American Public Diplomacy from the Military in Iraq," *Middle East Journal*, 2012.
12. US Department of Defense, Joint Chiefs of Staff, "Information Operations," Joint Publication 3–13, February 13, 2006, p.I-6, http://www.fas.org/irp/doddir/dod/jp3_13.pdf.
13. US Department of Defense, "Quadrennial Defense Review Report," February 2010, http://www.defense.gov/qdr/images/QDR_as_of_12Feb10_1000.pdf, pp. 7, 25–26 and 57.
14. Petraeus and Mattis, section 2–8.
15. Petraeus, Amos, and Nagl, p.2.
16. Ibid., pp.2–11.
17. Quoted in David Hoffmann, "Beyond Public Diplomacy," *Foreign Affairs*, March/April 2002.

18. Retired senior American diplomat, comment to the author by email, July 2013.
19. US DOD, "Information Operations Roadmap," August 14, 2006, p.25.
20. US DOD, Joint Chiefs, "Information Operations," February 13, 2006, p.3.
21. Robert M. Gates, Secretary of Defense, address delivered at Kansas State University, Manhattan, Kansas, November 26, 2007, www.defenselink.mil/speeches/speech/aspx?speechid=1199/.
22. Peter Cary, *The Pentagon Information Operations, and International Media Development*, Center for International Media Assistance: October 19, 2010. Available online at http://cima.ned.org/publications/ research-reports/pentagon-information-operations-and-media-development/.
23. Cary, pp.5–6, 9.
24. The Associated Press, "Number of U.S. Forces in Afghanistan Exceeds Total in Iraq for First Time," Published in *The Washington Post*, May 25, 2010, available at: http://www.washingtonpost.com/wp-dyn/content/article/2010/05/24/AR2010052403842.html. Accessed October 31, 2010.
25. State Department Office of the Inspector General, "Report of Inspection Embassy Baghdad, Iraq," July 2009, available at: http://oig.state.gov/documents/organization/126600.pdf. Accessed November 15, 2010; and US Embassy Baghdad website.
26. Richard Schmierer, Minister-Counselor for Public Affairs at US Embassy Baghdad from 2004–2005. Personal email quoted in Duggan.
27. State Department Special Inspector General, "Report of Inspection: Compliance Follow-up Review of U.S. Embassy Baghdad," October 2010, available at: http://oig.state.gov/documents/organization/150507.pdf. Accessed November 15, 2010.
28. US Department of State and the Broadcasting Board of Governors Office of Inspector General, Report of Inspection: Embassy Kabul, Afghanistan. February, 2010, 49.
29. David Ignatius, "Caution Lights for the Military's 'Information War'," *Washington Post*, March 24, 2010
30. DOD, Department of the Army, "Counterinsurgency," December 2006.
31. Ibid.
32. Ibid., Appendix B.
33. US Department of Defense, Office of the Undersecretary of Defense for Acquisition, Technology and Logistics, "Report of the Defense Science Board Task Force on Strategic Communication," September 2004, pp.2–3.
34. US Department of Defense, "Report of the Defense Science Board Task Force on Strategic Communication," January 2008, pp. ix–xxi.
35. US Secretary of Defense, "Report on Strategic Communication," December 2009. Transmitted to the House Committee on Armed Services by Secretary Gates, February 11, 2010, p.5.
36. Roberto J. Gonzalez, *American Counterinsurgency: Human Science and the Human Terrain*, Chicago: University of Chicago Press, 2009.
37. Anonymous reliable source, December 6, 2010.
38. DeCarvalho, Kivett, and Lindsey, pp.87–94.

39. Linton Wells II, "Strategic Communications and the Battle of Ideas: Winning the Hearts and Minds in the Global War Against Terrorists," Statement before the Subcommittee on Terrorism and Unconventional Threats and Capabilities, House Armed Services Committee, July 11, 2007., p.5.
40. Petraeus and Mattis, Section 1–21.
41. Wells, p.9.
42. Wells II, p.7.
43. US DOD, Defense Science Board, "Report of the Task Force on Strategic Communication," September 2004, p.38.
44. Bill Cavness, public diplomacy officer, in Iraq 2006–07, on the Iraq desk at State Department Headquarters, telephone interview November 3, 2010, quoted in Duggan.
45. Ambassador Richard Schmierer, private email quoted in Duggan.
46. Matt Lussenhop, PAO in Afghanistan 2010–12, interview with the author, April 25, 2012.
47. Richard Schmierer, interview quoted in Duggan.
48. Army Captain Christopher Ophardt, US Army Public Affairs Officer in Iraq from 2004–2005, from 2006–2007 and from 2009–2010, interview quoted in Duggan.
49. Rachel Greenspan, "Public Diplomacy in Uniform," *American Diplomacy,* March 11, 2011.
50. Lussenhop interview.
51. Anonymous source, interview quoted in Duggan.
52. Ambassador Richard Schmierer, Email November 25, 2010, quoted in Duggan.
53. Mark Mazetti and Borzou Daragahi, "U.S. Military Covertly Pays to Run Stories in Iraqi Press," *Los Angeles Times,* November 30, 2005, available at: http://www.latimes.com/news/nationworld/nation/wire/ny-la-woiraq1130,0,290135,full.story. Accessed November 25, 2010.
54. Bill Cavness, US official, interview quoted in Duggan
55. Guy Farmer, "Pentagon Gets Best Press its Money Can Buy," Nevada Appeal, December 18, 2005.
56. Michael Schrage, "Use Every Article in the Arsenal: Good Press Is a Legitimate Weapon," *Washington Post,* January 15, 2006, p.B3.
57. Bill Cavness, telephone interview November 3, 2010, quoted in Duggan.
58. Lussenhop interview, April 25, 2012.
59. Congressional Research Service, "Private Security Contractors in Iraq: Background, Legal Status and other Issues," August 2008, available at: http://www.fas.org/sgp/crs/natsec/RL32419.pdf.
60. Aaron Snipe, Deputy Spokesman, US Embassy Baghdad, 2008–09, phone interview November 2, 2010 quoted in Duggan. See also Aaron Snipe, "Walk: Front Lines to Main Street," *Wing Tips on the Ground* Blog, March 21, 2009. Accessed November 7, 2010.
61. DOD, Department of the Army, "Counterinsurgency," December 2006.
62. Lussenhop interview.

63. *Foreign Affairs* January/February 2012, p.179; previously, US soldiers had been instructed that contact with local women was culturally inappropriate.
64. Lussenhop interview.
65. Captain Jeanne Hull, "Iraq: Strategic Reconciliation, Targeting, and Key Leader Engagement," Strategic Studies Institute, September 2009, available here: http://www.strategicstudiesinstitute.army.mil/pdffiles/pub938.pdf. DOD does have a short course at the Military Information School at Ft. Meade MD.
66. Donald Rumsfeld, Secretary of Defense, "New realities of the Media Age," address delivered at the Council on Foreign Relations, New York, February 17, 2006.
67. Anonymous reliable source, December 6, 2010.
68. Information in this paragraph provided by a public diplomacy professional who served in Afghanistan, email June 2013.
69. See for example, Vanessa M. Gezari, *The Tender Soldier: A True Story of War and Sacrifice*, New York: Simon and Schuster, 2013, and *New York Times*, August 28, 2013, p.C2.
70. Robert J. Callahan, "A View from the Embassy," *American Journalism Review*, April/May 2006.
71. US Department of Defense, "Joint Information Operations Orientation Course (JIOOC)," http://www.jfsc.ndu.edu/schools_programs/jc2ios/io/jiooc.asp.
72. Information from an experienced retired senior public diplomacy officer, email, June 2013.
73. Robert Gates, Secretary of Defense, Landon Lecture, Kansas State University, November 26, 2007.
74. Rumsfeld address, February 17, 2006.
75. Thomas E. McNamara, "Rebalancing National Security Policy After Afghanistan and Iraq," *The Foreign Service Journal*, October 2013, p.35.
76. DOD, Department of the Army, "Counterinsurgency," December 2006,
77. Mark Davidson, US official, quoted in Greenspan.
78. American Academy of Diplomacy and Stimson Center, "A Foreign Affairs Budget for the Future: Fixing the Crisis in Diplomatic Readiness," Washington DC, October 2008, p.4.
79. Davidson interview.
80. J. Anthony Holmes, "Where Are the Civilians? How to Rebuild the U.S. Foreign Service," *Foreign Affairs*, vol.88, no.1, Jan/Feb 2009, pp.149–51.
81. Gates lecture, November 26, 2007.
82. Mike Mullen, US Admiral, lecture, Kansas State University, March 3, 2010. www.cfr.org/publication/21590/ admiral_mullens_speech_on_military_strategy_kansas_state_university_march_2010.html/.
83. US DOD, "Report on Strategic Communication," December 2009, p.3 http://www.au.af.mil/au/awc/awcgate/dod/dod_report_strategic_communication/.
84. US Department of Defense, "Report on Strategic Communication," December 2009, transmitted to Congress on February 11, 2010 by Secretary Robert M. Gates.

85. US DOD, "Report on Strategic Communication," December 2009.
86. Department of Defense, "Quadrennial Defense Review Report," February 2010, http://www.defense.gov/qdr/images/QDR_as_of_12Feb10_1000.pdf, pp. 7, 25–26, and 57.
87. President Barack Obama, remarks in the East Room of the White House, June 22, 2011.

## 13 Changes and Enduring Principles

1. For example, see Kristin M. Lord, "Voices of America: U.S. Public Diplomacy for the 21st Century," Washington, DC: Brookings, November 2008; Council on Foreign Relations, "Finding America's Voice: A Strategy for Reinvigorating U.S. Public Diplomacy," New York: Council on Foreign Relations, 2005; Keith Reinhard, "American Business and Its Role in Public Diplomacy," chapter 16 in Nancy Snow and Philip Taylor, Eds., *The Routledge Handbook of Public Diplomacy*, New York: Routledge, 2009, pp.195–200; Susan Epstein and Lisa Mages. *Public Diplomacy: A Review of Past Recommendations,* Congressional Reference Service, October 31, 2005. crs_publicdipl_reviewofpastrecomm_rl33062_02sep05.pdf/.
2. Leonard H. Marks, Charles Z. Wick, Bruce Gelb, and Henry E. Catto, "America Needs a Voice Abroad," *The Washington Post*, February 26, 2005, op-ed, p.A19.
3. Fred A. Coffey Jr., William A. Rugh, Stan Silverman, and William Maurer, "Making Public Diplomacy Effective: Crippled State Department Public Diplomacy Must Be Restructured," January 23, 2009, unpublished—a proposal presented to Undersecretaries for Public Diplomacy Charlotte Beers, Karen Hughes, Margaret Tutwiler, and Judith McHale, as well as Secretary Powell, and supported by former USIA director Charles Wick, but senior officials at State did not support it (author's personal information).
4. http://learningenglish.voanews.com/; http://americanenglish.state.gov/.
5. http://www.gallup.com/poll/162854/americans-oppose-military-involvement-syria.aspx; http://www.gallup.com/poll/116236/iran.aspx/.

# INDEX

(public diplomacy is abbreviated ad PD, the Department of Defense as DOD)

9/11, the 9/11/2001 terrorist attack on the US, 2, 4
  impact on PD programs, 46, 54–8, 163–4, 172
  impact on DOD, 186–7, 194–201, 209, 218, 222, 232
  impact on anti-terrorism and security, 62, 67

Access Microscholarships, 138–9
Afghanistan
  DOD programs in, 184–7, 191–4, 202–8
  PD programs in, 48, 57–9, 86, 112, 155, 170, 192–3
  State compared to DOD in, 24, 46, 188, 194–6, 201, 205–6
Africa
  DOD in, 197–8
  PD personnel in, 24
  PD programs in, 57, 116, 140, 151, 176
  *see also* individual countries
Agency for International Development, US (USAID), 60, 62, 85, 183–6, 193–5, 205, 216
ambassadors
  and cultural and education programs, 132, 168, 172
  and interviews, 90, 110
  and social media, 108–12, 120, 124

American spaces, 145–60
  *see also* American centers, American corners, IRCs, BNCs
al Qaida, 86, 197, 203, 205
Albright, Secretary of State Madeleine, 19
al-Jazeera television, 86–9, 194, 228
America-Mideast Education and Training Services (AMIDEAST), 137, 175–6
American speakers program, 72, 130–2
Anderson, Michael, as PAO in Indonesia, 157–8, 255–6
Armed Forces Radio and Television Services, 182

Bahrain, 46, 119–20, 137
Beyrle, John as ambassador to Russia (2008–12), 110, 124, 135
binational centers (BNCs)
  changes in, 151
  examples, 146–7, 151, 153, 156
  origin, 146–7
  purpose, 137, 152, 155, 159
blogging, bloggers, 93, 97, 98, 106–7, 112, 114–15
book translations, 12, 140
books about public diplomacy, 1, 2
Boyce, Ralph, as ambassador to Thailand (2004–07), 110

Brazil, 47, 84, 102
Broadcasting Board of Governors (BBG), 4, 20, 192, 222
Brown, John H., 89–90, 227
budgets, public diplomacy
  at DOD, 185, 205
  at State, 20, 46, 130, 193, 197, 238
  at USIA, 16, 18, 21, 137, 147, 206
Burma, 10, 149
Bush, President George W.,
  and al-Jazeera, 86–7
  and DOD, 188, 194, 201, 206, 216–18
  foreign view of, 27, 49–50, 83
  and Global War on Terrorism, 62, 222
  and language learning, 18, 27
  and PD programs, 163–4, 167, 188

career tracks, 23, 33–6, 69, 116
  cross-track assignments, 34–5, 38
  *see also* cones
cell phones, 67, 105, 150, 191
centers, American
  changes in, 147–8, 152, 156–9
  examples of, 109, 146, 152–3, 156, 192
  management of, 43–4
  mandated in law, 10, 12
  origins, 8, 9
  purpose, 69, 145–9, 154–8, 223
Central Intelligence Agency, 72
Chile, 103, 109, 153
China
  importance to US of, 46, 114
  media in, 15, 105, 107, 113–14
  PD programs and staff in, 46, 114, 133–4, 138, 141, 171
  public opinion in, 50
  restrictions by, 60, 84, 230
Civil and Humanitarian Affairs (CAHA) by DOD, 185–6
clearances, security, 121
Clinton, Secretary of State Hillary, 124, 250

Clinton administration, 17, 19, 21
Clune, Daniel, as ambassador to Laos (since 2013), 111
co-financing, 155, 171, 173
CO.NX, 101, 118
cones, 23, 69, 116
  *see also* career tracks
coordination of PD, 44
  with DOD, 183, 185–6, 194–9, 205
  within the embassy, 60–2
  *see also* MIST, PRTs
corners, American
  benefits and problems, 152–6
  examples, 152–6
  origin, 151–2
  *see also* American centers, American spaces, IRCs, BNCs
counterinsurgency (COIN)
  operations, 197, 199
  policy, 187, 191, 201–6
counter-terrorism. *See* terrorism
covert activities, 183–4, 190, 227
Crane, Elise, x
Cuba, 59, 114–15
Cull, Nicholas, 2
Cultural Affairs Officer (CAO), 4, 34, 43–4, 55, 81, 157
cultural awareness, 53, 206, 209, 214, 218, 225
cultural programming, 22, 130, 132–7, 142, 149, 155–8, 163–7
culture
  American, 38, 50, 58, 62, 85, 91–2, 129
  cultural officials, 73, 75
  defined, 12, 14, 18, 129
  and DOD, 185, 208, 214–15
  in educational exchanges, 139
  foreign, 26–7, 29–32, 44, 53–4, 63, 67
  importance of understanding, 224–5, 232
  in Iraq and Afghanistan, 192–3, 197, 208

# Index

deception, 183–4, 199, 199, 212, 227
  *see also* truth
Department of Defense, US (DOD), 181–220
  after 9/11, 2, 181, 201–8, 214–17, 222, 232, 225
  before 9/11, 9, 199
  budget and manpower, 24, 223
  compared with State, 218
  under Obama, 218, 223
Department of State, US (DOS)
  budget, 205
  and DOD, 9, 187
  field assignments, 60
  as lead PD agency, 205
  merger with USIA, 33
  Washington bureaus, 8, 9, 52, 54, 56, 98
dialogue
  examples of, 56, 99, 101–2, 152, 170, 209, 211
  importance of, 1, 29, 65–7, 71, 78, 99, 134, 207, 226
  State compared with DOD on, 182, 212–13
Digital Outreach Team, 93
disagreement with policy, 83, 89–90, 227

educational advising, 146, 175–6, 229
Educational and Cultural Affairs, Bureau of, Department of State, 19, 23, 31, 101, 137
educational exchanges, 9, 161–80
  by DOD, 184, 192, 211
  examples of, 103, 171, 173
  legal basis of, 12
  management of, 38, 131
  purpose of, 99, 110
  *see also* Fulbright program, International Visitor Leader Program
Egypt
  Muslim issues in, 56–7

PD programs in, 55, 76, 136, 172, 177
public opinion in, 48
social media in, 55, 100, 105, 108
embeds, 194
English Access Microscholarship Program, 139, 193, 253
English teaching
  changes in, 137
  examples of, 115, 131, 193
  PD value of, 136–7, 142, 210–11, 232
  Regional English Teaching Officers and English Teaching Fellows, 138
exhibitions, 8, 12, 141–2
  in Moscow, 16
  in Shanghai, 141

Facebook, 65, 96–104, 107–10, 115–16, 119–23, 139, 158, 193
  for English learning, 139
  problems with, 113, 11, 119–23
  in specific countries, 102, 105, 108–12, 115–16, 158, 193
  use by ambassadors, 112
Fernandez, Alberto, 88–9
field operations, importance of, 1–4, 224
first and second tour (FAST) officers, 36, 38
Foreign Service Nationals, 25, 45
  *see also* Locally Employed Staff
Foreign Service Officer (FSO)
  assignments, 121, 211, 214
  career entry, 24, 25
  career tracks, 23, 33–6, 38
  resignation from, 89, 227
  skills, 26, 26–7, 29–30, 35, 37–8, 215
France
  PD programs in, 54, 57, 132, 162–3, 171
  social media in, 103
Fulbright, Senator J. William, 11

Fulbright program
  commissions, 161, 163, 171
  management and budget of, 35, 154, 161, 164, 169
  purpose of, 9, 72, 92
  Secretary Kerry on, 167
  in specific countries, 56, 161–2, 169–72, 178, 189, 206
Fulbright-Hayes Act (Mutual Cultural and Educational Exchange Act of 1961), 12
*Future Leaders Exchange* program (FLEX), 163

Gates, Secretary of Defense Robert, 21, 24, 208, 214–16
Germany
  PD program rationale in, 8, 46, 169
  PD programs in, 112, 146–7
  public opinion in, 49
Gersten, Bridget, ix–x, 76, 142
Global Ties, 175
  *see also* National Council on International Visitors
Global War on Terror (GWOT), 8, 201–2, 210, 167
  *see also* terrorism
guidance, policy, 88–90
Gullion, Edmund, 12

Helms, Senator Jesse, 19
Huebner, David, as ambassador to New Zealand (2009–14), 112
Hughes, Karen, Undersecretary for Public Diplomacy and Public Affairs (2005–07)
  on educational exchange, 167
  on foreign media, 69, 87–8, 93, 102, 243
  on PD professionals, 36, 89
  on social media, 93, 106
Hungary, 61, 152, 242
Hurley, Michael, as Public Affairs Officer in Hungary and Moscow, 61, 168

India, importance of, 45
  media in, 105, 108, 123
  PD management in, 45, 104, 108, 169
  PD programs in, 108, 123, 136, 139, 172
  public opinion in, 55
Indonesia, importance of, 45
  Muslim audience in, 56, 62
  PD management in, 45, 108
  PD programs in, 155–8, 176
  social media in, 108
Information Officer, 4, 43–4, 71, 81
Information Resource Centers (IRCs)
  benefits and problems, 150–3, 159
  changes, 151
  examples, 115–16, 149–53
  purpose, 149, 152–3, 159
International Information Programs, Bureau of, Department of State
  function of, 20, 23, 31, 98–9, 115
  program management by, 83, 90, 97–8, 102–4, 107, 121–3, 141, 156, 159
International Military Education and Training (IMET), 184–5
Iran, 47, 50–1, 60, 71, 115, 170, 223
Iraq
  DOD role in, 187–91, 194, 196–203, 206, 208–27
  Islamic factor in, 2, 57, 205
  other foreign opinion of, 50, 120, 136
  PD programs in, 189, 194, 203, 205–6, 214
  public opinion in, 28, 48
  State-DOD coordination in, 194–5, 208

Japan
  PD by ambassador and DCM, 111–12, 117, 132
  PD programs in, 132, 146, 149, 153, 162, 172, 230
journalists, talking to, 82, 87–9

# Index

Keith, Kenton, as PAO in Egypt, 75
Kenney, Kristie, as ambassador to Thailand, 110–11
Kenya, 55, 58, 91, 111, 119, 147
Kerry, Secretary of State John, 124, 137, 167
Kiesling, John Brady, 89, 227
Kwan, Michelle, as Special Envoy, 133

languages, foreign
 importance of for PD, 44, 52, 90
 in radio, 198
 in social media, 99–100, 104, 106, 112, 193
 study of, 27, 38
 use by DOD, 198
 use by PD staff, 52, 93, 121, 123
 use in publications, 14–15, 90, 100, 107, 140–2
Laos, 111, 138
last three feet rule, the
 Murrow quote about, 65
 PD use of, 65, 72, 96, 116, 157, 225
Lebanon, 50, 55, 59
libraries. *See* American spaces, American centers, American corners, IRCs, BNCs
Locally Employed Staff (LES), 25, 43–4
 see *also* Foreign Service Nationals
Lugar, Senator Richard, 21
Lugar Report. *See* American spaces, American centers, American corners, IRCs, BNCs
Lussenhop, Matt, PAO in Afghanistan
Lynch, Marc, 88–9

McCall, Dawn, as head of the International Information Policy Bureau (2010–13), 98
MacInnes, Duncan, 100
McHale, Judith, Undersecretary for Public Diplomacy and Public Affairs (2009–2011), 156–7

measurement, 212–13
media hubs, 93, 230, 232
merger, of USIA with the State Department, 19–21, 33–7
 impact on field planning, 53, 61, 105, 218, 232
 impact on personnel, 35–9
Mexico, 14, 146–9, 173
Military Information Support Operations (MISO), 187
 see *also* psychological operations
Military Information Support Team (MIST), 195–8, 217
mobile phones. *See* cell phones
Munter, Cameron, as ambassador to Serbia, 111
Murphy, Philip, ambassador to Germany, 112
Murrow, Edward R., as Director of the U.S. Information Agency, 38, 65
 quotations of, 65, 77, 116, 225, 227

National Council on International Visitors (NCIV), 175, 229
 see *also* Global Ties
New Zealand, 112, 118
non-governmental organizations (NGOs), 30, 133, 137, 175–6, 195
Nye, Joseph, 12
 see *also* soft power

Obama, Barack, President of the United States
 foreign opinion of, 49–51
 policies of, 51, 57, 89, 217, 222
 use of media by, 106, 108, 116, 141
opinion polls, 52, 226

Pakistan
 media in, 52, 108, 118
 PD programs in, 136, 198, 202
 public opinion in, 51, 135, 177

partnerships for PD
  with foreign institutions, 28, 106, 137, 165, 173, 176, 193, 229
  with US organizations, 28, 76, 136–8, 141–2, 174–5
Pentagon. *See* Department of Defense
personnel, public diplomacy
  assignments, 33–5, 37
  contrasted with other tracks, 39
  recruitment, 35
  skills, 33, 37
planning for PD, 37, 73, 98, 130, 145, 213
  Mission Strategic Plan, 61
Powell, Secretary of State Colin, 87
print media editors, 43, 83–4, 86, 227
printed materials, 16, 21, 38, 90, 98, 101, 137, 178, 191
  by DOD, 181, 184
private Americans, 61, 71, 171, 229
private organizations. *See* partnerships
propaganda
  by CIA, 16
  defined, 10, 183, 187, 202, 208
  foreign, 8, 15, 46, 107
Provincial Reconstruction Team (PRT), 195, 206
psychological operations (PSYOP)
  contrasted with PD and public affairs, 183–4, 202, 227
  definition of, 182–4, 187, 202, 206, 208
  *see also* MISO
public affairs, 12, 98
  as defined by DOD, 181–7, 213–15
Public Affairs Bureau, U.S. Department of State (PA/State)
Public Affairs Officer, 3, 12, 43, 60–2, 67, 117, 232
  tasks of, 53–63, 73, 81, 90–2
Public Affairs Section (PAS), 12, 15, 43–5, 108
  management of, 25–31, 38, 51, 55, 98, 104, 175
public diplomacy defined, 3–4, 7

Qatar, 86–7
Qutb, Sayyid, Egyptian political figure, 168

radio
  access to foreign stations, 81, 85–6, 91, 116, 181, 189–90
  importance of foreign radio stations, 4, 10, 27, 58, 73, 86, 94, 124, 191
  monitoring foreign stations, 30, 43, 52
  US government radio broadcasts, 182–4, 191–2, 195–7, 222, 230
Ranneberger, Michael, as ambassador to Kenya (2006–11), 111
rapid response bulletin, 93, 102, 112, 215, 230, 232
restrictions on public diplomacy
  by foreign governments, 46, 59–60, 71, 78, 113–14, 170–2, 225
  as a management problem, 3, 58
  social and cultural, 58
  technical, 58, 95, 113
  by the US for security reasons, 147, 228, 242, 189
Rivkin, Charles, as ambassador to France (2009–13), 108, 132
Roos, John, as ambassador to Japan, 117
Rumsfeld, Donald, Secretary of Defense, 213–15, 267
Russia
  PD programs in, 76, 101–2, 134, 153–5, 163, 169
  PD staff in, 152
  restrictions on PD, 169
  social media in, 110, 124
  *see also* Soviet Union

Saudi Arabia, 58, 82, 120–2, 130, 142, 225
Secure Embassy Construction and Counterterrorism Act (SECCA), 147, 148, 152, 156–7

security
  problems for PD, 2, 59, 117, 133, 148, 150, 154, 157–8, 212, 223
  special problems in war zones, 189, 192, 195, 203–6, 217
  US security clearances, 24
  US security measures, 2, 31, 59–61, 67, 117, 156
  *see also* Secure Embassy Construction and Counterterrorism Act
Serbia
  PD programs in, 15, 153, 170
  public opinion in, 135
  social media in, 108, 111 (2012–13)
short messaging service (SMS)
  defined, 104
  PD use of, 14, 96, 104–6, 115–16, 118, 230
  start of, 95
Sierra Leone
  barriers to communication, 58, 116, 153
  PD audience, 56–7
Smith-Mundt Act (1948), 10, 76, 174
Smith-Mundt domestic ban, 205
social networking media, 95–128
soft power, 12, 39, 216
Sonenshine, Tara, Undersecretary for Public Diplomacy and Public Affairs(2012–13), 156, 167
South Korea
  public opinion in, 48
  reporters in, 77
  social media in, 102, 111, 120, 122
Soviet Union, 10, 15, 17–18, 55, 151, 163, 169
  *see also* Russia
specialists, compared with FSO generalists, 1, 22, 35
sports envoys, 133–4, 232
Stephens, Kathleen, as ambassador to South Korea (2008–11), 111, 120
Syria
  obstacles to PD, 60, 85
  PD programs, 115, 132, 136–7

television
  access by DOD to foreign television, 182, 191, 195, 204
  al Jazeera, 86, 88, 228
  impact of satellite television, 17, 94, 124, 137, 191
  limits on, 73, 86
  monitoring foreign television, 27, 52
  PD access to foreign television, 30, 58, 81, 85–8, 91–3, 103–4, 230
terrorism, 2, 56, 86, 187, 196, 223
  counter-terrorism policy, 8, 62, 196–7, 204, 212, 215, 232
  and DOD, 2, 181, 187, 196, 199, 201
  in Iraq and Afghanistan, 49, 222
  and Obama, 218, 223, 232
  and PD, 8
  and social media, 209
Thailand, 55, 57, 102–3, 108–11, 117, 138, 152, 161–2
training
  cross training, 34
  by DOD, 184–5, 187, 197, 213–15
  for foreigners, 192, 195
  optimal, 34–8, 44, 49, 130, 133, 138
  for PD, 12, 24, 26
truth
  and credibility, 183, 227
  importance of, 9, 10, 227
  and loyalty, 68, 77, 227
Tuch, Tom, 2
Twitter
  importance of, 65, 96–7, 105, 108–9, 116, 119
  problems in use of, 89, 96, 114–15, 122
  use and promotion by Washington, 97–100, 104
  use by ambassadors, 117, 119, 124
  use by field posts, 102, 110–14, 122–3, 158, 193

U.S. Agency for International Development (USAID), 60, 62, 85, 183
  budget of, 205, 216
  and DOD, 186, 195
U.S. Information Agency (USIA)
  establishment of, 11
  histories of, 2
  merger with State Department, 19–21, 33–9, 105, 130, 218, 232
  programs, 13–16
  staff and budget, 16–19
Undersecretary for Public Diplomacy and Public Affairs
  establishment of the position, 20, 31
  Judith McHale as, 156–7
  Karen Hughes as, 36, 69, 87, 93, 102
  Tara Sonenshine as, 156, 167
United Kingdom (UK), 50, 84–5, 102, 138

Venezuela, 121
Vietnam, 16, 138, 182, 186
Voice of America (VOA), 9, 20, 148, 184, 194, 198, 222
Voluntary Visitor Program, 163

Washington File, Wireless File, 8, 13–14, 90, 99
websites
  in foreign languages, 101, 122–3
  managed by DOD, 190, 198–9
  managed by US embassies, 100–3, 105, 109, 122–3, 138, 149, 158
  managed by VOA, 184
  managed by Washington, 101, 139, 176–7
  *see also* CO.NX

Yemen, 72, 75, 137, 197
youth
  field post focus on, 49, 55–6, 103, 108, 132–3, 163–4
  and social media, 2, 100, 103
  Washington focus on, 54, 62, 164, 173
Youtube
  importance of, 96–100, 113
  use at posts, 102–3, 107, 110, 119–22, 193
  use by ambassadors, 110, 111
  use by Washington, 54, 62, 164, 173
Yugoslavia, 170